BETH HENLEY
Collected Plays Volume II

1990–1999

A Smith and Kraus Book
Published by Smith and Kraus, Inc.
PO Box 127, Lyme, NH 03768

First Edition: February 2000
10 9 8 7 6 5 4 3 2 1

The Library of Congress Cataloging-In-Publication Data
Henley, Beth.
[Plays]
Beth Henley: collected plays / Beth Henley. —1st ed.
p. cm. — (Contemporary playwrights series)

Contents: v.2: Abundance. Control Freaks. Signature. Revelers. L-Play. Impossible Marriage.

ISBN 1-57525-200-7 (cloth) — ISBN 1-57525-201-5 (pbk.)
I. Series.
PS3558.E4962 A6 1999
812'.54—dc21   99-052209

BETH HENLEY

Collected Plays Volume II
1990–1999

CONTEMPORARY PLAYWRIGHTS
SERIES

SK
A Smith and Kraus Book

BETH HENLEY was awarded the Pulitzer Prize in Drama and the New York Drama Critics Circle Award for Best American Play for her first full-length play, *Crimes of the Heart,* which was the co-winner in 1979 of the Great American Play Contest sponsored by the Actors Theatre of Louisville prior to its move to New York. *Crimes of the Heart* has since been produced in many of our leading resident theatres, on a major national tour, and in many countries throughout the world. Ms. Henley's second play, *The Miss Firecracker Contest,* has been produced in several regional theatres in the United States and in London at the Bush Theatre and opened in the spring of 1984 at the Manhattan Theatre Club. It subsequently transferred for an extended run off-Broadway, and was published in the Ten Best Plays of 1983–84. Ms. Henley's third play, *The Wake of Jamey Foster,* had its premiere at the Hartford Stage Company prior to its presentation on Broadway, directed by Ulu Grosbard. Ms. Henley's one-act play *Am I Blue?* was produced at the Circle Repertory Company in New York. It is included in the Best Short Plays of 1983. Her play *The Debutante Ball* was presented in the spring of 1985 at the South Coast Repertory in Costa Mesa, California, and was presented in a substantially revised version at the Manhattan Theatre Club and the New York Stage and Film Company in the spring and summer of 1988, respectively. Subsequently, it was presented in London at the Hampstead Theatre Club in the spring of 1989. Her play, *The Lucky Spot,* was presented at the Williamstown Theatre Festival in the summer of 1986 and had its New York premiere at the Manhattan Theatre Club in 1987. It had its London premiere in the spring of 1991. *Abundance* had its premiere at the South Coast Repertory and opened at the Manhattan Theatre Club in the fall of 1990 and was produced at The Riverside Theatre in London in the fall of 1995. Her play *Signature* was given a workshop at the New York Stage and Film Company in the summer of 1990 and had a full production at the Charlotte Repertory Theatre in the spring of 1995. *Control Freaks* premiered at Chicago's Center Theatre in 1992 and opened at the Met Theatre in Los Angeles in July, 1993, under the direction of Ms. Henley. Her play *Revelers* had a production in the summer of 1994 under the auspices of New York Stage and Film at Poughkeepsie, N.Y. Ms. Henley's newest play, *Impossible Marriage,* is currently running at the Roundabout Theatre.

Ms. Henley wrote the screenplay for the acclaimed film version of *Crimes of the Heart* for which she was nominated for an Academy Award. The film was directed by Bruce Beresford and starred Diane Keaton, Jessica Lange, Sissy Spacek, and Sam Shepard. She also wrote the screenplay for *Miss Firecracker* starring Holly Hunter, Mary Steenburgen, and Tim Robbins. She wrote the screenplay for *Nobody's Fool,* which starred Rosanna Arquette and Eric Roberts, and a teleplay for the PBS series, *Trying Times.*

She was born and raised in Mississippi, graduated from Southern Methodist University, and lives in Los Angeles with her son Patrick.

CONTENTS

INTRODUCTION

I'd like to continue the introduction for Volume Two in the same vein as Volume One: with my own memories and impressions of each play, followed by remembrances of treasured and wildly generous colleagues. There is, however, one thing that somehow interests me concerning geography. The first five plays in Volume One take place in the present/past. By that I mean they are contemporary plays but not quite set in the here and now. They deal essentially with obsessions and concerns from roughly the first twenty years of my life. All of them, with the exception of *Am I Blue* (set in New Orleans) are set in Mississippi, the place I grew up. These plays seem to have an amber quality to them; they search to make sense of observations made long ago. To nick a term from Tennessee Williams, they are memory plays.

The final play in Volume One, *The Lucky Spot*, takes place in Louisiana in 1933. The first play in this volume takes place in the Wyoming territory beginning in the 1860s. By setting these plays in period, I was able to take some active control of the amber glow, move out of Mississippi, and start heading west. These are plays written about parts of my life that occurred after leaving Mississippi...the struggle to revive love betrayed (*The Lucky Spot*); the conflict between our need for love and security pitted against our desire for rapture and danger (*Abundance*).

After completing two plays that had required a lot of research, I was anxious to write something completely from my imagination with no concern for history or fact. I set the new play, *Signature*, in Los Angeles, where I had been living for many years but catapulted past the present into the year 2052, when I would be a hundred years old. I actually have a daydream about hobbling in to see a production of this play on my hundredth birthday.

It was after *Signature* I finally wrote a play set in Los Angeles, the time: NOW. All these years I had been peeling off layers to get to a place where my past and present met face to face out of the amber glow under fluorescent lights. After *Control Freaks* I faltered a bit. Witness *L-Play* where the central theme is: Nothing is central, all is fragmented and a mess because there are just too many styles, times, characters, and chaos to choose from.

Impossible Marriage, the final play in this volume, and *Family Week*, my newest play, seem fairly sturdy. I feel both plays are written from somewhere in me that is vital and present, without the veil of nostalgia or historic period. I believe I'm catching up with myself, but life keeps running ahead. Thank God.

One more point. I do not judge the strength or value of any of these plays by how or from where they came into being. I feel grateful for them all. I only wanted to explain something about the journey.

ABUNDANCE

The first day of rehearsal for *Abundance* in the first production at South Coast Repertory, I was ecstatically eager. Generally I am not verbose in rehearsals. I tend to lie on my side watching or listening while doing leg lifts with strapped on weights. However, I knew the two actors, Belita Moreno and Bruce Wright, who were working on the scene, very well and for a long time. I was impatient for results and jumped to my feet declaring, "This encounter must be much more brutal. Bruce, don't push her away, sling her away! We're out west. Things are tough, fierce, barbaric." They began the scene again and a split-second later Belita was on her back with a broken wrist. The director and stage manager glared at me. I went with Belita to the hospital to set her arm. She got the cast off the last week of previews. The lesson: restraint rather than results in rehearsal.

BELITA MORENO, ACTRESS, DIRECTOR
A wondrous event is the first-ever read-through of a Beth Henley play, usually in her living room, surrounded by friends, old and new, who have come to hear the material for the first time. Like musicians at a jam session, the actors riff and bounce off each other trying to find the right tempo, rhythm, and dynamics of the piece. As one who has been fortunate enough to have performed in a number of Beth Henley plays, I find those living room readings integral to my process. I spend much of my time in rehearsals trying to relocate my original living room interpretation of the writer's words.

MAX NEMTSOV, RUSSIAN TRANSLATOR, EDITOR
I first saw *Abundance* on paper. But I remember the vivid starkness and aus- terity of the staged play (the Blackfriars' production in Vladivostok) and those living characters that drew me irresistibly to that work. I remember their vibrant speech. For me it was quite a challenge to recreate *Abundance* in Russian, preserving the rhythms and patterns of their speech. I couldn't let go of it until I finished the translation (in a month)—that was a month of fine, almost jeweller's work and one of the best I've ever had.

SIGNATURE

The inspiration for *Signature* came one night walking down Melrose Avenue with a friend from London. I was in a dark place and hadn't written for some time. Out on the sidewalk was a man with a chair and box set up with a sign reading "Graphologist." He could read your life through your handwriting. "Just write any two sentences." He'd be able to tell.

My friend wrote two sentences and was praised for his "courage, nobil- ity, creative brilliance, good heart, and good looks." I eagerly paid my ten dollars and wrote two sentences. My handwriting was indicative of a "petty, selfish, measly, talentless egotist." The graphologist added, "I don't mean any of this as a value judgment."

I went away consumed with grief. Later I pondered why and how I had so eagerly given over my power, had paid ten dollars to give over to some stranger who would interpret my signature. My essence. My mark on the world.

Keats had inscribed on his tombstone, "Here lies one whose name was writ on water." I thought what I'd like on my own grave was, "Here lies one whose name was drilled in granite." I started to write the play.

JIM MCGRATH, WRITER, DIRECTOR
The characters of *Signature* live in the future at a time when the forces of death would seem to have won. Many citizens die young from an omnipresent plague. The government has conquered individual liberty and severely hampered free will. Addictions abound, the strongest being to the Warhol fifteen minutes. The Springer cult has turned every breakup of every personal relationship into a televised event. A tar-like substance is eating the

environment alive. Every man is a Job, every woman a Joan of Arc. In such a world, hearts have reason to be heavy.

But the hearts of Henley's characters rise like the Phoenix with more love than guile, more hilarity than pathos, and more courage than care. Boswell and his crowd speak their own language. As the play progresses they teach it to us. By the end of the play we are fluent. The language teaches us about the particulars of this other world and about ourselves. Some of the characters break our hearts with their bold strokes in a fragile universe. Others we overlook, or worse discount, only to be astonished at the warmth of their kisses.

When I began the process of directing this magnificent work, I distracted myself too long with the glittering externals. Toward the end of the rehearsal period, when the artists involved had done their jobs so beautifully, I came to know that all of the craft in the creation of Beth Henley's alternate universe is put to the purpose of distracting from self-involvement long enough to show truth. The world of this play is not difficult to understand simply because it is so much like our own.

CONTROL FREAKS

Control Freaks was the first and only play of mine I have directed. I did a workshop of the play in Chicago at the Center Theater followed by a full production before doing the play in Los Angeles. As I worked on the piece in Chicago, it became clear that I needed to move very far from a realistic interpretation. The set needed to be utilitarian and expressionistic. The actors would need to do nothing less than invent a style of moving and relating that was wholly original, existing only in the world of this play. *Control Freaks* needed to be performed like a choreographed, choral poem, flowing seamlessly from excruciating control to bludgeoning chaos. The problem being to create chaos, it takes a great deal of fearlessness, daring, precision, and of course, control. For a neophyte director it was an overwhelming challenge.

The first day of rehearsal at the Met Theatre in Los Angeles I was nervously churning over how in the hell I was going to achieve any of this. I shuffled from the audience to the stage with a load of notebooks and a tattered script, only to trip on the rim of the stage, stumble to the ground, falling flat on my face. There was a moment of awkward mortification as I lay among clutter strewn from my purse, only a moment before Bill Pullman nose-dived onto the stage, crashing down helter-skelter next to me. Without a thought the rest of the cast riffed out, falling and whirling to the ground like drunken lunatics, ridiculously writhing to redeem me. One thing I know: Actors don't get any better than this.

HOLLY HUNTER. ACTRESS
Some of Beth's characters have rebellion at their core. Some of her characters are afflicted with desires that cannot be contained within the conventional settings of their world. But *Control Freaks* is a play that gets down on the floor to kick and scream, and the characters, by God, inhabit that rant. It was a scary challenge to meet the life of the rant head-on. In rehearsals, I used to hope I would have a car wreck so my psychological torment would be over. It was the most disorienting rehearsal period I've ever been through. The distress was relentless. But when we finally began to catch a glimpse of the *Control Freaks* landscape stretching out before us, there was a freedom sometimes to be had onstage that I had never felt. For an hour and a half every night we would writhe. The play gets down to "Yes" and "No." And sex. And acrobatics fit in there with no effort at all. I love when Beth raves on, and there's plenty of that in *Control Freaks*. Anger spews, and what's next? Poison drinks all around. An antidote chaser for some, not for others. Last stop: Triumph. Liberation. Forgiveness of Self. We had a blast.

BILL PULLMAN, ACTOR, DIRECTOR
Beth Henley had her director's notepad still wet in her hand and she was dancing full bore with the four of us *Control Freaks* in the backstage/greenroom of the upstairs 99-seat theater on Oxford Street in Hollywood's east side. What a wiggly, wombat dance we could do in that ten-minute countdown to curtain. The soundtrack of choice was Los Lobos' "In The Neighborhood" album, and "Take Me to the River" was just the warm-up. Was it the outfits, the pull of polyester that got us stretching nasty around the room? Maybe Holly and I just enjoyed the aching groove of brotherly and sisterly affection, Carol just could tingle instantly with succulent sauciness, and Wayne could easily trip into his Cheshire-cat poisoning pride. And we could all get ratcheted up by Beth—that Southern Madam of Murder and Mischief—with her eyes beaming ecstatic around the room of writhing *Control Freaks*.

CAMILLA CARR, ACTRESS, WRITER

I could never pick a favorite play, but if I had to pick a favorite production, it would be *Control Freaks*, which I saw night after night at the Met Theatre in Hollywood with utterly heartbreakingly brilliant Holly Hunter as "Sister." Whimsical, mocking, defiant, defeated and triumphant, she seeks escape from self, fleeing and merging from persona to persona, before completely abandoning the tortured "Sister" in a final breathtaking flight. Bill Pullman's "Carl" was simply magnificent. Frightening and funny, sinister and loveable, that confusing breed of humanity: a charming, compelling, revolting demonic paradox. And Carol Kane's "Betty" was ingenious. Hilarious, scary, sexy, appealing and appalling! Caught in the midst of this messy bunch of control freaks was Wayne Pere's "Paul," deliciously heading for disaster. It was the most delicate balance I have ever seen on any stage. The most horrifying. And the most moving. And, of course, Beth Henley directed it herself. Friendships *strained*. (And remain!) I still shudder, both thrilled and terrorized, when I visualize this production—and the triumphant realization of the monumental demands of its text—because that kind of balancing of talent, artistry, craft and perfection of execution is seldom ever seen ANYTIME, ANYWHERE. O! how I would love to see it again… And AGAIN!

REVELERS

I got the idea for *Revelers* when I was in Chicago workshopping *Control Freaks* and staying in a small room at Dale Calander's apartment. I'd met Dale years ago at the University of Illinois. In 1976, the bicentennial, we'd acted together in an outdoor drama, *Your Obedient Servant A. Lincoln*. Dale now helped run Center Theater where I was generously allowed to work on work.

I had become obsessed with the Woody Allen/Mia Farrow scandal. It fascinated and terrified me, how close relationships and treasured beliefs can utterly transform with circumstance and time. Dale came into my room to bring me his early edition of *People* magazine with the scandal on the cover. I was greedy for it, but Dale lounged down on the bed and started telling me about our former acting teacher's memorial. A group of Chicago thespians went to a cottage on the shore of Lake Michigan, prepared a meal with all of the deceased's favorite food, had an elaborate memorial, and sprinkled the ashes around the lake at sunset. It struck me that the mentor had never been to the cottage where he would rest for eternity. He had only hoped to go there.

I had mixed feelings in that I had feared and hated the acting teacher. He had advised me to return to Mississippi, get married, and stay south. In a fit of rebellion I'd thrown his final assessment of me unread into the trash bin at Arby's Roast Beef. The unsettling thing was I had learned much from this tyrant: ways of looking into characters by asking vital questions. What is the character's greatest dream, greatest fear? What smell do they like best? Questions I still ask in my work today. I can't say how but all of this figured in to a need to write *Revelers*.

Later Dale Calander starred in the role of Jasper Dale in the Chicago production.

DALE CALANDER, ACTOR, DIRECTOR
I reveled in playing Jasper Dale in *Revelers*. It's a dark comedy about coming to terms with one's fate—and how our lives change when we choose to move on. Beth drops little gems of life into all of her characters. Actors love working in her plays because she doesn't take the conventional route.

L-PLAY

I had several notebooks with interesting bits of dialogue, evocative images, compelling settings, and so forth. The problem was nothing was jelling. Generally, in some mysterious, organic way a play will begin to make an appearance, to rise from the rubble. This play was elusive. I'd start out with a Christmas scene set in 1930 and next be noodling on a contemporary scene about a drunken couple in Los Angeles.

I was distraught. I wanted to be figuring out a new play in my head. When I'm not working on a play, I get anxious in the grocery line, or numbingly bored in the shower. Life is grim when there is nothing to turn tedious moments into private creative struggles.

I finally got the idea for the play when I realized I had no idea. I felt fragmented, decentralized, clueless. I had become confused over who was more truthful, more enlightened: Sophocles, the Three Stooges, Edgar Allan Poe, Elvis, Nero?? There are so many worldviews, endless realities, tones, messages. I decided to go with it—the mosaic of life. I wrote a variety of different scenes in different styles and different characters. The only unifying element would be that the title of each scene would begin with an L. An L is half a box. It is a letter that is searching to connect, to link.

COLLEEN DODSON-BAKER, ACTRESS, WRITER

I was in the first reading of *L-Play*. It was in a living room in Chicago. I was based in New York at the time and Beth was in Los Angeles, but we would meet up at the Center Theater in Chicago (a theater company founded by friends of ours from the University of Illinois) and work on our plays. This particular trip Beth was dramaturging a play of mine and I was acting in her play, *Revelers*, when Beth mentioned that she had a "new play" that she'd love to hear read. I was one of the lucky ones who was handed a script and told "you'll be playing…" When I first read the play I was struck by how unlike "Beth" it was. The playlet form went against her usual linear structure, actors were playing multiple roles, and the use of highly contrasting styles and tones created a strangely disconnected musicality. I had no idea what to make of it. And yet when the play was read it all came together like an amazing patch-work quilt. The bold comedic strokes of one play only made the deeper darker tones of another more compelling.

ALFRE WOODARD, ACTRESS

I became an actor for the rush of total freedom the "act" affords. And I believe one cannot have a complete life as an actor without having performed or explored a Beth Henley piece. It is certainly the experience of being turned out at full gallop. Which is not to marginalize her writing as simply a great workout for the actor—but that full tilt is where real human beings live and flounder and occasionally triumph. Her unselfconscious approach to circumstance and character honors the flesh and blood folk that populate our families, our romances, and the four directions—especially the South.

In the climate of false control, cool minimalism, and forced glibness that often characterizes today's writing, Henley fearlessly lets fly emotionally unashamed material and allows us to feel, to question, to argue, to hoot, to mourn.

When you step up to this work as the actor or director, you can't fake it. Her people are trying for all they're worth to make life work. And for a measure of eternal grace.

I was elated going to meet Scott Ellis to discuss doing a play commission for the Roundabout Theatre in New York. Scott told me there would be no stipulations on what I wrote and the money was (for a play commission) very generous. The only bit I was worried about was the time. They wanted a first draft in a year. Normally this would not be a problem, but I was completing work on a screenplay, I hadn't any notion or clue of what to write, what I had to say, and I was expecting a baby in August. Being childless I had no sense of how much that might hold me up. A week? A month? Ten years?

When my mother heard I had been commissioned to write a play, she pleaded for: "A happy play! You shouldn't put that baby under stress." I agreed I would like to write a "happy play." I'd certainly never tried it. Something effortlessly brilliant with keen, incisive wit. Something like *The Importance of Being Earnest*, except by me.

For the first time I read all of Wilde's plays. What a good time that was. I started looking at drawings by Aubrey Beardsley: sensual, formal, and forbiddenly erotic. When the play started to come together, I realized the characters' insides were vastly different from their facades. I began staring at Chagall's circus figures, blue flying lovers, red horses with wings, green angels with horns... I tried to imagine these feelings inhabiting the Beardsley figures.

I was able to write parts one and two before my son was born. After that I was transformed into a sleep-deprived, anxious, fearful, inadequate scullery maid. I would never finish this play or any other. Impossible, or at least very tricky.

STEPHEN WADSWORTH, DIRECTOR, TRANSLATOR
Beth had seen a Marivaux play I directed at the Mark Taper Forum in Los Angeles and suggested that I do her new play *Impossible Marriage* at the Roundabout. The leap from eighteenth-century French comedy to the world of her plays seemed like, well, a leap. What she wanted was a combination of things she had been drawn to in the Marivaux show: an envelope-pushing, heightened, theatrical style that was somehow grounded, truthful, very emotional. My favorite line in *Impossible Marriage*, a short one (and it could have been written by Marivaux), seems like the epicenter of Beth: "But my heart..."

ABUNDANCE

DEDICATED TO ROBERT DARNELL
AND THE SPIRIT OF DARNELLI POINTS

I

Belita Moreno, Bruce Wright, Jimmie Ray Weeks, and O-Lan Jones
in South Coast Repertory's 1989 production of
Abundance.

photo by Charlaine Brown

ORIGINAL PRODUCTION

Abundance was produced by the Manhattan Theatre Club (Lynne Meadow, Artistic Director; Barry Grove, Managing Director) in New York City on October 4, 1990. It was directed by Ron Lagomarsino; the set design was by Adrianne Lobel; the costume design was by Robert Wojewodski; the lighting design was by Paulie Jenkins; music and sound were by Michael Roth; the fight director was J. Allen Suddeth; and the production stage manager was Ruth Kreshka. The cast was as follows:

Bess Johnson . . . . Amanda Plummer
Macon Hill. . . . . Tess Harper
Jack Flan. . . . . Michael Rooker
William Curtis . . . . Lanny Flaherty
Elmore Crome . . . . Keith Reddin

World premiere of *Abundance* was produced by the South Coast Repertory (David Emmes, Producing Artistic Director; Martin Benson, Artistic Director), Costa Mesa, California, on April 21, 1989. It was directed by Ron Lagomarsino; the set design was by Adrianne Lobel; the costume design was by Robert Wojewodski; the lighting design was by Paulie Jenkins; music and sound were by Michael Roth; and the production manager was Paul Hammond. The cast was as follows:

Bess Johnson . . . . O-Lan Jones
Macon Hill. . . . . Belita Moreno
Jack Flan . . . . Bruce Wright
William Curtis . . . . Jimmie Ray Weeks
Elmore Crome . . . . John Walcutt

THE CHARACTERS
BESS JOHNSON
MACON HILL
JACK FLAN
WILLIAM CURTIS
PROFESSOR ELMORE CROME

THE SETTING
Wyoming Territory and later in St. Louis, Missouri.

THE TIME
The play spans twenty-five years, starting in the late 1860s.

ACT I
SCENE I

Late 1860s. Morning. Spring. Outside a stagecoach ranché in the Wyoming Territory. Bess Johnson, a young woman, sits on a bench. There is a bag at her feet. She wears a dirty traveling suit that has no buttons.

BESS: *(Singing to herself.)* Roses love sunshine
　　Violets love dew
　　Angels in heaven
　　Know I love you.
　　Build me a castle forty
　　feet high
　　So I can see him as he
　　rides by
　　(Bess stops singing and speaks softly to herself.)
　　The size of the sky. The size of the sky.
　　(Macon Hill enters wearing green goggles and a cape. She is covered with road dust and carries a satchel and green biscuits on a platter. She is whistling. She stops when she sees Bess.)
MACON: Lord Almighty.
BESS: What?
MACON: You're like me.
BESS: Huh?
MACON: Sure. You're like me. Biscuit?
BESS: Please.
MACON: Go ahead. Help yourself. What's mine is yours; what's yours is mine. After all, you're like me. You've come out west to see the elephant. Hey, true or no?
BESS: Elephant. No.
MACON: To see what's out there; whatever's out there. *(Beat.)* What do you guess is out there?
BESS: Don't know.
MACON: Right. Could be anything. I savor the boundlessness of it all. The wild flavor. I'm drunk with western fever. Have you ever seen a map of the world?
BESS: Uh huh.
MACON: Well, it stopped my heart. There are oceans out there. Oceans aplenty, and I swear to you I'm gonna see one and walk in one and swim

in one for sure. I love water, it never stops moving. I want to discover gold and be rich. I want to erect an ice palace and kill an Indian with a hot bullet. I'm ready for some sweeping changes. How about you? We could be friends throughout it all. It's part of our destiny. I can smell destiny. One day I'm gonna write a novel about it all and put you in it. What's your name? *(Macon produces a pad and pencil.)*

BESS: Bess Johnson.

MACON: *(Writing down the name.)* Good. That's a good name for a novel. Bess Johnson. Will you be my friend?

BESS: It'd be a pleasure. A true pleasure. Could I—could I trouble you for another biscuit?

MACON: Why sure. Sure, I hate stinginess. You'll never get anywhere watching every egg, nickel, and biscuit. Ya gotta let it go! Let it go! Go! And I don't give a damn if ya never pay me back.

BESS: Thanks kindly. I'm near pined t'death with famine. These green biscuits taste heaven to me.

MACON: Why, how long ya been at the ranché?

BESS: Ten days, I been waiting here. My travel money's all spent. Yesterday I traded French Pete my buttons for an extra night's lodging. I'm at my rope's end if Mr. Flan don't get here real soon; I don't know what.

MACON: Who's Mr. Flan?

BESS: He's the man who's coming t'pick me up. We're to be wed.

MACON: Wed? A wedding?

BESS: That's right. It's been arranged.

MACON: Then you're a bride-to-be?

BESS: Yeah.

MACON: Lord Almighty! Angels sing; devils dance! I'm a bride-to-be, too. It's like I said, you're like me. It's true! It's true! Tell me, do ya know your husband or is he a stranger to ya?

BESS: We had…correspondence.

MACON: Correspondence. Me too. And he sent you the fare?

BESS: Partial.

MACON: Me too! Me too! *(She whistles a few notes.)* Ya know what I hope? I hope our husbands don't turn out t'be just too damn ugly t'stand.

BESS: You think they'll be ugly?

MACON: Maybe. Maybe. But I hear divorce is cheap and easily obtainable out here in the West.

BESS: I'd never get no divorce.

MACON: Honey, I'd rip the wings off an angel if I thought they'd help me fly!

You may find this hard to believe, but back home they considered me the runt of the family. See, those folks are all full, large-bodied people, and to them I appeared to be some sort of runt. But out here I can be whoever I want. Nobody knows me. I'm gonna make everything up as I go. It's gonna be a whole new experience. We're dealing with the lure of the unknown. Yeah, we're hunting down the elephant! Bang! Bang! Bang! What's wrong with you? You're looking morose.

BESS: I—I'm just hoping my husband ain't gonna be real terrible ugly.

MACON: Well, Bess, I hope so too.

BESS: It don't mention nothing about his looks in the matrimonial ad.

MACON: Well, now that ain't good news. Folks generally like t'feature their good qualities in them advertisements.

BESS: 'Course I know I'm no prize. I got nice hair, but my eyes are too close together and my nerves are somewhat aggravated. Still, I was hoping we'd be in love like people in them stories. The ones about princesses and chimney sweeps and dragon slayers.

MACON: Oh, them stories ain't true. They ain't factual. Catapult them stories out of your brain. Do it! Do it! Catapult 'em!

BESS: I don't know, I—well, I bet he's gonna like me some.

MACON: Sure. Maybe he'll be cordial at Christmas.

BESS: I promise I'll be a good wife, patient and submissive. If only he'd come. I hope he ain't forgotten. He sent partial fare. Three letters and partial fare. Three letters all about the size of the western sky.

MACON: Damn! What size is it?

BESS: The largest he has witnessed.

MACON: Glory be.

BESS: And he loves singing. I can sing real pretty. Oh, I'm betting we're gonna be a match made in heaven, if only I ain't left stranded. See, 'cause, well, I don't know how I'll get by. I can't do nothing. I don't know nothing. I oughta know something by now. I went t'school. They must have taught me something there. But I can't even recall what my favorite color is. Maybe it's blue, but I'm just guessing.

MACON: Well, the fact is, if ya know too much, it's just gonna limit your thinking. Take me, I got this brown dress and I don't even get upset about it 'cause I got no recollection in my mind that my favorite color is blue. I mean, it may be, but I don't know it. Have another biscuit.

BESS: It's your last one.

MACON: I saved it for you.

(Jack Flan enters. He is handsome, with an air of wild danger.)

JACK: 'Morning.

MACON: 'Morning.

JACK: I'm looking for—Is one of you Bess Johnson?

BESS: That's me. That's me. I'm here. I'm here. That's me.

JACK: Uh huh.

BESS: Are you Mr. Michael Flan?

JACK: No, I'm Jack Flan, Mike's brother.

BESS: Oh well, well, pleased t'meet you, Mr. Jack Flan. Would you do me the great favor of taking me t'meet Mr. Michael Flan?

JACK: Mike's dead.

BESS: What?

JACK: Got killed in an accident and died.

BESS: Are you saying Mr. Michael Flan is no longer living?

JACK: That's right; he's dead.

BESS: Dead. Oh my. Oh my. Lord, Lord, Lord.

JACK: What's wrong with you? You never laid eyes on him. You're just some stranger.

MACON: Hey, hey, don't be so grim.

BESS: *(Crying with fury.)* I wanna go home. I'll die if I stay here. I don't wanna die in this miserable, filthy territory!

JACK: Look at her crying. She's a woman alright.

BESS: Oh, how can this be? My husband's dead. He's gone. He's dead. I never even got to meet him or shake his hand or say, "I do." "I do, I do." I worked on saying them words the whole way here. Over cliffs, across streams, in the rain, in the dust. "I do, I do." Every dream I ever had I said in them words. "I do, I do, I do, I do…"

JACK: I'm gonna knock her down.

MACON: Don't do that.

(Jack shoves Macon aside, then goes and knocks down Bess. Macon comes at him with a knife. He takes her by the hair and slings her to the ground.)

JACK: *(To Macon.)* You're out west now. Things are different here. *(To Bess.)* Come on with me. I'm gonna marry you. But I won't have you crying. Never again. You got that clear?

BESS: Yes.

JACK: Let's go.

(They exit. Macon gets to her feet.)

MACON: That was something. I didn't mind that. That was something.

(Macon whistles to herself. William Curtis enters. He is neatly dressed. He wears a patch over the left eye. There is a scar down the same side of his face.)

WILL: Hello. Are you Miss Macon Hill?

MACON: Yes, I am.

WILL: I'm Mr. William Curtis. I've come for you. You're to be my wife.

MACON: Well, here I am. I'm ready to ride.

(They exit.)

SCENE II

Later that day. Jack's cabin. Jack sits in a chair. Bess is pulling filth-covered blankets off the floor.

BESS: This is a beautiful home. Some women get squeamish over fleas and ticks and lice, not me. We'll root 'em out by bathing with plenty of sheep-dip and then we'll add kerosene to the sheep-dip and boil all our clothes and bedding in the sheep-dip and kerosene. That'll root 'em out. Kill 'em all for sure. I'm gonna be happy here. I can feel it coming.

JACK: Don't start messing with things around here. That's not my way.

BESS: Uh huh. Uh huh.

JACK: *(A beat.)* I'm not used to you being here.

BESS: *(A beat.)* I can—I can cook something.

JACK: There's nothing t'cook. Got some dried beef on the shelf.

BESS: I'll fetch it. *(She gets the dried beef and brings it back to the table.)* Here.

JACK: Thanks.

BESS: Welcome. You're welcome.

(They chew on the dried beef in silence.)

BESS: Mr. Flan.

JACK: Yeah?

BESS: Do you like singing?

JACK: No. *(A beat.)*

BESS: Your brother said he liked singing.

JACK: You never met my brother.

BESS: He wrote it in his letters.

JACK: That he liked singing?

BESS: Yes.

JACK: Never said nothing to me about it.

BESS: I got his letters, if ya wanna look at 'em.

(Jack nods.)

BESS: Here they are. He wrote three of 'em.

(Jack takes the letters and looks at all three of them.)

BESS: In each one of 'em he mentions something about singing. Says there's not much music out here, but for the birds. I was hoping to change things for him. See, me, well, I sing—

(Jack tosses down the letters.)

BESS: Pretty letters, ain't they?

JACK: I don't read writing.

BESS: Oh, well, I could read 'em for ya. *(Bess picks up one of the letters and starts to read it.)* "Dear Miss Bess Johnson, I was overjoyed to receive your correspondence accepting my humble proposal of marriage. I sincerely believe you will not be disappointed living in the west. The skies out here are the largest I have witnessed. The stars hang so low you feel you could reach up and touch them with your hand—"

(Jack grabs the letter out of her hand. He tears up the letters.)

JACK: Hey! You don't read t'me! I ain't no baby. You ain't no schoolmarm. You got that clear?! Nobody reads me nothing! Nothing! Nothing at all!

BESS: *(Overlapping.)* Don't tear 'em! Please, don't tear 'em!

JACK: I did! I tore 'em! They're torn! And I don't want you singing. There'll be no singing. I don't tolerate no singing never. You hear me?

BESS: I do.

JACK: Hey, you better not start crying. Remember what I warned you about crying?

BESS: I won't. I won't never be crying. I'm telling ya. I can do things right.

SCENE III

Same day. William's cabin. Will and Macon enter.

WILL: Come on in. Here we are.

MACON: I see.

WILL: What do you mean by that, Miss Hill?

MACON: Nothing. I just see—Here we are.

WILL: I lost it in a mining accident.

MACON: What?

WILL: No need playing coy. I see you see it's missing.

MACON: Oh, your eye.

WILL: Yeah.

MACON: Oh, well, I did observe it'd been removed.

WILL: Man knocked it out with a mining pick. It was an honest mistake. There was no violence or malice intended.

MACON: Hmm. Well, I bet you wish it didn't happen.

WILL: I intend to order a glass one just as soon as finances permit. It'll be brown, same color as the one I have left.

MACON: Uh huh.

WILL: You can tell me right now if this makes a difference. I'll send you back if it does.

MACON: I ain't going back.

WILL: Alright. *(Pause.)* Miss Hill?

MACON: Yeah?

WILL: I got something for you.

MACON: What?

WILL: It's a ring. A ruby ring. *(He takes out a ring.)*

MACON: Oh, I cherish rings.

WILL: It was my wife's.

MACON: Your wife's.

WILL: Yes, she died.

MACON: Oh.

WILL: Last winter. It was snowing. *(Pause.)* She once had a photograph taken of her. Would you like to see it?

MACON: Alright.

WILL: *(He hands her a photograph.)* Her name was Barbara Jane.

MACON: What'd she die from?

WILL: No one could say for sure. She took to bed. A long time I stood by her. One night she coughed up both her lungs. There was nothing to be done.

MACON: She looks pretty sickly.

WILL: I thought she was beautiful.

MACON: Well, I don't think I want her ring.

WILL: Why not?

MACON: Could have her sickness on it. I don't want no part of it.

WILL: She never wore the ring when she was sick. She only wore it the first year of our marriage.

MACON: Why's that?

WILL: She lost three fingers in a sheep-shearing accident. One of 'em was the ring finger.

MACON: Well, y'all certainly seem t'be plagued with all sorts of disfiguring misfortunes around here.

WILL: If the ring won't do, I'll get a piece of tin and bend it around for ya. Maybe in time I can get ya another ring with a stone in it.

MACON: I'd appreciate it.

WILL: The Marrying Squire will be here at the end of the month. At that time we'll be wed.

MACON: Uh huh.

(They glance at each other, then turn away in silence.)

SCENE IV

Three months later. A summer's night. In a field. Bess is calling out to Macon who has disappeared into the night.

BESS: Macon! Macon, you out there? Where are you? Where'd you go? Indians could be lurking! Come back! Macon!

(Macon runs onstage, breathless with excitement.)

MACON: I almost touched it!

BESS: I thought you was lost in the dark.

MACON: I almost did.

BESS: Indians might a' captured you.

MACON: From the top of that far-off hill I almost felt it.

BESS: What?

MACON: That little silver star. The one sitting there so low in the sky. See it?

BESS: Uh-huh.

MACON: Stars send off chills. Closer you get, the more chill you feel. Go on, try it. Go on, reach up for it.

(Bess reaches up to touch a star.)

MACON: There you go! Jump! Jump! Did ya feel the chill?

BESS: Maybe I might a' felt some sort of small chill.

MACON: The thing we gotta look out for is a falling star. You ever seen a falling star?

BESS: No.

MACON: Well, now, when we see one of them, we gotta run for it. I know I can touch one of them. *(Macon whistles.)*

BESS: That's a nice tune. I never heard it.

MACON: It's a good song. You wanna learn it?

BESS: Oh, I don't sing no more. Jack don't like it.

MACON: Jack don't like singing?

BESS: His brother, Michael, liked singing. But Jack don't.

(Macon whistles a moment.)

MACON: I don't mean t'speak out, but your husband, well, he don't seem t'got a whole lot to recommend him.

BESS: Oh, he suits me fine. Why, I ain't sure we ain't a match made in heaven. Soon as we get the inheritance money Mr. Michael Flan left. Everything'll be rosy.

MACON: Well, I sure hope things work out for you. I got doubts about my own predicament.

BESS: Don't ya get on with your new husband? He seems a good man t'me.

MACON: Well, I hate to criticize Mr. Curtis. I know he does try; but, well, frankly, I'm allergic to him physically.

BESS: Is it 'cause of his eye?

MACON: Could be part of it. But even with one more eye, I might find him repulsive. *(Macon whistles.)*

BESS: Show me how t'do that.

MACON: What? Whistle?

BESS: Yeah.

MACON: Easiest thing in the world. Just watch me. I'll show ya how.

(Macon whistles. Bess tries to imitate her. She fails. Macon starts to laugh.)

BESS: I can't get it!

MACON: You will!

BESS: When?

MACON: Soon! *(Running off.)* Come on! I wanna show you the white jasmine. They're in bloom now down by the pond.

(They exit.)

SCENE V

Three months later. Autumn. Jack is walking down a path near his property. He carries a load of mining equipment. He sees something coming. He hides behind a rock. Macon appears carrying a bundle. She wears a cape and is whistling. Jack takes out his six-shooter, aims it at Macon, and fires. Macon screams in horror and throws the bundle up in the air.

MACON: *Aah!*

(Jack saunters out from behind the rock brandishing the pistol.)

MACON: You trying to kill me?!

JACK: If I was, you'd be dead. *(A beat.)* Better watch out. Bullets make me
smile.

*(Jack shoots off the gun and then exits. Macon stands frozen with fear and
fury. Bess enters.)*

BESS: Macon, you alright?

MACON: Yeah. It was Jack. He seen a snake.

BESS: He kill it?

MACON: Scared it away. Here, I got two small items for ya. Coffee and some
shoes.

BESS: Thank you, Macon, but I don't need t'take things from you no more.
Me and Jack, well, everything has turned around.

MACON: You talking on account of Lockwood's mine?

BESS: That's right. Jack purchased it last night with all the inheritance money
Mr. Michael Flan left. It's sugared with pure gold like a town of fairies
been dancing there.

(Macon whistles for a moment, then stops.)

MACON: Pause a moment, Bess. Use the round thing above your shoulders
and tell me why anyone in this world would sell a mine laden with pure
gold?

BESS: —Mr. Lockwood's very old. His eyesight's poor.

MACON: Well, his mind is sharp.

BESS: What're you telling?

MACON: I know that mine. It's dry as a parched tongue. Lockwood salted that
claim with gold dust just to lead greedy fools astray.

BESS: I hope that ain't so. 'Cause we paid him for it. We paid him all we had.
Oh, what's gonna become of us now? Times is already harder than hard.

MACON: I know. I seen it coming. Now it's arriving at the front door.

BESS: Not at your door. Things are going good for you and Will Curtis.

MACON: Maybe in your eyes you see it that way. But me, I've come to a
staunch conclusion. We gotta go. We gotta go now. We could leave here
tonight.

BESS: Where'd we go?

MACON: West. We'd be going west.

BESS: Which way west?

MACON: Out past the Jack pine and yellow cedar, off through the grass that
grows scarlet red across the plains, and on and on and onward.

BESS: We'd die of thirst and famine.

MACON: We'll drink plentiful before starting out, then chew constantly on small sticks to help prevent parching. Wild fruits grow all in abundance. Ripe plums will cool our fevered lips.

BESS: What about the Indians?

MACON: I got a cup of cayenne pepper and a corn knife t'take care of 'em. Whatever happens it don't matter. Why limit the limitless. I'll write a novel about it all and put you in it. Go with me.

BESS: I can't go.

MACON: Why not?

BESS: I'm married.

MACON: He don't treat ya no good.

BESS: I'll learn t'make him.

MACON: You can't change his nature.

BESS: I'm here to try. You go on. You go without me. Please. Ya don't need me.

MACON: You're my one friend.

BESS: I ain't special.

MACON: You looked my way.

BESS: I can't go. I gave out my oath.

MACON: *(A beat.)* Here's the coffee. It's from parched corn and sorghum sweetening, but better than the dried carrot variety you been drinking. And take these shoes; those flaps of skin will never get you through the winter.

BESS: I'll pay ya back someday.

MACON: Don't mention it. I like giving gifts. It's who I am.

SCENE VI

A year later. Fall. A clearing.

WILL: *(Offstage.)* Hey, let go of that wood! You ain't stealing no more of my wood!

JACK: *(Offstage.)* Stealing? I ain't stealing nothing!
(A crack of wood offstage.)

JACK: Ow! *(Jack is thrown onstage.)*

WILL: I'll kill you, you son of a bitch!

JACK: You calling me a thief?

WILL: That's my wood. Pay me for it fair.

JACK: Miser.

WILL: Shiftless.

JACK: Blind mouse, one-eyed, scar-faced farmer—

WILL: *(Overlapping.)* Lazy, no-good, fool's gold miner—

(Jack and Will tear into each other. The fight is brutal. Macon enters. She carries a walking stick and wears field glasses around her neck. She dives into the fight, knocking the men apart with her stick.)

MACON: Hey, hey, what's going on here? Stop it! Please! Hey! We're all neighbors here. Will Curtis, what is wrong?

WILL: He wants to freeload more of our wood. Hasn't paid me for the last five bundles. He ain't getting nothing else for free.

MACON: Will. Please! There's a bobcat caught in the trap line. Better go check on it before it gets loose. I don't want it on our hands.

WILL: *(To Jack.)* You get off my place. *(Will exits.)*

JACK: Good thing he went off. I might a' had t'kill him.

MACON: You come here looking for wood?

(Jack looks away from her.)

MACON: You know where the woodpile is. You take some and haul it on home.

JACK: Just so you'll know, I got things in the works, irons in the fire. Nothing worries me.

MACON: You oughta look to salted pork. Last year we put up 1,560 pounds at three-and-a-half cents a pound.

JACK: It don't interest me. I'd rather gamble for the high stakes. Afternoon, May Ann.

MACON: What?

JACK: May Ann. It's a prettier name than Macon. Its suits you better. I think I'll call you that.

MACON: Tell Bess she can keep the needle she borrowed. I won't need it back till Monday.

JACK: Uh huh.

MACON: She's had a hard summer, losing that baby. You need t'watch after her.

JACK: Is that what I need? Is that what I need, May Ann?

MACON: That's not my name.

JACK: It is to me.

(Jack exits. Macon pauses a moment, then looks after Jack through the field glasses. Will enters.)

WILL: Bobcat got loose. Chewed off its paw.

(Macon quickly stops looking through the field glasses.)

MACON: Will.

WILL: What?

MACON: I told him t'take some wood.

WILL: You what?

MACON: All they got t' burn is green twigs.

WILL: I don't like that, Macon. Why, that man's a freeloading ne'er-do-well. We don't want nothing to do with him.

MACON: Still I gotta look out for Bess. She's a friend of mine.

WILL: I don't understand about her and you. She's not special. Just some joyless creature with sawdust for brains.

MACON: Don't say that.

WILL: Look, I've observed in her strong symptoms of derangement that just ain't healthy. That ain't right.

MACON: Don't you got one drop of human kindness inside your whole bloodstream. It was just last summer she buried her infant child in a soap box under a prickly pear tree and wolves dug it up for supper.

WILL: Things haven't gone her way, that's true. Still, I cannot agree with her strange and gruesome behavior. How she dresses up that prairie dog of hers in a calico bonnet and shawl; sits there rocking it on the porch, talking to it just like it was a somebody.

MACON: People do strange things t'get by.

WILL: That may be. But everybody's got to make their own way. If they drop down, it ain't for you to carry them.

(Macon turns away from him and looks through the field glasses into the distance.)

WILL: I just don't like being exploited. I don't like the exploitation. People should earn what they get. What're you looking at?

MACON: Checking the cows.

WILL: How're the cows? Can you see the cows?

MACON: I see 'em.

WILL: Anyway, what's a load of wood? After all, we seem to be prospering. Last year we sold 1,560 pounds of salt pork at three-and-a-half cents a pound. Friday I'll go into town and see if the copper kettle you ordered from St. Louis has been delivered in the mail. After all, they're the ones with problems and burdens. If their luck doesn't change, they won't make it through the winter. They'll starve to death by Christmas. When the copper kettle comes, it will improve the looks of our cabin. You spoke about it before. You said it would add cheerfulness.

SCENE VII

Christmas, months later. Night. Jack's cabin. It is snowing. The wind is howling. Jack sits staring. Bess is on the floor, picking shreds of wheat out of the straw mattress.

BESS: You know what, Jack? Jack, you know what? I think it's Christmas. I've been thinking that all day.

JACK: I don't know.

BESS: I could be wrong. But I might be right. There's not much wheat in all this straw. Not much wheat to speak of. Would you agree it could be Christmas?

JACK: Where's the prairie dog?

BESS: Of course, Macon would have been here by now if it'd been Christmas. She was planning to bring us a galore of a spread. I was looking forward to it. Maybe the bad weather's put her off. The blizzards. Blinding blizzards for weeks now. Keeping Christmas from our front door. Jack, something happened to Prairie Dog.

JACK: It did?

BESS: It was when you went out trying to kill us something this morning.

JACK: Yeah.

BESS: This man came by. Some wandering sort of vagabond dressed in rags. Dirt rags. He wanted a handout. Food, you know.

JACK: We don't have anything.

BESS: I told him. I sent him on his way. "We don't have anything," I said. "I gotta go through the straw in the bed mattress picking out slivers of wheat so we won't starve here to death. I don't have food to spare some unknown wanderer." He asked me for just a cup of warm water, but I said no. Not because we couldn't spare it, but just because I didn't want him around here on the premises anymore. Something about him. His face was red and dirty. His mouth was like a hole. *(About the wheat.)* This is not gonna be enough for supper, this right here.

JACK: So what happened to the dog?

BESS: As he, as the vagabond was leaving, Prairie Dog followed after him barking. He picked up a stone and grabbed her by the throat and beat her head in with it. With the rock. She's out back in a flour sack. I'd burn her to ashes, if only we could spare the wood.

JACK: This is your fault.

BESS: Yes it is.

JACK: You're so weak. You make me sick. Christ, you're useless. I may just have to kill you.

BESS: You know what? I think it is Christmas. It's Christmas, after all. And you know what? I got something for you. I been saving it for Christmas. A surprise for you. A present. A Christmas gift. I been hoarding it away for you, but the time has come. The day has arrived. Merry Christmas, Jack. *(She produces a sack of cornmeal.)*

JACK: What is that?

BESS: Cornmeal.

JACK: Cornmeal. What're you gonna do with that?

BESS: Make you some cornbread. Cornbread for Christmas. A surprise.

JACK: Yeah. Yeah, a real big surprise. Boo! Surprise! Boo!

BESS: It's special. It's a treat. Hot cornbread. A lot better than that ash-baked bread we used to have.

JACK: Yeah, sure. But I ain't gonna choke t'death on no ash-baked bread. I ain't gonna turn blue and purple and green till I die eating no ash-baked bread.

BESS: You ain't gonna die eating no cornbread neither.

JACK: You tell that to Mike. You tell that to my brother, Mike, who had himself a big hunk of cornbread and choked t'death on it while riding bareback over the swinging bridge.

BESS: I never knew about that. I never knew how he died. I swear it, I didn't.

JACK: You might not have known it. Possibly you never was told it. But I bet you guessed it. I bet you dreamed it up. First Mike, then the baby, next Prairie Dog, now me. You want us all dead, don't you? You like things dead. You want it all for yourself. Well, here, have it. Take it. *(He throws a handful of cornmeal in her face.)*

BESS: No—

JACK: *(He continues throwing the cornmeal at her.)* There. There you go.

BESS: Stop.

JACK: Take it all!

BESS: I wanted this to be good. I wanted to be your true one.

SCENE VIII

Same night. Will's cabin. Macon and Will are drinking cordials. It is Christmas.

MACON: I don't think so, Mr. Curtis. I don't believe so in the slightest. We're in no agreement, whatsoever.

WILL: Reliance on one crop is too risky. I'll say no more.

MACON: I'm telling you wheat promises the largest cash return and there's nothing comparable to it.

WILL: Besides there're other cautions to attend. We don't wanna expand too rapidly. We oughtn't get ahead of ourselves.

MACON: But there's no way to get ahead of ourselves. Not with the Union Pacific track-laying crew coming through. We gotta look to the future. Did I steer you wrong about the pork prices? No, I did not. We bought up Dan Raymond's east field with the profits from salt pork. Turn that over in your head a minute.

WILL: Listen here—

MACON: Ssh! Ssh. Just turn it over. Churn it around. Let it fester. Here, now, I'll pour both of us another cordial. After all, it's Christmas. *(She pours out two drinks.)*

WILL: You have a nice way of pouring that drink. It looks delicate.

MACON: It's got a pretty color. The liquor.

WILL: Macon.

MACON: Huh?

WILL: There's, there's something for you. St. Nicholas left it, I guess.
(He hands her a gift with a card. She starts to open it.)

MACON: A present for me.

WILL: Wait, wait. There's a card. Read the card.

MACON: Oh, yeah. "Merry Christmas, Mrs. Curtis. You are sweet as honey. From Brown Spot." Brown Spot?

WILL: *(He laughs.)* Yeah.

MACON: Brown Spot, the cow?

WILL: She's your favorite one, ain't she?

MACON: Not really, I prefer Whitey.

WILL: Oh, oh, well, pretend it was from Whitey. It was supposed to be from Whitey. Alright, now open the gift. But first, tell me, what do you guess it's gonna be?

MACON: I don't know. I'm hoping for a thing.

WILL: I got a feeling it's what you're hoping for.
(She opens the gift.)
WILL: Well?
MACON: What is it?
WILL: It's an eye. A glass eye. It's brown, see?
MACON: Oh, yeah.
WILL: I promised you I'd get one and I've kept that promise. Want me to put it in?
MACON: Alright.
WILL: I need a looking glass. *(He goes to put in the eye.)* I tried it on before, right when it arrived. I been saving it five weeks now. It ain't real... *(He groans.)* ...comfortable, but it makes a difference in my appearance. I think you'll appreciate it. *(He turns to her, wearing the eye.)* Hello.
MACON: Hi.
WILL: What do you think? Looks pretty real, huh?
MACON: Uh-huh.
WILL: If it wasn't for the scar, no one could guess which was real and which was glass.
MACON: Don't it hurt inside there?
WILL: Sure, but that's part of it. I'll adjust. Give me another cordial. That'll help it.
(Macon pours him another drink.)
WILL: I like to watch that pouring. Your hands. Delicate.
(She brings him the drink and starts to leave.)
WILL: *(He gently holds her arm.)* Stay here. *(He drinks the drink.)* Macon, I know most times you don't feel like being nice to me. But I thought tonight since I got this new eye, maybe you would.
MACON: *(A beat.)* Alright. *(Macon unbuttons her top and takes it off.)* Mr. Curtis?
WILL: Yes?
MACON: Have you thought any more about planting wheat in the east field?
WILL: Not much.
MACON: It'd be a good idea.
WILL: Alright if that's what you think. We'll do it that way.
(There is a loud, desperate knocking at the door.)
BESS: *(Offstage.)* Macon! Macon, let me in. Please. Let me in. Please, please.
(Macon rushes to the door. Bess enters. She wears a thin coat. She is covered with snow, wheat and cornmeal. Frozen blood is caked to her forehead.)
MACON: Bess, Bess, come in. Get in. Look at you. You've been hurt.

BESS: You've got to help. My husband Jack—he's in an insane condition.

MACON: She's freezing. Bring a blanket. My God. My God, Bess.

BESS: He took a torch and set our cabin on fire. It's burning hot, hot in the snow.

MACON: Will, we gotta go see to Jack Flan.

WILL: I'll see to him. I'll go. Both of you stay here. I'll handle his derangement. *(Will exits.)*

MACON: Here, get outta these wet boots. How in the world did you get here? How did you cross the gulch in this blizzard and not freeze to death?

BESS: Freeze t'death. Freeze t'death. I like the sound of that prediction. I long for the flutter of angel's wings.

MACON: Calm down. You're in a fit of delirium. Let me wash off your face for you.

BESS: It's all uncoiling. The springs in my mind. In my body. They're all loose and jumping out. Rusted and twisted.

MACON: I should have come to you. I should have braved the storm. I had your Christmas spread all packed up, I just been waiting for a break in the weather.

BESS: I wish you'd come. I been so lonely. I been going outside and hugging icy trees, clinging to them like they was alive and could hold me back. I feel so empty sometimes I eat warm mud, trying to fill up the craving.

MACON: Hush now. You're with me now. Let me brush out your hair. You got straw and sticks in your hair.

BESS: I just wanna say—I just wanna say—

MACON: What?

BESS: Early disappointments are embittering my life.

MACON: I'll draw you a bath of herbs and water. Sleep will fall on you. It'll restore your peace.

BESS: Macon?

MACON: Huh?

BESS: Let's go west.

MACON: West?

BESS: Let's start all over. Let's start from scratch. See, I've tried and I've tried, but I'm starting to believe Jack, he's just not in my stars.

MACON: I have to say—I have to remember—I did, I always thought I'd make much more of myself than this. My husband gave me a Christmas card from our cow. Still, I need to think things out. There's a lot we don't know. Practical knowledge, reality and facts.

BESS: But we will go?

MACON: Oh yes, we'll go. Soon we'll go.

BESS: I realize now—now that you're brushing my hair, that I love you so much more—so much more than anyone else.

SCENE IX

Over two years have passed. It is spring. Outside Will's cabin. Bright sun shines down on Jack who is sitting on a fence eating a large piece of pound cake. He wears dress pants, but is barefoot and bare-chested. His hair is slicked back. Will enters, barefoot and bare-chested. He carries two freshly pressed dress shirts.

WILL: Here're the shirts.

JACK: Thanks.

WILL: It's gonna be some feast we're having, some celebration.

(Will puts on his shirt. Jack eats cake.)

WILL: Can you believe it's been four years since the Marrying Squire came through here and joined us all together in holy matrimony?

JACK: Happy anniversary.

WILL: I don't know. Time travels.

JACK: Well, what else can it do?

WILL: Yeah…Have you checked into that new land that's opened up for homesteaders?

JACK: I hear there ain't nothing available that ain't worthless.

WILL: Huh. Well, have you given any more thought to rebuilding on your own property?

JACK: Everything's burnt up over there.

WILL: Then what're ya gonna do?

JACK: About what?

WILL: This is supposed to be the deadline. Our anniversary. We made a deal, remember? You and your wife could stay here until this anniversary, then your time was up.

JACK: Fine. Our time's up. Fine.

WILL: You have been living here over two years now. I know you was sick for a time, but we've been more than generous. That cabin's damn small.

JACK: Alright, we'll go.

WILL: When?

JACK: Now. Right now.

WILL: Where're you gonna go?

JACK: Don't know. What do you care?

WILL: Well, don't go tonight. Wait a while more. Tonight's a celebration. Macon's been preparing all week. We best not spoil it.

JACK: Have it your way. *(Jack finishes the pound cake.)*

WILL: Was that the pound cake Macon brought out for us to sample?

JACK: Yeah. Damn good cake. Warm and moist, right outta the oven. *(Will hunts around for another piece of cake.)*

WILL: Where's my piece?

JACK: It's all gone.

WILL: She said she left a piece for me. She said she left two pieces.

JACK: Oh, well, I ate both of 'em.

WILL: Both of 'em. You ate both of 'em. But one of 'em was for me. One of 'em was my piece.

JACK: Sorry, I was hungry.

WILL: Well, damnation, I'm hungry, too! I'm hungry, too!

JACK: Look, you don't wanna ruin your supper. We're having a huge supper. It'd be a shame to spoil it.

WILL: Well, you didn't mind spoiling your supper. It didn't bother you none. Damn, I wish I had that cake.

JACK: Well, ya don't. It's gone. I hogged it. What can ya do?

WILL: Nothing. Just nothing. Not a damn thing.

JACK: Here, some crumbs. There's some crumbs left.

WILL: Forget it. I don't want it. Forget it. *(Will picks up some crumbs with his fingers and sticks them into his mouth.)*

SCENE X

Same day. Inside Will's cabin. Bess wears a cape. She is walking around the room whistling and waving a list in the air. Macon sits at a table putting a waterfall hairpiece on her head.

BESS: The list is complete. Completely complete. The day has arrived. The time has come. We have it all here: tallow, rice, tea, chip beef, grease bucket, water barrel, one kettle, one fry pan, powder, lead, shot—check it out. See for yourself. The list is complete.

MACON: Do we have heavy rope?

BESS: Yes, we do. There it is right there.

MACON: And a tar bucket.

BESS: Tar bucket, tar bucket, right there. Right there. *(A beat.)* We should go tonight.

MACON: On our wedding anniversary?

BESS: Why drag things out?

MACON: It would be a cruel blow to our husbands, leaving them on our marriage day.

BESS: They'll adjust. They have each other.

MACON: I think we should wait a little.

BESS: It's just we've been waiting so long.

MACON: I wanna see what the pumpkin patch produces. I suspect, it's gonna yield a phenomenal crop.

BESS: I don't care about the pumpkins.

MACON: And I got that rainbow-colored petticoat ordered. I can't leave before it arrives. And next month I'm to be the judge of the baking contest. Last year I won first prize. I got t'stay here and judge. It's your duty if ya win first prize.

BESS: I got this feeling that you're putting me off. You swore last time soon as I got the new items on the list we'd go. Please, I can't stay here no longer.

MACON: Things aren't so bad for you now that you and Jack have moved in here with us. You seem content most of the time.

BESS: I try not to show my hurt. I hide it in different parts of the house. I bury jars of it in the cellar, throw buckets of it down the well, iron streaks of it into the starched clothes and hang them in the closet. I just can't hide it no more. We got t'go now. You promised. You swore.

MACON: Stop pushing at me. I got things here. Out there, I don't know what.
(Jack enters wearing his clean shirt. He is still barefoot.)

JACK: *(To Macon.)* Hi.

MACON: Hi.

JACK: Good pound cake.

MACON: Thanks.

JACK: Will's out there upset. Says I ate his piece a' cake.

MACON: I told you one was for him.

JACK: I was hungry.

MACON: Shame on you, Jack Flan. I'll go take this bowl out to him. He can lick the batter.
(Macon exits. There is a horrible moment of silence. Bess gets Jack's boots and takes them to him.)

BESS: I polished your boots, Jack.

(Jack puts on a boot. Bess stands staring at the floor.)

JACK: I can't see myself in the toe.

(Bess kneels down and slowly starts to shine the boot. Jack gives her a glance filled with cold-blooded disdain.)

SCENE XI

That night. Will's cabin, after the anniversary supper. Will, Macon, Jack, and Bess are all gathered.

JACK: Listen to me. I'm asking you. I'm making a point. Why do we have to be hungry? Why do we have to be hot or cold? Why do we have to stink? If someone could find a cure, a potion, an elixir for one of these conditions or possibly all four of 'em, that person could make a whole lot of money. Picture a killing. Picture money to burn. The facts are simple. Nobody wants to stink. Not really. Not if they thought about it. They'd come to me; I'd give them the potion; they'd cross my palm with silver; thank you very much, next customer.

MACON: It sounds like an exciting prospect.

JACK: It's how my mind works.

WILL: Well, he's right about one thing, nobody wants to stink.

BESS: I know I don't. I used to put vanilla behind my ears, but Jack said I smelt like food.

JACK: I'd love another piece of that delicious pound cake. It melts like butter in my mouth.

(Macon takes the last piece of cake and pushes it onto Jack's plate.)

MACON: Well, I'm delighted nothing's going to waste.

WILL: Was that the last piece?

MACON: *(Nods.)* Uh huh.

JACK: *(Biting into the cake.)* Mmm, mmm. You cook better than anybody I ever knew.

MACON: Thank you, Jack, but Bess helped out a lot.

BESS: Not much really.

JACK: She's good at scrubbing dishes, but all her cakes fall flat as nickels.

MACON: Why, that's not true, Jack Flan. Why, that two-layer strawberry cake she made for my birthday was a sensation.

BESS: Oh, no, Macon, you don't remember. It was a five-layer carrot cake I made for you, but it only rose half an inch high. We all got such a big laugh out of it.

MACON: Oh, that's right. I remember now.

WILL: Your wife sure is good for a laugh, I'll say that. Remember when she asked me, "How'd I get my eye t'grow back?"
(Everyone laughs.)

WILL: She thought this glass eye was a real eye that just sprouted back there in the socket like a radish.

JACK: She's a howl alright.

BESS: *(Cheerfully.)* I guess I've just been dreadfully stupid all my life.

MACON: Don't listen to them. They're only having fun. It's all foolishness. Why, no one's even noticed the bow in Bess's hair. Turn around, please. Now isn't that a lovely sight?

JACK: Yes, it is. She's got pretty hair. Her eyes are too close together. But she's got pretty hair. *(To Macon.)* What about you? Your hair looks different tonight. What happened to it?

MACON: Waterfall curls. I ordered them from Boston. They're the latest sensation.

JACK: Ain't they something.

WILL: Delicate.

JACK: Lovely, lovely, lovely.

BESS: The ribbon's my favorite color. It's blue. Macon lent it to me. It's her favorite color, too. We're alike, us two. *(Bess points to a bucket of daisies.)* Both of us love daisies. They're our favorite flower.

MACON: Oh, daisies aren't my favorite flower. My favorite flowers are tulips.

BESS: Tulips?

MACON: They grow in this small country called Holland. They're the most beautiful flowers in the world. Daisies don't compare. Why, daisies are really nothing more than common weeds.

BESS: Well, I'm sure, if I ever got to see a tulip, they'd be my favorite flower, too.

MACON: Maybe someday we'll all go over to Holland and pick rows and rows of tulips. That would be a time to remember. Filling our skirts with golden tulips and tossing 'em up in the sky! Ho! Oh, I feel like being boisterous, let's have some celebrating! I wanna dance!

JACK: Alright!

WILL: Go ahead!

BESS: *(Overlapping.)* Me too! Me too! I love to dance!

MACON: I have a step I know. It's from the quadrille. It's the latest dancing fashion.

JACK: Let's see it!

MACON: Everyone's gotta clap!

(Macon, Bess, and Will all start clapping.)

MACON: Come on, get the rhythm going! That's good! Keep it going! Jack Flan, why aren't you clapping?

JACK: I don't do anything to music. I don't dance to it. I don't clap to it. I like to watch it, but I won't join it.

MACON: You are as ridiculous as ever, surely more so. Here, hold my combs for me. Hold them, silly. Hold my combs.

(Macon gives her hair combs to Jack. He holds them for her.)

MACON: *(To Will and Bess.)* Clap for me now. Louder, please! Louder! *(Macon does some fancy dance steps to the clapping.)*

BESS: Bravo! Bravo!

WILL: She's delicate! Look how delicate!

JACK: Look at her go! Swing them curls.

BESS: Oh, I wanna join in!

MACON: Come on, Bess! Take a turn!

(Bess starts dancing wildly.)

MACON: That's it! Go now! Wow! What a dancer!

WILL: Watch out! Watch out! Oh, let it ride! Yes sir, yes sir, let it ride!

(Bess kicks her foot up high and falls on her butt.)

BESS: Oops!

MACON: Oh, well, that was good! That was good! Give her a hand!

BESS: I fell down. I can't do things right. I think I'm clumsy.

WILL: You took a spill alright. Up in the air you went and down again.

JACK: Try to be more ladylike. Everyone saw all your things under there.

MACON: Come on, take another spin.

BESS: I don't wanna dance anymore.

MACON: Come on. You can do it.

BESS: No, please, let me be.

MACON: Well, I know, why don't you sing for us?

BESS: I don't sing. You know I don't sing.

JACK: That's right. She told me when we got married that she never sang. Didn't you mention that the very first day we met?

BESS: That's right. At one time I did sing, but I don't anymore.

MACON: Well, if you sang once, you can sing again. Why, I believe I've even heard you singing when you wash the clothes.

BESS: Oh, that's not singing; that's more like humming.

MACON: Well, if you can hum, you can sing. Please, sing a song for us. I'd like to hear it.

BESS: Can I, Jack?

JACK: I don't know, can you?

BESS: Well, I do remember this one tune.

MACON: Good, let's hear it. You're on stage now. The stage is set for your song. The curtain is rising on you. Welcome Bess Flan and her singing! *(Macon claps.)*

BESS: *(Singing.)* Down in the valley
The valley so low
Hang your head over
Hear the wind blow
Hear the wind blow, dear
Hear the wind blow
Angels in Heaven
I love you so
Roses are blue, dear
Roses are blue
Roses are blue
They're so, so blue
Blue, real, real blue…

MACON: That was wonderful.

BESS: I—I guess I've forgotten the song. Some of it. How it goes.

WILL: I know that song. I've heard it before. It didn't sound right.

MACON: Do you know another one?

JACK: She didn't know that one.

MACON: She knew most of it and she's got such a lovely voice.

JACK: I don't know a thing about singing, but it seems to me, if you're gonna sing a song, you need to know the words to the song you pick.

BESS: I used to know a lot of songs. I knew 'em all by heart. It's just I haven't sung ever since I come out here. It felt funny opening up my throat to sing. Like it was somebody else who was singing. Somebody else who wasn't me. I think I'm gonna go outside in the moonlight and pick some night-blooming jasmine out by the pond. Their fragrance draws me to 'em. The smell of 'em and the moonlight. *(Bess exits.)*

JACK: For no apparent reason, she seems to have lost her mind.

MACON: I think you hurt her feelings about her singing.

JACK: What? I did not. I didn't say anything against her singing except she should brush up on the words.

MACON: Maybe you should go see to her.

JACK: She don't want me to see to her.

MACON: Why not?

JACK: She's mad at me about her damn singing.

WILL: All the cake's gone, I suppose.

MACON: Yes.

WILL: My eye's burning. I'm ready to take it out for the evening.
    (Macon starts for the door.)

WILL: Where're you going?

MACON: Out to see to her. *(Macon exits. Offstage.)* Bess...Bess... *(etc.)*

WILL: *(A beat.)* Think they'll be alright out there in the dark?

JACK: I don't know.

WILL: There're wild animals out there this time of night. Coyotes for sure. Bears and wolves.

JACK: Indians, maybe.

WILL: Macon! Macon! *(Will exits.)*

MACON: *(Offstage.)* What? Huh?

WILL: *(Offstage.)* Macon, come back in here. I'll get Bess.
    (Jack gets up, goes and pours himself a drink. Macon enters. Jack looks at her, then downs the drink.)

JACK: Whiskey?

MACON: No.

JACK: *(Pouring himself another drink.)* Are you sure...May Ann?

MACON: Don't you call me that. Ever.

JACK: Alright. Here're your combs back. I been holding them for you. Pretty combs. Lucky, too. Lucky to be running all through your hair.

MACON: Don't talk to me. Sit there and don't talk to me.

JACK: *(A beat.)* May Ann; May Ann; May Ann.

MACON: Shut up.

JACK: You been circulating in my head. All through my head. You're more vivid to me than any other thought. I can't get you outta here. Can't knock you out; can't drink you out; can't scream you out. Never, never. You always here.

MACON: Stop it. Don't do this. Stop it.

JACK: Can't you see that I am outta control of my feelings over you?

MACON: Look, I don't want anything to do with you. I got a husband, Will. You got a wife, Bess, who is my dearest friend of mine. I would never,

ever imagine betraying her feelings. Never, ever, even if I did care for you, which I do not and never will and never could; 'cause in all honesty, there's absolutely not one thing about you I can bear to stand. You're mean and selfish and a liar and a snake; I spit on your grave, which can't get dug up fast enough and deep enough to suit me just fine.

JACK: *(A beat.)* Well, I just wanna know one thing. You tell me one thing. Why did you ask me to hold your combs for you? You chose me to hold your combs. You placed them in my hand. Why'd you do that? Huh?

MACON: Because I—you were standing there nearest to me, and I realized how I was afraid when I danced the combs would fly out of my hair and get lost in some faraway, far off corner of the room. You must know, I mean it is common knowledge, that you can have somebody hold your combs for you and still believe with your whole being and heart that you hate them and they're worse than bad, but you just need your combs held and they happen to be standing in arm's reach.

JACK: You certainly are talking a lot. Rambling on. Why's that?

MACON: I—I don't know. I'm just talking. I just feel like talking. I got this sensation that keeps on telling me that silence ain't safe.

JACK: Hush now.

MACON: No, I can't allow no silence 'cause then something real terrible's gonna happen. The world might stop moving and that could start the earth shaking and everything'll just fall into cracks and openings and horrible holes—

JACK: Just hush a moment.

MACON: No, I won't, I can't, the world will break open; the oceans will disappear; the sky will be gone; I won't; I can't; I won't—

JACK: Hush or I'll have to gag you.

MACON: It won't do no good. I'll still go on mumbling and moaning all under the gag.

JACK: Maybe then, I'll just have to break your neck. *(Jack grabs her and holds his hand to her throat.)* There now. Be very still.
(Macon freezes.)

JACK: Hear that? The world's not falling apart. Hear that?
(She nods her head.)

JACK: You can handle it, can't you?

MACON: Yes.

JACK: *(He removes his hand from her throat.)* You can handle it just fine. *(He puts his hand on her breast.)* Tell me how you can handle it.

MACON: I can.

JACK: Just fine.

MACON: Yes.

> *(They embrace with a terrible passion, tearing at each other like beasts. Finally, Macon breaks away. Tears of rage stream down her face.)*

MACON: Stay away. You viper. You twisted snake.

> *(Jack looks at her helplessly. He goes to get a drink. Macon straightens her dress and hair, then sits in a chair with her arms folded. Will comes in the door carrying Bess's cape and an arrow. His face is white. He is in a panic.)*

MACON: Will?

WILL: She's not out there by the pond. She's disappeared.

MACON: That's her cape.

WILL: I found it on the ground. And this. *(Will produces an Indian arrow from under the cape.)*

MACON: Oh my God. Where is she? What's happened?

JACK: Who's is it?

WILL: Looks like Oglala.

JACK: You think Indians got her?

> *(Macon runs to the door and calls out in the night.)*

MACON: Oh God! Bess! Bess!

> *(Will grabs Macon in the doorway.)*

WILL: Macon!

MACON: Please, God! Bess!

> *(Blackout.)*

END OF ACT I

ACT II
SCENE I

Five years later. Will's cabin. A spring night. Macon is drinking whiskey. Will and Jack are eating huge pieces of cake. Jack has a mustache.

JACK: I love this cake.

WILL: It's got a delicate flavor.

MACON: I know it's both your favorite. Happy anniversary, everyone.

WILL: Happy anniversary.

JACK: Happy anniversary.

MACON: Can you believe how fast time travels? Nine years I been living out here on this plain. Youth isn't really all that fleeting like they say. I mean, it seems solid, like it was there, the time you spend being youthful. The rest here, it just flies by, like everything'll be over before you can breathe.

JACK: I don't like to discuss time. It's not my favorite subject, I'd as soon not hear about it.

MACON: I'm sorry, Jack. I know anniversaries are hard for you. Here, let's hand out the presents.

WILL: They're some major presents this year. Some major surprises.
    (Macon hands out two gifts that are wrapped identically.)

MACON: Here you go. I ordered them from the catalogue. I hope you like 'em.

JACK: Thanks.

WILL: Thanks, Macon. *(After opening the gift.)* Well, that's nice. A fancy cup.

MACON: It's a mustache cup. So you won't get your mustache wet when you drink.

JACK: Well, that's a crafty idea. It oughta come in real handy.

WILL: I ain't got no mustache.

MACON: Oh, well, maybe you'll grow one. Jack's looks real nice on him. I think mustaches are the coming thing.

JACK: Here, pour me some cordial. Let me test mine out.

MACON: Alright, let's see.

WILL: Anyway, I could still use it. I'll just drink out of this other side.
    (Macon pours Jack a cordial. He drinks from his mustache cup successfully.)

MACON: Oh, look!

JACK: Pretty handy. Pretty handy.

WILL: Macon, I know there's concern now that the railroad's being rerouted, but I went on and splurged. I got these for you. I know they're what ya wanted. *(Will presents Macon with two red pillows.)* Scarlet plush sofa pillows. Two of 'em.

MACON: Oh, thank you, Will. Thank you! They're so pretty; aren't they pretty!

WILL: They'll cheer up the place.

MACON: They will. Oh, I appreciate it, thank you. Now, if only I could get a new room built, I'd be satisfied. But perhaps not. Seems like I've always something to wish for.

WILL: You do like the pillows though?

MACON: Uh huh.

JACK: I got a gift for you, May Ann.

MACON: You do? Why thank you, Jack.

WILL: *(About the gift.)* It looks kinda small.

(Macon opens the gift.)

MACON: A ring. It's a ring. I cherish rings.

JACK: It's sapphire blue. The color you like best.

MACON: *(Trying the ring on.)* Look, how it fits.

JACK: Just right.

WILL: I don't like him giving you a ring. I'm your husband. You're supposed t'wear my ring.

MACON: Will, I wore that tin band ya gave me till it tore right off.

WILL: I always figured to get ya another one. And now he comes in with this sapphire ring, knowing blue is your favorite color just like you was his wife or something. *(To Jack.)* It's not right! You set your own house on fire, set it aflame, burn it t'ashes and then move in here with us. Just come t'stay and don't ever leave; start giving out rings. Rings are what you give to your wife and she's not your wife. She's my wife. She don't want this ring. Save it for your own damn wife.

MACON: Will, what's wrong with you? You know he ain't got no wife.

WILL: I wouldn't be so sure about that.

MACON: I don't wanna be sure about it. I sure don't wanna be sure. But we've hunted all over for her for years.

JACK: We sent out searching parties.

MACON: We put articles in broadsides, and made inquiries to U.S. Army officers.

JACK: I never wanted to give up hope, but when that hunter from the trading post brought us that scalp...

MACON: She had such beautiful hair.

JACK: It's all I got left of her. My darling Bess. How I miss her apple butter cheeks now that they're gone.

WILL: People don't always die when they're scalped. You know that, don't ya?

JACK: Yeah.

WILL: Sometimes, they take the scalping knife and cut just a small tuft off at the crown of the head. People recover. It happens a lot. Happy anniversary, Jack. *(Will hands an official-looking letter to Jack.)*

JACK: What's this?

WILL: A letter from the U.S. Army. They got your wife. They're gonna deliver her to ya in an Army ambulance.

(Jack grabs the letter. He realizes he can't read it. Macon grabs the letter.)

WILL: A Mexican fur trader tipped off a Captain Patch at Fort Sully. The Captain says they had to threaten the Chief, Ottawa, with a massacre 'fore he'd sell her back. They got her for two horses, three blankets, a box of bullets, and a sack of glass beads.

MACON: I don't believe this. She's alive.

JACK: I wonder what she'll look like? How do people look when they've been scalped?

MACON: It says here, she's been tattooed on her arms and on her chin.

JACK: Tattooed?

MACON: It don't matter. She won't have changed that much. She's alive. They're bringing her to us and she's still alive.

SCENE II

A few days later. Bess stands rooted in the center of the room. She is barefoot. Her skin is dark and burnt; her hair is thin and sun-bleached; her chin has been tattooed. She wears an enormous dress that was lent to her at the fort. Macon and Will stand around her. Jack stands alone gazing at her from the corner of the room.

MACON: Bess. Bess. Welcome back. Welcome home. We've missed you. We've prayed for your return and here you are back from the vale of death. Fresh from pandemonium.

WILL: I don't think she likes being inside. I bet, you ain't used to having a roof over your head? It agitates ya, don't it?

JACK: No point in pumping her. She don't wanna talk.

MACON: Well, I'm sure it was an awful experience but it's over. Right now you probably could use a bath. Will, go bring a couple of buckets of water for me from the well. Jack, you go fetch the washtub.

JACK: Alright, but I bet she don't remember what a bath is.

(Will and Jack exit.)

MACON: Everything's gonna be fine. Just fine. Just very fine. In honor of your homecoming we're having a big juicy ham.

(Bess retches.)

MACON: What's wrong?

BESS: Thought of hog eaters make me choke.

MACON: What's wrong with hog? It's just pig. It's just pork.

BESS: *(Fiercely.)* Mud and water animal, bad.

MACON: Well, we could have something else. Vegetables. A lot of vegetables and pumpkin pie for dessert. You remember our pumpkin patch? Well, anyway, it's doing real well. People come by at Halloween time and pick out their own jackerlanterns. We make a little money from that venture. It comes in handy. It's not like times are flush around here. Wheat prices have dropped and the railroad's been rerouted. We're in bad debt 'cause of purchasing three fields we don't have the resources to work. But like they say, trouble comes in twos. I'm hoping someday things'll be different and we'll have an abundance. Don't you remember me at all? I'm your friend. I taught you how to whistle. *(Macon whistles.)* Don't ya remember?

(Macon whistles again; she stops. Bess looks at her. Macon whistles with a desperate intent. Bess whistles back to her, very softly.)

BESS: Friend.

MACON: Right. Yes. It's gonna be alright. Everything'll be just like it was. Sour milk will help bleach down that dark skin, and we'll get ya a brand-new dress. A blue one.

BESS: Blue.

MACON: Yeah, one that'll fit ya just right. Lord, that captain's wife musta been bigger than a mule. A real mud and water animal, that captain's wife.

BESS: Oh, big.

(They laugh.)

MACON: I don't know but somehow, you survived it.

BESS: I picture you.

MACON: What? You pictured me?

BESS: Hunt the elephant.

MACON: The elephant?

BESS: Bang, bang, bang.

MACON: I think you're gonna need some false curls. And maybe some corn-starch over that chin. Or veils. Sweet little net veils.

(Bess feels her chin.)

BESS: Ottawa.

MACON: What?

BESS: To be his bride. They mark me.

MACON: You were a bride?

BESS: *(She nods.)* Two…two children. Chante, Hunke-she. Ottawa. I thought he was true one. He gave me black horse.

MACON: No, no. He was bad. He was an Indian. He was bad.

BESS: Yes, bad. Sold me. Sold me cheap. Two horses, blanket, beads, bullets. Cheap.

MACON: Bess, you can't—don't ever tell Jack.

BESS: No.

MACON: No one else. Don't tell anyone else.

(Jack enters with the washtub.)

MACON: Jack. Jack, she's talking. She don't like pork, but she's talking.

BESS: Jack.

JACK: Look at her. She's disgusting.

MACON: Jack, don't—

JACK: *(Running on.)* She smells like old cheese.

MACON: Stop it!

JACK: *(Running on.)* I wish they'd never found her.

MACON: Hush up! Hush!

(Jack grabs Macon passionately in his arms, smelling and caressing her. He rams his fingers through her hair, tearing out her combs.)

JACK: I want you. Not her. Only you. Understand me?

MACON: *(Overlapping.)* Let me go. Let go. Get away. *(Macon pushes him away.)*

JACK: She may be back. But nothing's changed.

(Jack exits. Macon turns to Bess who stares at her with anguished eyes.)

MACON: Bess, please, he—I'm sorry. I never—You must believe me. I thought you were dead. They brought us your scalp. You were gone so long. So many years.

BESS: No. You. I saw. *(Pointing to Macon's combs.)* Combs. You gave him. He held them. I saw.

MACON: It'll be over now. I promise. I'll make it up to you. I'll make it right, I swear. Everything will be just the same.

SCENE III

A week later. A hot summer night. Will sits outside the barn hammering together a chain. He now has a mustache. Macon enters.

MACON: Have you finished?

WILL: Not yet.

MACON: It's always hot. Summer's almost over and it hasn't rained once. There's no relief.

WILL: I think you're working the ox too hard. It needs more rest. More water.

MACON: We have to work the fields.

WILL: If the ox gets sick, it'll be over for us.

MACON: What do you want? The bank is breathing down our necks. When will you finish that?

WILL: I don't know.

MACON: I need it by morning. I can't chase her and be in the fields. Not in this heat.

WILL: I don't like the idea of this.

MACON: I don't know how else to stop her from running away. She bites through rope.

WILL: Why not let her go?

MACON: She's my friend, I have to save her. We got to be patient. We got to wean her from her savage ways. She'll come around in time. God, you look—

WILL: What?

MACON: I don't know, old, I guess.

WILL: Maybe it's the mustache.

MACON: Oh yeah. You have a—you grew one.
(Macon exits. Will continues hammering on the chain.)

SCENE IV

A month later. A hot day. Outside Will's cabin. Jack aims his six-shooter at an offstage target. He fires the gun. He misses his target.

JACK: Damn. *(Jacks shoots two more bullets. He keeps missing his offstage target. This puts him in a rage.)* Damn, hell, damn.
(Macon appears from the direction of the barn.)

MACON: What are ya shooting at?

JACK: Playing cards. I used t'could split 'em at thirty paces.

MACON: Stop wasting powder.

(*Jack turns around and points the gun at her.*)

MACON: You don't scare me anymore.

JACK: And you don't make me smile. (*Jack lowers his gun.*)

MACON: Your wife's here for that.

JACK: Uh huh.

MACON: (*Softly, intensely.*) It's all over between us.

JACK: It wasn't over in the barn last night.

MACON: Well, now it is.

JACK: You been telling me that for some time. I'm starting to doubt your word.

MACON: Go clean out the chicken coop. Earn your keep.

JACK: I still smell you.

(*Jack embraces Macon. She responds.*)

MACON: (*With loathing.*) I wanna be rid of you. Why can't I be rid of you?
(*Bess appears. She wears a blue dress and is barefoot. She has a shackle around her foot and is chained to an offstage stake. Macon and Jack break apart. They stare at her for a brief moment before Jack exits toward the barn.*)

MACON: Where're your shoes? You have to wear shoes. We all wear shoes around here. And you need to keep that veil on to cover your face. Those tattoos are not proper. People frown on 'em.
(*Will enters. He looks very glum.*)

MACON: Will! Will, you're back. How'd it go? Not good? Not so good? What? Huh? Speak! Will you speak!

WILL: They won't renew the note. They're repossessing the steel-tipped plow and the barbwire. They want our horse and mule and hogs, even our ox. Everything we used as security.

MACON: They can't take our livelihood. The last two years, there's been a drought.

WILL: They've heard all about the drought.

MACON: I'll go into town. I'll fix this myself. You can never get anything done. You're incapable. I'll get my hat and gloves. I'll get this settled.
(*Macon goes into the cabin.*)

WILL: (*To Bess.*) I understand why you wanna run away. I'd let you go, but she keeps the key. Me, I'm not sure why I stay. I don't know what I expect to get. She used to be nice to me sometimes for very short intervals of time. Not anymore. I don't know what I expect to get now. I mean, from now on.

(Macon appears from the cabin wearing a hat and gloves. She carries Bess's shoes and veil.)

MACON: Have you hitched the wagon?

WILL: Not yet.

MACON: Go do it.

(Will exits for the barn. Throughout the following, Macon dresses Bess in the shoes and veil.)

MACON: Will Curtis is a very commonplace type man. Really, anyone who would spend money to buy a glass eye makes me laugh. You'll see, I'll go into that bank and come out with a loan for a windmill, a gang plow, and twenty cord of barbwire. Great invention, barbwire. Keeps what you want in and all the rest of it out. There, that's better. That blue dress looks good. You look pretty in it. I sacrificed a lot to get it for you. I want to make you happy. I'd take these chains off, if only you would stay. Will you stay? Bess. Bess. *(A beat.)* I wish you'd speak to me. *(A beat.)* No. Alright. I'll bring some daisies back for you, if I see them on the road. *(Macon exits. Bess jerks violently at her chain. She struggles with fierce rage pounding the chain. She moans with unbearable despair and finally sinks to the ground exhausted. Jack and Professor Elmore Crome, a distinguished-looking young man, enter from the barn road. Jack holds money in his hand.)*

JACK: *(Indicating Bess.)* Here she is. Right there. Go ahead. Look at her. *(Jack removes her veiled hat.)*

ELMORE: Why is she chained up?

JACK: We've had to restrain her to prevent her from returning to the wilds.

ELMORE: I see. Mrs. Flan?

JACK: I didn't say you could talk to her.

(Elmore hands Jack another bill.)

JACK: Alright. But she don't talk back.

ELMORE: How do you do, Mrs. Flan. I'm Professor Elmore Crome. It's an honor to make your acquaintance. I read about your brutal capture in a broadside. What an amazing feat to have survived such an ordeal. You're a remarkable woman. I'm in awe of your strength and courage.

JACK: She don't understand nothing you say.

ELMORE: One more word, please. I just—I just wish so much I could hear about your experiences from your own lips. I was hoping we could write a book together. A book that would help prevent others from falling prey to similar atrocities.

JACK: Write a book. Why she ain't spoke one word since they brought her back. *(Sympathetically.)* She's just a pitiful specimen.

ELMORE: Please, I have a gift for you. I brought a gift.

(He hands her a silver mirror wrapped in a handkerchief. She looks at herself in the mirror. She touches the tattoos on her chin.)

ELMORE: I know people would want to read about you. People all over the world. I'm sure you have so much to tell. So many adventures to impart. You must know a great deal about Indian ways. About their lives; about their treachery.

JACK: That's enough now.

(Bess looks Elmore in the eye. He looks back at her.)

JACK: I said time to go.

ELMORE: Good afternoon, Mrs. Flan. In all honesty, I must say, you have the bravest eyes I have ever witnessed.

(Jack and Elmore start to leave.)

BESS: Don't—

ELMORE: *(Stopping.)* What?

BESS: Go.

ELMORE: Yes.

BESS: I do. I know treachery. I could write book. A big book. All about treachery.

ELMORE: Excellent.

SCENE V

Two months later. The yard in front of Will's cabin. Will rushes onstage. He is breathing hard. His eyes are grief-stricken. He stops, sits down, and puts his hands over his face. Jack appears from the cabin carrying a pitcher of cool punch and two tin cups.

JACK: 'Morning, Will. How're things going?

WILL: The wheat's burnt dead. There's no saving it. The ox just collapsed down in the dirt. He's alive, he's struggling but he can't get back up. Could I have a drink? I'm parched.

JACK: I made this beverage for the Professor and Bess. They get real thirsty working on the book.

WILL: I just want a sip.

JACK: Sorry.

(Macon appears from the fields. She hauls a load of wilted corn. She is in a state of mad frenzy.)

MACON: Christ. Will. The ox. The look in his eyes. God, how he's suffering. Did you get the gun?

WILL: Not yet.

MACON: Go get it. Shoot him! Kill him! Blow out his brains! I can't bear it! He keeps looking at me like I owe him something!!!

(Will goes into the cabin to get a gun.)

MACON: Where were you last night?

JACK: I didn't come.

MACON: I waited for you.

JACK: I couldn't get away.

MACON: Why not?

(Bess is heard singing "Down In The Valley.")

JACK: Because of her.

MACON: Her.

JACK: Yeah.

MACON: Did you stay with her?

JACK: What could I do? She's my wife.

(Bess and Elmore enter. Bess carries a parasol. She wears a cape and new shoes. She doesn't wear her veil. We see her tattoos. Elmore has a pad and pen. He is constantly taking notes.)

ELMORE: What a voice you have! Like an angel!

BESS: Every time the Oglalas raised scalps on a pole and threatened to slay me, I'd sing for them. They'd fall to their knees and listen to my song, entranced, like charmed wolves. Ottawa, the head man, gave me strings of beads; others gave me acorns, seeds, ground nuts, feathers. Any treasure they possessed so I would favor them with my singing.

ELMORE: Amazing. Quite a provocative tale. Ah! The punch! Please serve Mrs. Flan a glass. I'm sure she must be parched.

(Jack serves punch, then holds Bess's parasol to shade her.)

BESS: Oh, no. Why I often went months without a drop of any drink during my stay in captivity.

ELMORE: Fascinating. How did you survive?

BESS: I'd chew constantly on a small stick to help prevent parching, or I'd hunt for wild fruits that grow all in abundance. *(Bess whistles softly.)*

ELMORE: You are an amazing creation. How anyone could have endured such hardship.

MACON: She pictured me.

ELMORE: What?

MACON: She pictured me.

(Will comes out of the cabin with a gun.)

WILL: Macon, I have the gun.

MACON: Not now.

WILL: I—I'm going to shoot the ox. It has to be done. He's suffering. *(Will heads toward the field.)* Won't you please come?

MACON: Shoot it by yourself.

WILL: I'll need somebody to help me slaughter it. Jack, would you?

JACK: The Professor pays you for our room and board. I'm no hired hand. *(Will exits.)*

MACON: Bess, tell the Professor how you pictured me when you was captured.

BESS: I thought about ya. I thought about all my loved ones back home.

ELMORE: It must have been unbearable—your sorrow.

BESS: It's true, I've suffered. But I come out here drunk with western fever. I wanted to see the elephant. To hunt down the elephant. Bang! Bang! Bang! I savor the boundlessness of it all! The wild flavor!

ELMORE: You take my breath away. How powerfully you speak in your simple, unadorned language. When your book comes out we must send you on the lyceum lecture circuit. What a sensation you'd make.

BESS: You flatter me, really.

MACON: My Lord, yes. Just imagine Bess on a big stage in front of a whole room full of people. Such a shy little thing. She'd die of fright. You need somebody who's got a real knack for that sort of thing. Ya know, I once played the Virgin Mary in a Christmas pageant. I had such a saintly face, an unearthly glow. I cried real tears when the Innkeeper told us there was no room for us at his inn.

ELMORE: *(A beat.)* It seems to me, the sun's very bright here. Why don't we go work in the willow grove down by the pond.

BESS: Yes. I'll tell you all about how the horrid hell hounds tattooed my face with sharp sticks dipped in weed juices and the powder from blue mud stones.

ELMORE: Monstrous savages. Godless perpetrators of butchery. *(Elmore and Bess exit.)*

MACON: I wore a blue robe as the Virgin Mary. Blue looks good on me. It's my best color, although I did not know it at the time.

JACK: Something about you's changed. You've lost the stars in your shoes. You used to run everywhere you'd go.

MACON: Well, what about you? Look at you. Serving punch, toting parasols, bowing and scraping.

JACK: I do, what I do.

MACON: You live like a leech.

JACK: Would you give me back the ring I gave you? I want to give it to my wife.

(An offstage gunshot is heard.)

MACON: Take it. Here, take it.

WILL: *(Offstage.)* God, it's still alive. Macon!

MACON: Good, it's over. Good.

WILL: *(Offstage.)* It's looking at me.

MACON: I'll kill it. I'll blow it dead. I'll do it!

(Macon exits. Jack looks after her. He tosses the ring up in the air and starts offstage. As he goes toward Bess and the Professor, we hear one last shot.)

SCENE VI

The following spring. Will sits alone in the yard. Bess and Elmore are gathered in Will's cabin. Elmore is looking through a portfolio taking out letters, contracts, illustrations, etc. Bess is waving a check through the air.

ELMORE: A phenomenon. Your book is a phenomenon!

BESS: I've hit pay dirt!

ELMORE: *(Looking at a sheet of figures.)* It's astonishing! No one can believe it!

BESS: I must have a pet songbird! We'll sing a duet together!

ELMORE: Over sixty thousand copies sold!

BESS: Oh, and get me a giant harp with gold cherubs and an ice palace to keep it in.

ELMORE: Whatever your heart desires.

BESS: *(Singing.)* Roses are blue, oh, roses are blue...

ELMORE: *(Overlapping.)* Now I have some correspondence that requires your attention.

BESS: Yes, yes, proceed; proceed.

ELMORE: *(Presenting a letter.)* The President of Indian Affairs wants to dine with you at the White House the day you arrive in Washington.

BESS: Oh, delightful. I'm delighted. How thrilling! I hope they don't serve any pig.

ELMORE: No, of course not. I'll alert them to your wishes. All pig shall be banned. Now here's an inquiry from actor-manager-playwright Dion Boucicault. He wants to adapt your book into a hit play.

BESS: Dion Boucicault? Who's that?

ELMORE: He's very famous.

BESS: Oh, alright then, I consent.

(Jack enters carrying some luggage. He has shaved his mustache.)

ELMORE: *(Handing her an illustration.)* Now here's the portrait of you that we want to include in the second edition.

BESS: Oh, dear.

ELMORE: I find it very sensitive, yet I feel there's a deep sense of inner strength.

BESS: Hmm. My eyes are too close together. I've got beautiful hair, but my eyes are too close together. *(To Jack.)* Don't you agree?

JACK: No.

BESS: But they're closer together than an average person's eyes, wouldn't you say?

JACK: I don't know. No.

BESS: Well, how close together do you think an average person's eyes are?

JACK: I don't know.

BESS: Then stop offering opinions on subjects you're completely stupid on.

JACK: Alright.

BESS: Don't be so agreeable. Finish fetching our bags and move them out to the carriage. We don't want to miss our train.

(Jack exits into another room.)

BESS: Do we really have to bother with him?

ELMORE: Of course, it's entirely your decision, but I'm afraid an anguished, adoring husband makes for excellent pathos.

BESS: Yes. Well, then. I'll manage.

ELMORE: Good. Excellent. Now, according to this schedule, you'll be doing up to one hundred and fifty lectures this season. You stand to profit over twenty-five thousand dollars from the lecture circuit alone.

BESS: Angels sing, devils dance.

ELMORE: Mr. William Sutton is the promoter for the tour. He's a very successful land speculator who is deeply devoted to western expansion and the concept of manifest destiny. He'd like for you to sign this contract agreeing to expound certain philosophical beliefs from the podium.

BESS: Philosophical beliefs? I'm not sure I got any of them. Here, let me see the paper.

(Bess takes the contract and reads it thoroughly. Macon enters the area in front of the cabin. She spots Will.)

MACON: Repossession. Repossession. That one word they clung to like a pack of sick dogs. They're taking our home. There's nothing to be done, unless they get fifty dollars. Fifty dollars. I asked the man with the red beard if he'd accept potatoes as partial payment. He laughed at me like I was a brand-new joke.

WILL: I told you how it come out. Things are finished here. We'll have to go somewhere else. Start fresh.

MACON: I'd rather choke to death right here in the sun.

(Inside the cabin Jack enters with the bags. He starts for the cabin door. Bess stops him.)

BESS: Jack, don't forget that basket there, I packed us some food for the road.

JACK: Great. What is it?

BESS: Cornbread.

(Jack nods, picks up the basket, and leaves the cabin. He goes into the yard. Macon spots him.)

MACON: Jack, where're you going?

JACK: The Professor's come for us. Bess's book's selling like wildfire. We're going on a lecture circuit. We've become important people.

MACON: You're leaving right now?

JACK: That's right.

MACON: How long will you be gone?

JACK: For good, I hope.

MACON: God. How will I ever stand living in this great wasteland all alone.

JACK: *(Indicating Will.)* Ya still got him.

MACON: Yeah. Listen, Jack, I'm in trouble. I need fifty dollars to save the homestead.

JACK: I ain't got no money.

MACON: Well, would you talk to Bess for me? Would you put in a good word?

JACK: You talk to her. She's your friend.

MACON: That's right. You're right. She's my friend. I done a lot for her. A whole lot. Good-bye, Jack.

JACK: So long, May Ann.

MACON: I'll always remember you as the possessor of a very handsome pair of eyes.

(Jack exits. Will stares ahead, trying to decide why he doesn't care about killing these people. Macon goes into the cabin. Will exits.)

MACON: Bess. I need to talk to you. It's concerning a personal situation. Good afternoon, Professor.

ELMORE: Yes, well...good afternoon, Mrs. Curtis. *(Elmore gets up and goes into the yard.)*

MACON: I heard you're leaving. You're off. You've made it in the big time.

BESS: That's how it appears.

MACON: I don't begrudge you. I saw it coming. People lap up them atrocity stories. They read 'em all the time in them penny dreadfuls. Now you go and give 'em the real factualized version. Ya even got the marks t'prove it. People'll get up outta their homes and come down to them big halls to see them marks. Them tattoos. People thrive on seeing freaks.

BESS: Well, I'm glad you don't begrudge me.

MACON: No. Why would I?

BESS: No reason. I just thought you wanted to write a book, a novel. You spoke about it. But I guess that was more like a pipe dream, a childish fantasy. Nothing to be taken seriously.

MACON: I had a book in mind at one point. I was gonna write about my adventures.

BESS: I guess, you just never had any, did ya?

MACON: I had some. Some things happened to me.

BESS: Not that much, though.

MACON: Well, I never got my face scarred.

BESS: Do you wish you had?

MACON: Why would I?

BESS: Because, maybe you would like to be…remarkable. But you're not. You look forward to things by decades. You're settled, staid, and dreamless. I see it haunts you how ya just can't compare t'me. To Bess Johnson, the woman who survived five adventurous years of Indian captivity. Who returned to write the book of the century and be adored by throngs all over the globe.

MACON: You don't fool me. I know how ya done it all. You pictured me. You stole from me. You stole me. I showed you how to walk and speak and fight and dream. I should have written that book. People should be clamoring t'meet me, t'talk t'me. I'm the real thing; you're just a watered down milquetoast version. Them Indians stole the wrong woman.

BESS: Is that a fact?

MACON: Yeah, it is.

BESS: Well, maybe it ain't too late. Maybe you've got one more chance. Here, take this knife. Take this ink. Go ahead. Cut open your face. Pour in the ink. Go be me, if you think you can. If you think you're so brave. I'll let you be me. You can do my tour. People will rise to their feet and clamor for you. Go ahead. The Oglalas rejoice in wounding themselves. They do it for prayer. They do it to celebrate grief. Come on, do it, celebrate, rejoice, do it—all it is is your face.

MACON: Bess, please—I always cared for you. I always did.

BESS: Then do it. Cut it. To shreds; all to shreds.

MACON: I did, you know. I always did.

BESS: Then do it. Cut it; do it.

(Macon takes the knife. Holds it to her face, then sets it down.)

MACON: I'm not gonna cut myself up. I don't wanna be scarred for life.

BESS: *(A beat.)* No. That would cost too much. And you've gotten so measly you watch every egg, nickel, and biscuit. *(Bess starts putting on her hat and gloves.)*

MACON: I know we don't like each other. We used to be friends. But somehow we drifted apart. Still you have to admit, you have to see, that you owe me something.

BESS: What do I owe you?

MACON: You—well, you owe me—fifty dollars. At least, fifty dollars. I gave you shoes when you had none and food and coffee and clothes and lodging. I even brought you blue ribbons and a blue dress. Whatever your heart desired, I gave to you.

BESS: Maybe it never occurred t'you. Maybe you never realized the fact, but people don't like being beholding. They resent always needing and always owing. And pretty soon they come to resent whoever it is they been taking from.

MACON: I do. I know that. You've resented me all along.

BESS: Yeah, I believe I have and I don't want you resenting me. So why don't we just call it even.

MACON: But I gotta have it. The fifty dollars. I need it to save my homestead. They're gonna throw me out on the dusty road. You can't do this to me.

BESS: Honey, I'd rip the wings off an angel if I thought they'd help me fly.

(Bess leaves the cabin and goes out into the yard. Macon follows her.)

MACON: You owe me! I'm due! You can't deny me what's mine! I gave you green biscuits; I combed your hair; I taught you to whistle!

ELMORE: Are you ready?

BESS: Yeah.

ELMORE: Did you read the contract?

BESS: They want me to demand the immediate extermination of all Indian tribes.

ELMORE: That's correct.

BESS: I got no problem with that. Just make sure wherever we go I have a basket of golden tulips to greet me. They're my favorite flower, tulips.

(Bess and Elmore exit as Macon screams after them.)

MACON: You thief! Robber—thief! Tulips are mine! They belong to me! I seen the picture! You never did!

(Will enters wearing his eye patch and carrying a satchel.)

MACON: God, Will. God. She wouldn't give me the money. She wouldn't give me nothing. She owes me, too. She knows she does. I was her friend. God, I'd like to kill her. I'd like to tear off her head and feed her brains to rabid rats. The selfish, backbiting, stuck-up, black-hearted Indian whore!

WILL: Macon, I'm leaving here. I'm heading west.

MACON: West? Where west.

WILL: Don't know.

MACON: Maybe we'll try Idaho. They got that Turkey red wheat in Idaho. It's a hard-kerneled wheat. You can grow it all spring.

WILL: I don't want you with me.

MACON: What?

WILL: My first wife, Barbara Jane, well, I loved her. And I remember she loved me. But you never loved me and I never loved you. That's all it's been. I don't want it no more.

MACON: You leaving me here? With nothing?

WILL: This is yours. Catch.

(Will throws her his glass eye. She catches it.)

WILL: I bought it for you. It never done me no good.

(Will exits. Macon paces around the yard tossing the glass eye back and forth, from hand to hand.)

MACON: I got nothing. Nothing. After all this time. *(A beat.)* Nothing.

SCENE VII

Fifteen years later. A hotel suite in St. Louis. Bess drinks a glass of whiskey. Elmore holds a copy of the St. Louis Chronicle.

ELMORE: Are you sure you want to hear this?

BESS: Uh huh.

ELMORE: It's not very good.

BESS: That seems to be the trend.

ELMORE: It's appallingly written.

BESS: Go ahead, Elmore, it's the last one I'll ever get.

ELMORE: The St. Louis *Chronicle* says, "Mrs. Bess Johnson delivered her speech with impassioned fervor. However, the story seemed excessive and outdated like a worn-out melodrama one would read in a dime novel. The text lacked all orderly progressions and seemed to ramble and roam incoherently, as though perhaps Mrs. Johnson had had a drop too many."

BESS: A drop too many! They can't actually expect me to deliver those speeches sans intoxication. What a tight-lipped powder puff. What a worm-ridden toad.

ELMORE: *(Folding up the paper.)* Yes, well, let's put it away.

BESS: God. I can't tell you what a relief it will be to never again have to rhapsodize about writing with fish blood and being scantily clad in a thin bark skirt.

ELMORE: Yes. I'm well aware we have played ourselves out. People are no longer interested in hearing about the untamed savages. Times have changed. Indians today are beloved circus performers. Yesterday, I read in a broadside that they finally arrested your old friend, Ottawa, down by the Pecos River. They'd been hunting him for years. He was the last holdout. The lone one.

BESS: Ottawa, I didn't know he was still alive.

ELMORE: He's not. He drank a lantern of kerosene the night they captured him.

BESS: Oh.

ELMORE: *(Presenting her with contracts.)* Well, here are the final papers disbanding our long and lucrative union. They're all in order. You'll find everything's as we discussed.

BESS: I'm sure they are. I'll just have my attorneys read it over before I sign it.

ELMORE: I admire your consistency, Bess. All these years and you've never trusted me once.

BESS: Sorry, Elmore. I tried that. It never really worked out for me.

(Jack enters smoking a large black cigar. He is dressed dappperly.)

JACK: 'Afternoon.

ELMORE: Hello, Jack.

BESS: What's that awful thing?

JACK: A ten cent cigar. I won it betting on the comic mule races down at the tent show.

ELMORE: Ah, yes, how was the tent show?

JACK: Pathetic, small town dredge. The freaks were even third rate: armless boy, electric girl, skeleton dude. Oh, but you'll never guess who I ran into. What's her name? We used to know her back when. Her husband wore an eye patch.

BESS: Macon?

JACK: Yes, I think that was it.

BESS: Macon Hill.

JACK: You should see her. Disgusting. She's got some syphilitic disease. It's broken out all over her face. She was working at a little booth dispensing whiskey and tobacco and raisins. I bought some raisins from her. She didn't recognize me. I had to laugh when I saw she had newspaper stuck in her clothes to stay warm. I remember her always thinking she had it so good.

BESS: Your cigar is foul. Put it out. Get it out.

(Jack puts out the cigar.)

BESS: God, you're an imbecile. Coming in here, filling the room with your vile smoke. You've given me a sick head. I'm going out for some air. Clear out this room before I get back. *(Bess exits.)*

JACK: Christ, why am I ever nice to that woman? You're lucky you're getting out from under her. I'm stuck with her for life. Tomorrow we leave for our White Plains estate. We'll retire there together till the end of our days. What will it be like?

ELMORE: She can be difficult. But I think, underneath it all, she has real affection for you.

JACK: You think she does?

ELMORE: It's the sort of thing that's only apparent to an outsider.

JACK: Well, I'll say one thing, she'll never find anyone who'll treat her better than I do. She oughta know that by now. I'm her one true one.

SCENE VIII

A few hours later. Early evening. Macon's tent. Macon sits alone in the dimly lit tent drinking and playing solitaire. There are sores on her face.

BESS: *(Offstage.)* Hello? Anybody here?

MACON: Yeah.

(Bess enters.)

BESS: Macon?

MACON: Bess?

BESS: I heard you were here.

MACON: Jack tell you?

BESS: Yeah.

MACON: I seen him this afternoon. He bought some raisins. He wouldn't speak to me though.

BESS: Well, you know him.

MACON: Yeah. Why'd you come?

BESS: I—don't know. I was—remembering…

MACON: Uh huh.

BESS: So much.

MACON: Well.

BESS: How you been?

MACON: Great. Just great. Yeah, for a time I was raking in the green selling this Indian Remedy. A cure for your opium, morphine, liquor, and tobacco habit. Hell of a cure it was, too. Then I got this stuff coming out on my face and people kinda eased off on purchasing the cure. But for a time there, I was flush. How 'bout you?

BESS: I don't know. Maybe other people's lives have made more sense than mine.

MACON: It's always a possibility.

BESS: Oh, well. There it is, I guess.

MACON: Yeah, laid right out behind you like a lizard's tail.

BESS: Today I—Well, today I heard that Ottawa, the head man—my husband, was captured. He, ah, poisoned himself on a lantern of kerosene. I don't know why, but it's hard. I'd always thought I might—but now I won't—ever see him once more.

MACON: It's a shame how things turn out. I swear to God, I wish I knew how it could be different.

BESS: Uh huh. Me too.

MACON: 'Least ya got out there and saw the elephant.

BESS: Yeah. Yeah, the Oglalas knew such beautiful places. I saw rivers that were so clear you could see every pebble and fish. And the water was any color you could dream: pink and turquoise, gold and white, lime green.

MACON: Hell of a time you had with the Oglalas.

BESS: Beautiful time I had. Hey, you ever hear from Will Curtis?

MACON: Nah. Will got caught in a threshing machine back in '87. Got his leg cut off in the blade. Bled t'death in a field. Funny, I always figured he'd go piecemeal.

BESS: Yeah.

MACON: You know, when I was younger, I never knew who I was, what I wanted, where I was going or how to get there. Now that I'm older, I don't know none of that either.

BESS: Well, one thing I wanted, one thing I know I wanted was, well, I don't know, I guess you'd call it true love. And when I got them three letters from that man, that man, Michael Flan, who wrote to me about the size of the sky, I thought it was alright there, all within my grasp and all I had t'do was come out west and there it'd be.

MACON: Thought you'd just reach up and touch it like a star.

BESS: Yeah. Thought I might. *(Bess reaches her hand up as if she were grabbing a star.)* Aah!

MACON: Feel a chill?

BESS: Just a small one.

MACON: Bess?

BESS: Huh.

MACON: I, well, I've had a bad pain in my heart all day today. I'm scared and it troubles me, but I expect I'll die soon.

BESS: …What can I do?

MACON: Nothing t'do. I just wanted somebody t'tell, that's all. Someone to tell.

BESS: Well, you can tell me.

MACON: There ain't much t'tell.

BESS: Maybe not, but I'm glad you looked my way.

MACON: Uh huh. Well. Yeah.

BESS: Hey, do you still whistle?

MACON: Me? I—God—I— *(Then definitely.)* No.

(A long beat, then Macon whistles a tune, Bess whistles back. The women both laugh from deep in the bottom of their hearts. The lights fade to blackout.)

END OF PLAY

SIGNATURE

An Homage to Frederick Bailey

DEDICATED WITH BOUNDLESS LOVE
AND ENDLESS ADMIRATION
TO GREG GROVE

Christine Lahti
in New York Stage and Film Conpany's 1990 production of
Signature.

photo by Dixie Sheridan

ORIGINAL PRODUCTION

Signature was produced by New York Stage and Film Company in Poughkeepsie, New York, in 1990. The executive producer was Dixie Sheridan. It was directed by Thomas Schlamme; set design was by Anita Stewart; costume design was by Candice Donnelly; lighting design was by Donald Holder. The cast, in order of appearance, was as follows:

Boswell T-Thorp	Kurtwood Smith
Maxwell T-Thorp	Mark Linn-Baker
William Smit	Carol Kane
L-Tip T-Thorp	Christine Lahti
C-Boy	Damon Anderson
Reader	O-Lan Jones
TVP Personalities	Jennifer Cooley, Edward Enrique, and Stacy Rukeyser

Signature was produced by Charlotte Repertory Theatre in Charlotte, North Carolina, in 1995. It was produced by Keith Martin. It was directed by Steve Umberger; set and costume design was by Jan Chambers; lighting design was by Eric Winkenwerder; sound design was by Fred Story. The cast, in order of appearance, was as follows:

Boswell T-Thorp	Allan Hickle-Edwards
Maxwell T-Thorp	Graham Smith
William Smit	Wendy Hammond
L-Tip T-Thorp	Kathryn Knotts
C-Boy	Grant Perez Smith
Reader	Rebecca Koon

THE CAST

THE CAST

BOSWELL T-THORP: 40s, an art philosopher
MAXWELL T-THORP: 30s, Boswell's brother, a Tank Bureau worker
WILLIAM SMIT: 20s, a splatterer from the CTZ
L-TIP T-THORP: 30s, Max's wife, Boswell's manager
C-BOY: 11, a homeless Govenor ward
READER: 20–50s, a graphologist

THE SETTING

The play takes place in Los Angeles in the year 2052. Sets, lights, and sound should be expressionistic. We need to know, however, that we are in some form of Hollywood. Elements should be spare yet precise. The effect is a strange, chaotically horrifying, deathly beautiful, sadly silly world.

THE TIME

2052 A.D.

Note: Actors of any race who are suitable for the roles may be cast. Ideally, the company should be racially mixed, giving a cosmopolitan, universal feel to the play.

ACT I
SCENE I

We are in Boswell T-Thorp's apartment. It is nighttime. Boswell T-Thorp, a man in his forties, stands in colorful pants. He is bare-chested. Bright squares are painted around his breasts. There is a small purple square in the center of his forehead. Throughout the following, he dresses. He puts on a square shirt, a square tie, square shoes, a square wig, a square belt, and so forth. His box attire should be shabby, well-worn. Maxwell T-Thorp, Boswell's younger brother, follows him around in despair.

BOSWELL: *(To imaginary people.)* Good evening; good evening. I'm Boswell T-Thorp. The Box Theory? Yes, that was mine. I invented it. It came from me.

MAXWELL: I wish you could—I don't understand—I need someone to explain.

BOSWELL: *(To imaginary people.)* Quite right. Quite right. There's no place but box.

MAXWELL: Because, you see, I love her so much. Oh, why can't she love me?! What made her stop loving me?!

BOSWELL: Please, please, please! Can't you see I'm trying to get into the party mode?!

MAXWELL: Yes, of course. Go ahead. Forgive me.

BOSWELL: *(To imaginary people.)* Ho! Ho, ho! Of course I recall it. The Box Salute. *(He does the Box Salute.)*

MAXWELL: It's all so funny! It's funny. Because you never know how it will end. What it all will come to. I thought it was good. But it was not good. I was wrong. I was mistaken. A mistake was made!

BOSWELL: I'm thinking you should leave. Tab some ear fuel and dust.

MAXWELL: Please, you're my brother. I need a helping hand.

BOSWELL: I'm preparing for the party.

MAXWELL: No doubt you're a hobnob. No doubt.

BOSWELL: Ho, ho. Do you think I enjoy Hollywood? Do you imagine I revel in squealing like a pig? You must know how I suffer around the social scene.

MAXWELL: Yes, yes, of course.

BOSWELL: But a man must eat. After all, there are price tags to be paid. Bills to be swallowed.

MAXWELL: Yes, please, you must go on to the Celebrity Chase. You must return to the limelight.

BOSWELL: Well, I'm glad you comprehend. After all, tonight you are not on my menu. Now tab the fuel.

MAXWELL: *(Tabbing some ear fuel.)* They say this stuff'll eventually kill you.

BOSWELL: Yes, well, breathing will eventually kill you.

(William, a woman in her twenties, enters. She wears an orange splatter's suit, helmet, and boots.)

WILLIAM: Hello.

MAX: Is this your tenant?

BOSWELL: Yes, yes. I'm forced to take in government tenants now. Look at this one! A splatterer from the CTZ. I hope you're satisfied. If only you would lend me more. I need more.

MAX: *(Still dropping ear fuel.)* The Tank Bureau's cut back. What can I do?

BOSWELL: Personal sacrifice, more work hours, Lotto Dot! What do I care? Get me K! I need K!

MAX: Please, stop harping. I'm suffering here; I'm suffering. *(Max clutches his heart in agony.)* My God!

BOSWELL: What?

MAX: My heart is bleeding. Look, it's bleeding. Blood. Black blood. I'm dying. Oh my God. I'm dying.

BOSWELL: Let me see. Hold still! You are a swizzle-headed goat. This is an ink stain. It's ink. From a pen in your pocket.

MAX: It's the pen she gave me. It's my moon pen. Oh, how can I live without her?

BOSWELL: What is your problem? No one has died. No one's been maimed. No money has been lost. She noosed you. She shuttled you. She broke your heart like a match stick. Big fucking dose.

MAX: I loved her. I love her. I'm loving her still.

BOSWELL: Fine. You loved her. Good. Go love somebody else.

MAX: There's no one else I can love.

BOSWELL: Yo, yo, yo! Wake up! Love is cheaper than free. It grows all over your feet like yellow fungus in tent town. It drops like acid rain from the sky. Just go outside and open your mouth. Let it fall down your throat and burn up your insides. Aah. What do you think love is? Why, it's nothing more than an archaic form of egotism. A tawdry reflection of all the holes in your own shredded soul. Be a human being. Forget about love.

MAX: You're a monster.

BOSWELL: Rumba!

(The TVP [television phone] starts bleeping. L-Tip appears on the TVP screen. She is a tall, striking woman in her thirties. She is dressed in an array

of ghastly colored flowers. Strange antennas poke out of her headdress. She holds a portable TVP. She is looking at it, trying to get the picture of Boswell to click in.)

L-TIP: *(On the screen.)* Box? Are you there? Boswell, puppetto? I'm below, are you there?

MAX: It's her. Oh my God. It's her. She's there. My beloved.

L-TIP: *(On screen, waving two Day-glo tickets.)* I got us floor one chase passes. I pulled every pony I knew, but we're on the main rug. Hello?

MAX: She's going with you? She's escorting you to the great suckathon?

BOSWELL: Shut up. *(Talking into his TVP remote.)* I'm here, L-Tip.

L-TIP: *(On the screen.)* I can't see you on my TVP screen. Click in.

BOSWELL: I want to surprise you with my outfit.

MAX: Traitor. Hoodlum.

BOSWELL: Nick off.

L-TIP: *(On the screen.)* Yeah? Well, what do you think of my outfit? Don't I look sin? I'm dressed as Pansy Martin. Watch this. *(She does an impersonation of Pansy Martin the Fantasy Puppet.)* "I just love t'eat my platter of tulips in the morning dew. Jacka, jacka, jacka!" *(L-Tip drops character.)* I make a good Pansy Martin, don't I?

BOSWELL: Brill, dear.

L-TIP: *(On the screen.)* Oh, you reindeer you!

BOSWELL: Look, I'll be right down.

L-TIP: *(On the screen.)* Well, click, click, Box. We gotta go slide, spill, splatter, and burn! It's suck time. Jacka, jacka, jacka!
(L-Tip starts putting in some ear fuel. Boswell clicks L-Tip off the screen. There is a moment of silence.)

MAX: *(Stricken.)* She knows how to put on a front. You wouldn't know she was suffering. Unless you knew her very well, you might not be able to perceive it.

BOSWELL: I have to go.

MAX: She's going with you to the Celebrity Chase?

BOSWELL: She's my manager. That's all. You know that.

MAX: She's a rotten manager. You're her only client. You never work. You should fire her. I wish you would, Boz. I wish you would fire her.

BOSWELL: Maybe. I'll give it some thought. She does look ridiculous. *(Boswell exits.)*

MAX: *(To William.)* I didn't think she looked ridiculous. Did you?

WILLIAM: No. But the real Pansy Martin has pansy eyes and there are real flowers growing from her ears. Different kinds. All different kinds.

MAX: The real Pansy Martin is a Fantasy Puppet. L-Tip's a person.

WILLIAM: Righto.

MAX: I don't know. It's a problem. She's going to beg me to come back. And I don't want to be hard-hearted. But she has to see. I mean, there are certain consequences she should face. She baked her cake. Now she can choke it. I'm a proud man. I won't just come crawling back. That's not how things work. Not on my screen.

(As the lights fade to black, we hear the clatter, conversation, music, etc., of a strange cocktail party. On the TVP screen we see askew images of a decadent party.)

SCENE II

Boswell's apartment. Later that same night. William wears a green union suit. She lies on her mat. L-Tip and Boswell are heard coming up the stairway. The cocktail party noises begin to fade. The following scene is played fast.

L-TIP'S VOICE: *(Offstage.)* Doomed. I always thought you meant that we were doomed! Completely doomed.

BOSWELL'S VOICE: *(Offstage.)* That's a general misconception.

(Boswell and L-Tip enter. They bring in an air of exhilaration. They have been to a big party. They have been doing drugs.)

L-TIP: You see, to me, Boxdom translated: boxed in, cornered, trapped, limited by our own minds, resources, physical beings—

BOSWELL: No, no, no. The whole thesis is that one may put a box around anything: a circle, a rectangle, a triangle, a moving spill! If only the box is big enough, everything will fit. It's all so—so freeing!

L-TIP: Yes. Exactly. Yes. God, you are so brill. You make me sin, and sin and sin. Have one more vial.

(She produces two vials of a red liquid. Boswell takes one of the vials.)

BOSWELL: It would all be so apparent, if only you could have seen the original Boxdom poster. The lasomicrograph is simply not the same. It doesn't grasp the colors, the size, the shape. In the original, you could comprehend…it was all apparent.

L-TIP: It must have been an awful big dose when your great poster was destroyed.

BOSWELL: Actually, in some ways, I reveled in it. Me and Wanda stood on a balcony across the boulevard watching them smear and burn and cut it to ribbons. We were eating lemon snaps and drinking dirty water. She was crying. I was laughing in the face of it. Slinging lemon snaps up into the air. *(He demonstrates.)* "Ho! Ho!" That's how I was back then. Very ebullient.

L-TIP: And it did. It all turned around. The Opposition was overthrown. The No Good Solution Party came to power. You were awarded the Grand Poster Prize. Boxdom became a phenomenon.

BOSWELL: I was very confident. People were always seeking me out for appointments and dinners. Funny, so many people have forgotten all about it.

L-TIP: There were several members of the Old Guard who came up to you this evening. One of them gave you the Box Salute.

BOSWELL: *(Doing a Box Salute.)* Yes, yes.

L-TIP: And the little, pasty man serving decorative crackers, he asked for your autograph.

BOSWELL: God, what a pathetically hollow practice that is.

L-TIP: Also, you made a remarkable impression on M. Raffeyelle Movet.

BOSWELL: No. Not the lady I swiped with my boxed hairdo?

L-TIP: Yes, I spoke to her quite a while, all about you.

BOSWELL: Me?

L-TIP: Yes. She has her own channel.

BOSWELL: That woman with the rubber nose has her own channel?

L-TIP: It's on the Rehab Circuit.

BOSWELL: Oh.

L-TIP: But she's got good time slots. And I think—Well, she seemed very interested in having you on one of her shows.

BOSWELL: Me?

L-TIP: Yes!

BOSWELL: Which show?

L-TIP: The—well, it's called "The Whatever Happened To Show."

BOSWELL: "Whatever happened to?"

L-TIP: Yes! They do very few celebrities ! In fact, you'd be the only one on the show your week.

BOSWELL: I—I'm ill. This is an insult. Why, I'm not some out-fad Fantasy Puppet. I'm an art philosopher. What more do they want from me?!

L-TIP: They want you on the show.

BOSWELL: Never! Never! Never!

L-TIP: Look, I know what you've done. But you've been out of orbit for a very long time. Things change.

BOSWELL: I can't stomach it. Look who the Big Splash of the season is. That newcomer, K.Y. Von Ludwig. Him with his loathsome octagons and zigzags. He'd better hope he makes his mark before his hairdo unglues, the smug little toast.

L-TIP: Hey, now try not to unzap.

BOSWELL: I should have answered my fan mail; I should have consorted with celebrity swine; I should have been a grinning, glad-handing salt lick for the press.

L-TIP: *(Giving him a blue dot.)* Here, lap a blue dot.

BOSWELL: *(Lapping up the blue dot.)* So what else—who else would—would be on the show?

L-TIP: Oh, well, let's see. *(She produces a list.)* We got: whatever happened to a clear blue sky, good clean fun, a day at the beach, the open-stove policy, bloodbaths in China, anti-gravity gowns: micro pets, the downfall of capitalism, the coalition of fetuses, vulture hairdos, and things that last.

BOSWELL: How much do they pay?

L-TIP: Scale.

BOSWELL: When do they want me on the show?

L-TIP: Well, two weeks from Thursday. I mean—if—well. There's one thing.

BOSWELL: What?

L-TIP: You're kind of an alternate. You and "vulture hairdos" are alternates, in case any of the other stories drop out. But they always do. Always, it happens.

BOSWELL: Let me got this flat. I'm an alternate on "The Whatever Happened To Show?"

L-TIP: Well, for now: temporarily.

BOSWELL: Maybe I'll just call the Euthanasia Hot Line.

L-TIP: Please, try to be up. Up is in.

BOSWELL: *(Walking over to the TVP.)* They do it for free now. Government dole. Of course, I hear the paperwork's appalling.

L-TIP: You know they have this new ultra surgery where you can get your face fixed into a permanent smile. They say smiling twenty-four hours a day does wonders for your emotional health, as well as your appearance.

BOSWELL: Maybe you haven't grasped this, L-Tip, but I'm nicked, I'm busted, my plastic is pulp. I don't have money for fucking smile surgery.

L-TIP: Alright. Relax. That's what I'm here to remedy. Here, I'll turn on the galaxy satellite. There's supposed to be— *(She turns on the G.S. The screen lights up with a glorious view of the night's sky.)* Oh, look. There it is. The moon. A full moon.

BOSWELL: A cloud's passing over.

L-TIP: There's the Big Dipper.

BOSWELL: A band of stars.

L-TIP: The Milky Way.

BOSWELL: Luminous.

L-TIP: Boswell?

BOSWELL: Yes?

L-TIP: Are you available for sex?

BOSWELL: Um…no. I'm under surveillance.

L-TIP: Oh. I didn't know. So sorry.

BOSWELL: Nothing's definite. Nothing's at all definite.

L-TIP: Of course. Well, if you get a launch window, let me know.

BOSWELL: Sure. I'm sure I will, very soon.

L-TIP: Sin.

BOSWELL: What about Max?

L-TIP: I've made an appointment with Video Divorce for this Saturday. That'll be the end of it.

BOSWELL: Umm. Regrettable.

L-TIP: Yes. But he just—and we were—anyway, things don't always…

BOSWELL: Yes.

L-TIP: I have all these—and with him I never could—

BOSWELL: No.

L-TIP: Great moon. And stars. Always up there, right?

BOSWELL: I suppose.

L-TIP: Late. Better go.

BOSWELL: Good night.

L-TIP: I'll let you know about the show. Shine on, Boxey. Jacka, jacka, jacka.
(She exits. Boswell stares up at the stars. William sits up in bed.)

WILLIAM: Hello.

BOSWELL: Hi.

WILLIAM: Can I mix you your concoction?

BOSWELL: Yes.
(William gets up and goes to mix Boswell his medical concoction.)

WILLIAM: I just wanna know—at the party? What kinda food did they serve to eat?

BOSWELL: I don't really recall.

WILLIAM: Was it pretty food?

BOSWELL: I suppose.

WILLIAM: Tell me about it.

BOSWELL: I'm really not interested.

WILLIAM: Here's your concoction.

BOSWELL: Thanks. *(Boswell drinks the concoction.)*

WILLIAM: I'm sure it will make you well. I know it will. It's very good for you. *(Boswell hands her back the glass. She sets the glass down, then goes to her mat and sits down, hugging herself with both arms. Boswell has settled down on his own mat. He looks up at the stars, looks back at her, looks back to the stars.)*

BOSWELL: Why are you hugging yourself?

WILLIAM: Just 'cause I—just am.

BOSWELL: You—

WILLIAM: Huh?

BOSWELL: Umm.

WILLIAM: *(Softly.)* Can I? *(Boswell gives a nearly imperceivable nod. William moves over to his mat. Boswell keeps his arms folded. William sits near to him. She folds her arms. They do not touch.)*

BOSWELL: There were pink bubble shrimp served on a lavender platter surrounded by electric oysters. There was a marvelous blue dot dip, a crouton tray, some rainbow cheese balls garnished with yellow sea clover, sizzling clay steaks on a fried and refried tray, succulent duck bills... *(As Boswell talks, William slowly leans over and sets her head on his shoulder. The lights fade. Street noises come up. We hear the sound of wind and trash being blown down alleyways. Strange animals are howling.)*

SCENE III

The lights fade up on the stoop in front of L-Tip's apartment building. It is later that same night. There are two filthy, ragged homeless people sleeping out on the streets (Reader and C-Boy). They stay huddled under their rags throughout the following scene. L-Tip enters. She starts up the stoop. Max steps out of the shadows. His face is pale and his hands are trembling.

MAX: I just want to know. I just want you to tell me. About my fingers. What am I—I mean—my fingers?

L-TIP: I'm not—I won't—

MAX: These fingers on my hands. They're part of me, and yet they know where you dream. They've been all over you, journeyed through you and up you and in you. I can never change where they have traveled.

L-TIP: There are parts of me—parts of my life, that have nothing to do with you.

MAX: So you're just walking on. Walking right on over me. Stepping on my forehead with your highest heel. Impaling my heart with your red spiked shoe. Go on. I don't mind. I won't even squirm. Just please don't—please don't make that call.

L-TIP: …It's over.

MAX: Nothing is over. You know, nothing is over.

L-TIP: It is.

MAX: No. Not when I am willing to do anything. Any fucking thing. Stand here in the road and scream out your name. Lie down like a dog and let you kick in my brains. Or crawl, I will crawl; I will crawl at your feet. *(He gets down on all fours and starts crawling to her.)* Yes, I know, it's always better to kick someone who has risen to all fours than to pummel away at a motionless supine target. Come on. Kick me. I'm crawling. Kick in my gums, my lips, my face—whatever you want. Whatever you want.

(He crawls up to her and starts climbing up her legs. She kicks and shoves him away.)

L-TIP: *(Overlapping.)* Get away. Leave me. There is nothing I want from you. There is not one thing that belongs to you that I would have. Not a notion, not a smile, not the time of day, or a cut of gum. *(She stops kicking him.)*

(He looks up at her and wipes blood away from his mouth.)

MAX: Please…Forgive me. Please. This is not the way I normally behave. This is not who I am. I can't—I have never—And it is…killing me. I wish, for both our sakes, I wish I was dead.

(Max gets up and exits. L-Tip looks after him. She clutches her arms around herself and leans against the stoop; garbage whirls around her. There is the sound of rushing water and wind. The lights fade.)

SCENE IV

The lights fade up on Boswell's apartment. The sound of a shower is heard from behind the lavatory door. It is night. William stands at attention before the TVP screen. She wears her orange splatter pants over her green long johns. She wears a crisp white bow tie around her neck, white gloves, a white visor, and spotless white shoes. She is talking to an Official on the TVP screen. William speaks into the TVP remote.

OFFICIAL: *(On the screen; reading from an official report.)* "…rescue tab, par X; attitude par X; 129 O.T. hours." You could be headed for the W.Y. Badge.

WILLIAM: Thank you, sire. I intend to get it.

OFFICIAL: *(On the screen.)* Good work.

WILLIAM: Overall P.T. check, please, sire.

OFFICIAL: *(On the screen.)* One hundred and eighty-seven deuce.

WILLIAM: My tab shows one hundred eighty-nine.

OFFICIAL: *(On the screen.)* Let me reprocess. Oh, here it is, two of your rainbow ducks expired in tunnel release.

WILLIAM: I thought they'd make it.

OFFICIAL: *(On the screen.)* Nix. Good work, though. Good try.

WILLIAM: A personal request, sire. A click up into Freezer Dorm 380-T, beds 142 and 143.

OFFICIAL: *(On the screen.)* You're only on a two-minute window.

WILLIAM: Please, just whatever I got left.

OFFICIAL: *(On the screen.)* Approved. H.A.N.D.

WILLIAM: Yes, you too. Have a nice day!
   (The TVP screen changes to a Frozen Dorm. Many children and a few adults lie frozen in white compartments. The camera focuses in on William's two frozen children, Bonnie and Tabell.)

WILLIAM: *(Talking into her TVP remote.)* Hi. I'm here. I'm here. Mama's here. *(She walks up to the screen and touches her children.)* Oh, you both look so sweet. I miss you, Bonnie. I miss you, Tabell. Shall I finish the story? The one about the beautiful girl who ate the toxic apple given to her by the evil queen? I—
   (The screen flickers with zigzags, then goes dark.)

WILLIAM: Oh, oh. Good-bye, Tabell. Bonnie. Good-bye.
   (William puts down the TVP remote. She carefully begins removing her whites and placing them into the pristine box where they are kept. The water

stops running in the bathroom. The front doorbell buzzes, then we hear Max's voice over the door speaker.)

MAX'S VOICE: *(Offstage, from door speaker.)* Hello. This is Max. I stopped by. *(William clicks Max in with the laser remote. Max enters. He is pale and sweaty. His clothes are rumpled and dirty.)*

WILLIAM: Hello.

MAX: Hi. Where's Boswell?

WILLIAM: *(Indicating the lavatory.)* In there. He's washing.

MAX: I need to discuss something. A matter. With him. You're William, right?

WILLIAM: Yeah.

MAX: They bring you in from the CTZ?

WILLIAM: Yes.

MAX: They still got sheep there?

WILLIAM: Uh-huh.

MAX: I remember sheep. Wool trousers, lamb chops, bah, bah, bah? They got you working down on the shore?

WILLIAM: Uh-huh.

MAX: You Quake, Spill, Burn, or Splatter Crew?

WILLIAM: Splatter.

MAX: Big mess, all that. Hard to contain. A real job for somebody.

WILLIAM: I do my best.

MAX: This is not my day. I'm getting pasty. Melt-down. Oh, well.
(Boswell enters from the lavatory. His hair is wet and slicked back. He wears worn grey clothes.)

MAX: Boswell. Hello. I've come by.

BOSWELL: Yes?

MAX: I—there's something…Well. You know, trouble. Some. Nothing much. That job I had—I don't. And I—lost my place.

BOSWELL: You're homeless?

MAX: Who isn't? Really? These days.

BOSWELL: God.

MAX: I'm gonna be dish. I got irons in the fire. Daggers in the air. Rain on the way. I just—temporarily—need a loan.

BOSWELL: From me? From me?

MAX: You're my brother. I thought I'd ask.

BOSWELL: Look, I borrow from you. You don't borrow from me. You're the steady one. You earn the living. You know how that's done.

MAX: I've been fired, noosed, chucked! They let me go!

BOSWELL: For God's sake, why do you pick now to have this metaphysical malfunction?

MAX: She did it. It's her fault. She divorced me.

BOSWELL: Be that as it may, I have to eat my dinner.

MAX: Please, help me. I'm homeless. I could use anything. A tin cup. A cardboard box.

BOSWELL: I don't want to. I don't have any time. You have to go.

MAX: Is it because of the monkey? It is. Isn't it?

BOSWELL: What?

MAX: Our stuffed monkey, Mr. Yips. The one our father micro-charred, all because you wouldn't stop sucking your fingers. These two fingers here. He warned you. But you loved slurping them so much, you caused the torture death of our beloved Mr. Yips. That's why you hate me. Because I know you for the finger-slurping monkey killer you really are.

(The brothers glare at each other for several horrible moments. Then Boswell turns very slowly and deliberately to William.)

BOSWELL: William, what am I having for dinner?

MAX: Monstrous murderer!

(Max exits in a heartbroken fury.)

BOSWELL: I posed a question.

WILLIAM: Deluxe Banquet Festival.

BOSWELL: I'm ready to eat.

WILLIAM: Alright.

(William goes to the micro-meal machine. She punches a button.)

BOSWELL: What are you having?

WILLIAM: Dotted broccoli.

(Two micro meals come out, with disposable silverware and napkins included.)

BOSWELL: Don't you ever get sick of dotted broccoli?

WILLIAM: I like broccoli.

BOSWELL: But you have it repeatedly.

WILLIAM: Sometimes I'll vary. I have cauliflower, or brocflower, or flower-cauli.

BOSWELL: Never a dull moment with you.

WILLIAM: Every Sunday I have a sausage.

BOSWELL: I've seen that sausage you eat. It's a pitiful sausage. A sad little parsley sausage.

WILLIAM: *(Maintaining her dignity.)* I enjoy my sausage.

BOSWELL: I suppose it's all you can afford. You do the best with what you have. In a certain sense, you're to be applauded. Here, have a tomato.

WILLIAM: No, thank you.

BOSWELL: Come on, William. I know how much you like tomatoes. Go on, take it.

WILLIAM: I don't feel like a tomato.

BOSWELL: Don't be stubborn. Take the tomato. For God's sake, what is wrong with you? I'm telling you to take the tomato. I know you want it. Why are you treating me this way? For God's sake, take the tomato! I'm begging you, please, now, please.

WILLIAM: I'll take it. *(William takes the tomato.)*

BOSWELL: Fine. I just happen to know you like them. That's all. How was your day? Let's hear about your day. *(Quietly, desperate.)* I'd like for you to talk.

WILLIAM: Well, there was this sea lamb in the tubs out at the rescue center. Her eyes were sick and yellow and she was all covered in thick, black splatter. I put on my mask and gloves and started combing her with my furball remover fork. I combed and dug and scraped and tugged. It was tough going. Her eyes were frightened. This was a new experience for her. This furball remover procedure. But, eventually, I was able to scrape off most of the splat, and underneath I could see her skin was pink. A powder pink. I felt accomplishment, seeing that clean skin. It was a good day's work.

BOSWELL: A good day's work. My, how I've come to envy you, William. You with your non-skilled job. Picking lethal stickem off of dying plants and beasts. A mindless job, unglamorous, unrewarding, unbearably dull and useless.

WILLIAM: Some are saved.

BOSWELL: Saved? Saved for what? A miserable life in a filth-ridden world. One percent of one splatter is cleaned up before there is a whole new splat out. You save a thimbleful of sand on a blackened beach. You sit a legless dancer at a harp with no strings. Good work. Well done. *(About his dinner.)* This tastes like bile. I got the Final Report today.

WILLIAM: *(A beat.)* What did it say?

BOSWELL: It was unanimous.

WILLIAM: Oh.

BOSWELL: Um.

WILLIAM: Does that mean?

BOSWELL: Yes.

WILLIAM: How long do you have?

BOSWELL: Awhile.

WILLIAM: A good while?

BOSWELL: Not really.

WILLIAM: A year?

BOSWELL: Maybe less.

WILLIAM: Less. Oh. Oh. This is the worst thing ever. I don't want you to die. To leave. You'll be gone. And I got to see you. Every day I got to see you. Oh, where will they take you when you have died? Where will you be? I don't want you to be there. It's too far.

BOSWELL: Oblivion. I'll be in oblivion, where I'm sure I'll be perfectly dead and won't be plagued with any cares or woes. It's now, however, that's concerning me. It's now that's the problem. This time now when I'm alive and living with the burden of a mind, an imagination, and a trembling heart. Now, when I can lie awake nights picturing eons and eons of vast, dark deadness; where I'll be eternally alone, lost in nothingness without a book or a magazine or a smile from some stranger's child.

WILLIAM: This can't happen.

BOSWELL: It is.

WILLIAM: Oh, dear. Boswell—

BOSWELL: Stay away.

WILLIAM: Can't I come to you?

BOSWELL: No.

WILLIAM: Please—

BOSWELL: I said no.

WILLIAM: I want to.

BOSWELL: No.

(Boswell turns away from her. William stands alone, hugging herself. The chaotic sounds of the ocean roaring. The Reader, an ageless woman with fierce eyes, appears in space.)

READER: Come on. Come on. You wanna know? Come on. Up here. Eat with me. Mama took my cotton candy. But I found a wrapper. Pink sugar on the wrapper. Smell of peanuts. Smell of peanuts.

SCENE V

The stoop in front of L-Tip's apartment. Max, dressed in dirty rags, sits on the stoop. C-Boy, a boy of about eleven, sits on the edge of the curb. He is a filthy, emaciated waif. He wears an orange band around his waist and is eating from a government food box. It is an unnaturally hot day. The sun blares down. The smog is thick and green and brown. The chaotic sounds fade.

MAX: L.A. has changed. I can't quite put my finger on it, but things are different. Things are—not so good. You may not realize all this. You're sitting pretty. You get a government food box every day. What'd you get in there this time? Any Fig Bolts? You get a Fig Bolt?
(C-Boy moves away from Max, hovering over his food.)
MAX: Hey, I wasn't gonna ask for one. I just wanted to see. Christ, I'm not even interested in food. Food! Who needs food? I live on poetry, poems, and yearning. They flow from me like unkempt sewage. *(Max pulls various ratty pieces of paper from his pockets. He reads one of them to himself.)* *(L-Tip appears at the top of the stoop, carrying an air contraption. She is scantily clad and is perspiring heavily because of the relentless heat. There are green stripes painted up the back of her legs.)*
L-TIP: Hi.
MAX: Hi.
L-TIP: Hot day.
MAX: Yes.
L-TIP: Here's the air contraption.
MAX: Thanks.
L-TIP: I don't know how you're going to use it. You don't have a home.
MAX: It's part of the settlement.
L-TIP: Right. *(She turns to go.)*
MAX: *(Sincerely.)* Hey, I was wondering?
L-TIP: What?
MAX: *(Kindly.)* Just—How are things with you?
L-TIP: Sin, really sin. I've got five new clients. And I'm right on the verge of persuading K.Y. Von Ludwig to sign with me. He's the Big Splash of the season, you know.
MAX: So what makes you think he'll go with you?
L-TIP: You probably don't realize this, Max, but I'm starting to make a real

name for myself around this town. People are calling me "L-Tip the Hip Lip." I'm really dishing up.

MAX: Hmm. So this Von Ludwig's impressed with you?

L-TIP: Yeah.

MAX: Oh, then he doesn't realize you're really a nobody. I mean, in the scheme of things. In this town.

L-TIP: He thinks I'm sin.

MAX: Oh. What about you does he think is sin?

L-TIP: The green stripes I paint up the back of my legs. The ones you said were trash class. He says they suit me. He says I have legs like trees. Wilderness legs, he calls me.

MAX: What are you saying? Are you pogoing this toast? You out there hawking yourself like meat wrapped in tin foil down by the fucking bay?

L-TIP: Look at you. You're curling up with jeally and you got no track.

MAX: Hey, I'm not jeally. Not me. I'm not the type. And don't you zap labels on me. Don't zoom price tags on my forehead.

L-TIP: Chuck you. *(She starts up the steps.)*

MAX: Hey, L-Tip. There's one thing I forgot to tell you. There's one big thing I lied about. Our whole marriage I told one big lie.

L-TIP: What?

MAX: You are fat. You're a pig. Your thighs are pure blubber.

L-TIP: Bastard. You bastard. *(She exits up the stairs.)*

MAX: I knew that would cut her to the quick. Calling her a pig. That was a good one. It got her. It made an impression. I don't really need the air contraption. It was just an excuse to see her. To make some headway. I wanted to read her my poem. I think she would have been moved. Oh, why did I call her a pig? What a mistake. What a misguided blunder! *(He slaps himself in the face.)* What now? What now? I guess, I'll just—have to—grip on. Right. That's all. Grip on. Next time it will go better. Next time I'll do things right. Next time I'll be the way I should have been now.

SCENE VI

Boswell's apartment. Late afternoon. Boswell is anxiously sorting through a box of memorabilia. He is bare-chested. Grey sores are visible on his chest. William sits on her mat. She wears her splatter suit and helmet. She is cleaning black spill off of a strange creature with a wire brush.

BOSWELL: *(To himself.)* Very good. Very good. I must display important items from my memorabilia box. L-Tip will need to be familiarized with all facets of my career. *(Holding up a letter chip.)* What's this? Oh, a request for my autograph. *(Grandly.)* Someone once wanted a copy of my signature.

(There is a loud buzz.)

BOSWELL: L-Tip! Darling, please enter.

JENNIFER: *(Over loudspeaker.)* It's Jennifer.

BOSWELL: Who?

JENNIFER: *(Over loudspeaker.)* Jennifer T-Thorp. One of your daughters. The middle one.

BOSWELL: Shit. One of my swarmy brats.

(Boswell turns on the TVP. Jennifer, eight, appears on the screen. She wears a kerchief on her head and holds a Blue Dot Cactus.)

BOSWELL: What do you want?

JENNIFER: *(On the screen.)* I brought you a Blue Dot Cactus. Mum said you would like it.

BOSWELL: Oh, how sug. No doubt you read about my condition in the Up And Coming Obits.

JENNIFER: *(On the screen.)* Yes, we did. Can I come bring it up to you?

BOSWELL: No. Just put it in the laser box.

JENNIFER: *(On the screen.)* Oh. Alright.

(Boswell clicks her off the screen.)

BOSWELL: I'm sorry but I simply don't have time. After all I am someone whose face has been on a button. *(He holds up a square button with his face on it. A Blue Dot Cactus appears in the laser tray.)* Oh, very good, here it is. A Blue Dot Cactus. At one time Wanda and I had a whole garden of Blue Dot Cacti. Poor Wanda. She doesn't realize how I've grown. *(He picks up the cactus.)* I don't want this. I'm throwing it away.

(William lifts her face guard.)

WILLIAM: Could I have it?

(Boswell glares at her then throws the plant into the receptacle.)

BOSWELL: It's in the receptacle. Now get your clap back down. I've told you I can no longer tolerate the sight of your face.

(William lowers her face guard.)

BOSWELL: I do not like looking at your face.

(William goes back to cleaning the animal.)

BOSWELL: And another thing. I'm getting sick of you bringing in these wretched creatures. Picking away at them all through the night.

WILLIAM: I want to get selected Worker of the Year.

BOSWELL: God, how pathetic to live a life where every bone is a treasure.

WILLIAM: If I get the W.Y. badge, I'll be allowed a quarter cubicle. Then I'll be able to start the defrost on my kids.

BOSWELL: Forget about those kids. You don't know how lucky you are they've got them on ice.

(L-Tip's voice is heard over the door speaker.)

L-TIP'S VOICE: *(Through the door speaker.)* Boswell? Hi. Hi. It's L-Tip.

BOSWELL: Darling, darling, darling. Entree. Entree. *(Boswell clicks in L-Tip.)* *(L-Tip enters looking more trendy and today than ever. She wears a dress decorated with packages of food and drug vials. She is uncomfortable visiting her dying friend.)*

L-TIP: Boswell. Hi. Hi. Hi…My, don't you…you look good.

BOSWELL: Yes, and you're looking even more, more than ever.

L-TIP: *(About her dress.)* Isn't it sin? It's a fuel frock. Saves all sorts of time. You never have to stop for meals. *(Offering him food off of the dress.)* Here, are you hungry?

BOSWELL: No thanks.

L-TIP: Save it for later. I mean, well, soon later.

BOSWELL: Listen, L-Tip, I don't want your Fig Bolt, but I do have a proposal to make to you as my manager.

L-TIP: Whatever you want. Whatever I can do. *(Offering him grapes from her dress.)* Sure you—

BOSWELL: No.

L-TIP: *(Eating the grapes.)* I missed lunch.

BOSWELL: I just thought, in light of my present—state. That perhaps we could organize a salute to Boxdom. Something along the line of a Grand Memorial Dinner. Charge, say, two thousand K per tic. Get the elite satellites, get the V.I.P. press. The laser lead could read "Come See Box Before He's Boxed." I like that. It's thematic, yet witty…What are you thinking?

L-TIP: Hmm. I don't know. It's the future. Boxdom is way-out fad. It hasn't got any bite for today's market.

BOSWELL: No bite? I'm talking about handing you a dying artist's retrospective with the dying artist in tow, and you're telling me there's no bite?

L-TIP: If only you hadn't stopped so abruptly at the Box Theory. If only you'd done something more.

BOSWELL: Yes, well, due to my remarkable intelligence, I realized early on this world was not an oyster I wanted to try and swallow. Thus I went on to

other things. Like maintaining an image which was a vital part of secur-
ing government subsidy. I made replica posters, sold souvenir boxes. I
did that ad for box perfume…But I don't have to stand here and sell
myself to you. You're nothing more than a noodle pusher who used me
to worm her way into the Celebrity Chase. We went in there to get me
work, me! Instead, you come out with five new clients, while I'm still
standing here surrounded by the smell of zed.

L-TIP: Believe me, Boz. I've tried every sin in the book to got a job in Hollywood—

BOSWELL: I'm not asking for a job. I'm asking for a dinner.

L-TIP: Don't you understand, it's trash class to give a Grand Memorial Dinner
for yourself before you're really even dosed.

BOSWELL: Fine, fine. We'll just wait till I'm all dosed out, so we can leave it
up to you to make me look good. You who have the infallible fashion
sense to parade around town dressed up like a fucking Bee Jam's
Supermarket. *(He rips food off of her frock.)*

L-TIP: Hey, those are mine.

BOSWELL: Goo Goo Pops, indeed!

L-TIP: You got no track!

BOSWELL: You're fired! You know that? You're fused! *(Boswell exits.)*

L-TIP: *(Yelling after him.)* Yeah! Oh, yeah?! Yeah! Ding-a-roo. Look, he tore off
my snacks. I don't have to take this anymore. I got clients. I'm a professional woman. All my dreams are coming true.

WILLIAM: He thinks he's some big, fat bing. Well, he's not. If you wanna know
the truth, before I moved in here, I never even heard of Boxdom.

L-TIP: Oh, it had its day. It lived for about as long as a fish can breathe in
cement. But it's over, it's zapped, it's glue rot. He's not in step. I've got
this theory. I've developed it.

WILLIAM: Yeah?

L-TIP: Trend is life.

WILLIAM: Yeah?

L-TIP: If you're doing what's doing now, at least you know you're doing something. Even if it's stupid and fleeting, dangerous and dull, at least it's
happening. There's assurance in knowing you are participating in an era.
Have some Red Dogs.

*(L-Tip hands William some Red Dogs. Throughout the following, they eat
and drink from L-Tip's dress.)*

WILLIAM: Thanks.

L-TIP: Before I had this theory, I wasn't anybody. All I knew about myself was
I was in my thirties, I was Max's wife, I worked at a noodle stand, and

Chee Chee Kitty was my favorite Fantasy Puppet. I had all the Chee Chee Kitty fashion attire, laser dots, kitchen equipment, toiletries.

WILLIAM: Moe Zoe Beam is my favorite Fantasy Puppet. But I don't have any of his stuff.

L-TIP: The thing is, all that stuff doesn't make you happy, 'cause you're still sitting on the sidelines. I ultimately realized, what I really wanted to be doing was all the things the real Chee Chee Kitty was doing on Celeb Bites—wearing outfits made of sugar stars, lapping up the limelight, dancing at Cafe Who's Who with Count Tidbit. So, for the first time, I decided to turn my life around and become a manager.

WILLIAM: You just decided?

L-TIP: With every hair on my flesh. It thrills me knowing what I want, going out and getting it, taking it, swallowing it whole, wiping my lips and coming back for more. Mmm.

(L-Tip wipes her lips with her hand. William imitates her.)

WILLIAM: Mmm.

L-TIP: Ya gotta slurp up the stars. That's why they're up in the sky.

WILLIAM: Go. I feel like a puff next to you.

L-TIP: *(Showing her finger with a big laser ring on it.)* Tomorrow I'm marrying K.Y. Von Ludwig, the Big Splash of the season.

WILLIAM: Ding-a-roo. I saw his picture. He's dish.

L-TIP: Oh yeah, he's been on the front of five zill videozines this month. He's the Big Splash. I mean, he is unbearably conceited and self-sucking. But I don't think he can help that; he is a man. Anyway, this time I don't expect my marriage to work out. It's more like a career move. I'll do anything to get out ahead. 'Cause that's what I believe in. I mean, you gotta believe in something, right? Otherwise, what's the point?

(There is a loud banging at the door. Max's voice comes over the loudspeaker.)

MAX'S VOICE: *(Over speaker.)* L-Tip, I know you're in there. They told me you're in there. Open this door. Open this fucking door!

WILLIAM: *(Overlapping.)* It's Max. He sounds like he's detonating.

MAX'S VOICE: Click me in! Now, for fuck's sake! Now! Click me in! *(He continues banging.)*

L-TIP: *(Overlapping.)* I'll click him in. I'll show him what for. Calling me a pig. Come on, you bastard.

(L-Tip crawls to the remote and clicks Max in. Max enters. He has a large cut on his forehead. Blood has dried on his face and on his dirty garments.)

MAX: You gonna marry that fuck?

L-TIP: Yeah, I am.

MAX: But do you love him? You love that fuck? You think you're in love with him? It's—true love?

L-TIP: Yes.

MAX: You do? You love that fucking fuck?

L-TIP: Yes.

MAX: More than me?

L-TIP: Oh, yes.

MAX: But you did love me? At one time? You did?

L-TIP: I guess. I suppose.

MAX: But you stopped. It ended. You stopped loving me. Why did you stop? What made you stop? What? I—Look, I've written poems for you. *(He pulls out endless poems, all crumpled and dirty, from his pockets, shirt, shoes, etc.)* All these poems. Love poems. Passion notes, erotica. And these! And this! And that!

L-TIP: What? What? I don't want these. I gave you love. You had love. You held its fluttering wings in your hands and crushed it slowly to death. Now you hold up its breathless body, look at it and say you're very, very sad.

MAX: I didn't—I wouldn't crush—No—Untrue.

L-TIP: Yeah, well, the whole time we were together you never stopped pogo-ing every woman who ever gave you change.

MAX: You're the only one I loved.

L-TIP: Go. You didn't even know me. You thought you were married to Chee Chee Kitty. Remember how I always had to make those kitty whispers?

MAX: I thought you liked that.

L-TIP: I thought I did, too. We were both wrong. I'm leaving. *(She gathers herself together and heads for the door.)*

MAX: Please, tell me, I don't understand. What's happened to our love? Fourteen years of love. We were each other's lives. Can all that be wiped clean like dust across piano keys, and suddenly everything is silent? *(They look at each other speechlessly for several deafening moments of silence. Then L-Tip exits. Max starts to breathe heavily.)*

WILLIAM: You're bleeding.

MAX: I—Yes, I was hit by something. It was dropped on my head as I was walking down the street. A boulder, a Dr. Pop bottle, I don't know what? Something that could kill you.

WILLIAM: Did you hear the news? About M. Boswell?

MAX: Oh, yes, hasn't he always been the lucky one.

WILLIAM: I don't think it's lucky.

MAX: Maybe then you have something to live for.

WILLIAM: Sure. I do. I want a home to live in and I want my kids out of F.D. Then I want us all to learn to read and write and clap to music.

MAX: May I use your TVP?

WILLIAM: Uh-huh.

(Max goes to the TVP screen. Max's click goes through on the TVP. An amiable woman dressed in white surrounded by pink carnations, appears on the screen.)

WOMAN: *(On the TVP screen.)* Hello. Euthanasia Hot line. May I help you?

MAX: *(Into TVP.)* Yes. This is Maxwell T-Thorp. I want to be euthed.

WOMAN: *(On the TVP screen.)* So you're calling to euth yourself, not a friend or relative.

MAX: *(Into TVP.)* Yes. Correct.

WOMAN: *(On the TVP screen.)* Very well. If you'll just hold on a minute, I'll transfer you to the P.W. Department and we'll get started on your paperwork.

(Happy cartoons of people dying peacefully come up on the screen, as Max is put on hold.)

WILLIAM: Max, don't. Click off. Don't.

MAX: I can no longer live caked in this awful pain.

(A rosy, pink man appears on the TVP screen. He sits behind a computer.)

PINK MAN: *(On the TVP screen.)* Hello. M. Maxwell T-Thorp?

MAX: *(To the TVP screen.)* Yes.

PINK MAN: *(On the TVP screen.)* We're going to need some information.

MAX: *(To the TVP screen.)* Of course.

PINK MAN: *(On the TVP screen.)* Age?

MAX: *(To the TVP screen.)* Thirties.

PINK MAN: *(On the TVP screen.)* Residence.

MAX: *(To the TVP screen.)* Eighth box on Garbage Bag Row.

PINK MAN: *(On the TVP screen.)* Occupation.

MAX: *(To the TVP screen.)* Unemployed.

PINK MAN: *(On the TVP screen.)* Reason for euth request?

MAX: *(To the TVP screen.)* A broken heart.

(William picks the sea lamb up out of the box. It is clean and pink and glowing. She stands there holding it, rocking back and forth.)

SCENE VII

The Boardwalk at sunset. Later that same day. Sounds: ocean, wind, carnival noises, clean-up crews' machinery. There are two stools and a cardboard box set up. There is a sign on the box reading "Graphologist For Hire." Reader stands with one foot on a stool, hawking her talent. She has a mustache.

READER: One grain! One grain! One grain of sand. Magnified Magnify it. See if you can eat it whole. Time will tell. But I'll tell quicker. Let me read the writing; all the writing on your wall. Write your name on water. Sign your signature in the sand. I'll peek under your skin and tell you who's home.
(Boswell enters. He is distracted and pale.)
READER: Hey, M.! Right this way. Over here.
BOSWELL: What?
READER: You.
BOSWELL: Me?
READER: You.
BOSWELL: What do you want, you filthy arrangement of molecules?
READER: I read writing. I'll read yours.
BOSWELL: I don't think so. *(He stands and listens to the ocean roar endlessly.)*
READER: *(Whispering to him.)* I can tell you who you are, where you've been, where you're going, what you need, and what you'll get. For one extra quarter, I'll answer the big bonus question. You know the one.
BOSWELL: No.
READER: The big one. Why you are here. Why you're alive.
BOSWELL: I don't think I really need to know any of that.
READER: Suit yourself. But the truth is, you already know. It's all there, lurking in the writing.
BOSWELL: Writing?
READER: Handwriting.
BOSWELL: Oh.
READER: Look at the sunset. It's all green and gold and bloody blue. There's been a change in the atmosphere.
BOSWELL: How much do you charge?
READER: Ten K. Plus a quarter for the B.Q.
BOSWELL: B.Q.?
READER: Big Question.

BOSWELL: Oh. Well, why not? I have some time to spare.

(She hands him paper and pen.)

READER: Write two sentences.

(Boswell starts to write, then pauses.)

BOSWELL: What do I say?

READER: Makes no difference. Everything about you will be there. No matter what.

BOSWELL: Ha. This is silly. I've become a very silly man. *(He writes out two sentences.)*

READER: Now, sign your name. *(A beat.)* Write your signature.

BOSWELL: Well, yes. Alright. *(He writes his signature.)* There. I've finished.

(He pushes the paper over to her. She reads it over with a stunning intensity. She looks up at him for a moment with dark dread, then looks back at his writing. She studies the writing for several excruciating moments.)

BOSWELL: Well? What is it? What do you see? What's there?

READER: *(She looks up at him.)* I'm sorry.

BOSWELL: What for?

READER: The sores are grey now, slate grey. They'll soon be red, then black, and then—you'll be dead.

BOSWELL: I—I—Um.

READER: But that's not the worst of it. *(Referring to the paper.)* Your heart. It has shrunken and turned brown. You have a raisin for a heart. And your life. Your life is like an empty cereal box infested with microscopic bugs. Even in its heyday, all it held were Puffs. You're shallow, self-absorbed, antisocial, conceited, cruel, and cowardly. You let a minute early success paralyze you into doing, holding, and believing nothing. You're going to die unloved and unremembered. Why were you born? *(She rakes in the quarter.)* To prove how hollow and stupid life can be.

BOSWELL: I see.

READER: Please, I don't mean any of this as a value judgment. It's just—It's all right here. It's in the letters. It's in your signature.

BOSWELL: Where? How?

READER: Observe your shrunken *L*'s; your twisted *T*-crossings; the cowardly crest dots of your *I*'s; and the waywardness of your *P*'s.

BOSWELL: Oh. Hmm. I—but how should they be? How should the letters be?

READER: It depends on who you are.

BOSWELL: How about—How about, if you're someone who's lived—who's been—who is significant.

READER: Significant? Oh, well, everything would be completely different.

The *L*'s would be high. They would flow evenly. The loops would be daring and fluid, joyous and open.

BOSWELL: Show me.

(She demonstrates.)

READER: Like that. See? Like that.

BOSWELL: I can do that. *(He makes an L.)* How's that? Like that?

READER: Try again.

(Boswell tries three more L's. He shows them to the Reader with a desperate hope.)

BOSWELL: And now?

READER: There's no joy. You need joy.

BOSWELL: Joy. *(He tries again.)* How's that?

READER: Don't get frivolous.

BOSWELL: No.

READER: Think joy.

(Boswell tries again.)

BOSWELL: Joy.

READER: Closer.

BOSWELL: I must leave—I want to leave my signature. *(He writes his name with flourish.)*

READER: Very good.

BOSWELL: *(Encouraged, he writes again.)* Here lies one whose name was drilled in granite.

READER: Remarkable! That *T* crossing! Such heroic importance!

BOSWELL: Then it's not too late?

READER: Change your writing; change your life.

BOSWELL: I can still know everything; do everything; be everything I have always dreamt?

READER: Ah, what a profound dot to your *I*.

BOSWELL: *(Writing madly.)* All this time I didn't know; I didn't know I had everything right here in my hand. In my signature.

(The sunset turns blood red. Boswell continues to write. Blackout.)

END OF ACT I

ACT II
SCENE I

Boswell's apartment. Max wears an intricately patterned robe and a turban with a jewel. He is reading the galleys of his book of poetry. Boswell is in a frantic state of exhaustion. He is trying to learn everything there is to know in the universe. C-Boy, who is wearing filth-covered rags and his orange government belt, is clicking images of objects up onto the TVP screen, and then pointing to various parts of the object with a laser stick. It is Boswell's task to identify the object and the parts. Each time Boswell gets a correct answer, C-Boy takes his pointer and hits the correct button which flashes and makes a buzz noise. Slide A is the universe.

BOSWELL: Good one. Good one. It's the universe.
(C-Boy hits the correct button, then Boswell goes on to identify the various parts as C-Boy points to them with the laser stick.)
BOSWELL: Quasar. Quark. Doppler shift. Supernova.
(C-Boy clicks to Slide B. A clothespin.)
BOSWELL: Okay, I know that one. That's a—it's a—clothespin.
(C-Boy buzzes the correct button, then points with the stick.)
BOSWELL: Pinwood, gripping hole. Claw end. Spring slot.
(C-Boy clicks to Slide C. A nosebleed.)
BOSWELL: Easy, nosebleed.
(C-Boy buzzes the correct button, then points with the stick.)
BOSWELL: Nares. Nasopharynx. Leukocytes. Erythocytes.
(William enters. She is dressed in her splatter suit. She carries a pack on her back and limps slightly.)
BOSWELL: *(To William.)* Hello, William. How was the reef?
WILLIAM: Cold. Freezing. Lost a toe.
(Throughout the following, William removes her gear. She takes off her boots and puts on her shiny white shoes. Her foot has a bandage on it. C-Boy has clicked to Slide D. Pasta Dishes.)
BOSWELL: Go! It's Pasta Dishes!
(C-Boy buzzes the correct button, then points with stick.)
BOSWELL: Spaghetti Alla Puttanescan. Pasta Con Sarde. Penne Alla Arrabreta. Tubettini With Porcini And Cream Dots. My favorite!
(C-Boy buzzes correct button.)
BOSWELL: God, I'm a genius, a living genius. Oh, look at the time. I must rush to the Reader. Wait till she sees my new bounty. I have crossed a

new plateau of penmanship. There is no thing I cannot know! *(Handing C-Boy a list.)* C-Boy, when I return I want us to find the answers to these questions before dinner: How do you cook a fish? Who was Booker T. Washington? Are people supposed to be happy? If so, how, when, and at what cost? Also, if there is time, we could look into one more. *(He scans the list.)* Ah, here's a good one! Is there a God or is this all just a free lunch? Well, gotta run. Jacka, jacka, jacka! *(Boswell exits.)*

WILLIAM: I'm worried about Boswell.

MAX: His handwriting told him he must learn everything there is to know in the universe. I'm afraid he's gone completely mad. *(Showing her his manuscript with pride.)* Look, they X'd over the galleys for my book. Here are all my poems in print. I'm very prolific.

WILLIAM: Go. And they paid you?

MAX: Where do you think I got this charm suit?

WILLIAM: Things sure are going good for you.

MAX: *(Clicking his fingers.)* Rumba!

WILLIAM: Maybe you should click up the euth line and cancel your order.

MAX: What? No. I can't. The main reason they're publishing these poems is because of my back story. I'm the very first person to be euthed for love. I'll be remembered as the most romantic figure of the twenty-first century. I'll make history. It's part of the marketing.

WILLIAM: Max, I wish—please, don't.

MAX: Look, before I was gonna get euthed I had nothing to live for. Now that I'm getting euthed, everything's going my way. Why rock the shuttle?

WILLIAM: I don't know, it just seems stupid. It's dumb.

MAX: Well, hey, I've got to take the bubble over to my publishers. They want me to do some video pub. Look, I'm sorry about your toe.

WILLIAM: It's okay. It was…a small one.

(Max nods and starts to leave again.)

WILLIAM: Uh. Max?

MAX: What?

WILLIAM: *(About C-Boy.)* Who's that?

MAX: Oh, that. That's C-Boy. He's Boswell's ward. Don't ask me. Something in Boz's handwriting told him to reach out to the human species at large.

WILLIAM: *(About C-Boy.)* Well, what's wrong with him?

MAX: Parents did a lot of ear slack. But he's all the Gov. would award Boz because of Boz's failing health condition.

WILLIAM: *(About C-Boy.)* Does he talk?

MAX: Not to me. And he's really selfish with his Fig Bolts. See ya, Willie.

WILLIAM: 'Bye.

(Max exits. William goes over to talk to C-Boy.)

WILLIAM: Hi. I'm M. William Smit. Do you talk? No? What was it, the drugs that got ya? That's a nice belt. It's orange. Red and yellow together make orange. I know that 'cause it's my favorite color, orange. They say the sun is orange. My suit is orange. My favorite food is an orange. I give myself an orange every Holiday Day. Maybe that sounds strange to you, someone giving their own selves a present. But I believe on occasions it's worthwhile to do nice things for one's self. For instance, I always try and keep my shoes nice and buffed. That way I know I always got something shiny to look at as I'm walking down strange roads that may not be going my way.

(C-Boy looks at her. He looks down at his filthy, tattered shoes. He spits on one of his rags and slowly starts to rub dirt off the tip of his shoe.)

SCENE II

The Boardwalk. The Reader is looking over the pages of Boswell's mad handwriting. Boswell stands by sucking two of his fingers in a crazed despair.

READER: More chaos! Worse swill! Such a vast bonanza of garbage! Grotesque struggling, like vipers in a toilet bowl fighting to get shit on.

BOSWELL: Please, I wanted—I thought—is it too late?

READER: Too late for what? To race a rocker ship to Mars? To dance with Ginger Rogers? To dine with Wong Dong? To discover cures for cancer, cruelty, and loneliness? Is it too late? Maybe you should buy a watch.

BOSWELL: And yet I want to do all that. And much more. Everything, everything.

READER: Yet all this while, all this long while, you've never even looked at a pickle.

BOSWELL: A pickle? I've seen pickles.

READER: What kind?

BOSWELL: A—it was green.

READER: There're an awful lot of pickles. An awful lot of green ones. There are sweet pickles, garlic pickles, butter pickles, cucumber pickles, jalapeno pickles, midget pickles, gherkin pickles, kosher pickles, dot pickles, dill and baby dills. Whole shelves in stores hold nothing but pickles and we haven't even delved into your relish.

BOSWELL: Relish? Pickles? You've digressed. We were discussing something of import.

READER: I'm telling you, look to the pickle. Study its size, its shape, the colors, the smells, the ways it can be sliced. Take it into your heart. Sleep with it under your pillow. Walk with it in the dark.

BOSWELL: A pickle. Just one pickle.

READER: It's best not to spread yourself too thin. Write the word pickle ten thousand times in small, precise letters using green ink. That will be the start of everything.

BOSWELL: I—I can do that.

READER: I know you can.

BOSWELL: You—I—you…

READER: What?

BOSWELL: You soothe me.

READER: Do I?

BOSWELL: Um. *(A beat.)* Tell me something about yourself. I want to know something personal.

READER: I have strange orbs.

BOSWELL: You do?

READER: Warm milk and blood and mud all flow from my orbs. Which do you want to suck?

BOSWELL: From your orbs? I—none. Thank you.

READER: It's a horrible situation for me. It makes me peculiar.

BOSWELL: I—yes. It's…

READER: What?

BOSWELL: It's amazing to me how we all get by.

READER: I didn't know we all did.

BOSWELL: No, of course, *some* don't. *(He starts to leave, then turns to her.)* Pickle.

READER: Yes. And eat each pickle. Each pickle that you write. Taste it.

BOSWELL: Taste it.

READER: Yes. That's what I'd do.

BOSWELL: I'll do it then. I'll do it that way.

READER: Yes. Do.

(Boswell exits. Sound of a heartbeat. Reader twists like a viper as her breasts begin to ache. She clutches her right breast. It throbs with a painful longing, a longing for Boswell.)

READER: Oh. God. Oh. God. Boswell. Boswell T-Thorp. Boswell. How long till you are mine? How long?

(As the lights fade, we hear L-Tip's desperate voice and the sound of a clock ticking.)

L-TIP'S VOICE: God. Please. How long?

SCENE III

In front of the Pharmaceutical Distributors. Early morning. L-Tip is waiting for the store to open. She is distressed. She wears a black raincoat, no makeup, her hair is chaos.

L-TIP: Time. God. Time.
   (Max enters. He is formally attired. It is the end of his evening. He wears a wilted laser flower in his lapel. As Max strides by, L-Tip reaches out to him.)
L-TIP: The time?
MAX: Oh yes. Quarter till. *(Recognizing her.)* L-Tip.
L-TIP: *(Recognizing him.)* Max.
MAX: How—why, how are you?
L-TIP: Oh, I'm standing outside the Pharmaceutical Distributors waiting for them to open so I can get my emotional equalizers, soul sedatives, and pain executioners. That's how the fuck I am. How're you?
MAX: Fine.
L-TIP: Just coming from the big bang-a-roo over at Cafe Who's Who?
MAX: That's right.
L-TIP: Do tell.
MAX: Umm. Look, I have a blue dot, if you...
L-TIP: Thanks. I—good. Thanks.
   (He gives her a blue dot.)
L-TIP: Max. I—Those poems, I read. They were touching. You wrote some touching poems.
MAX: I—was inspired. So.
L-TIP: Yeah. My marriage ended.
MAX: I saw it on Night Bites.
L-TIP: Yeah? Well, it's a relief really. I mean, the only bad thing about the slice is now my career is, well, it's over. I'm through; I'm nicked; I'm glue rot. What time?
MAX: Twelve till.
L-TIP: I don't know how this happened. I don't see how. I mean, I am a human being. I've tried my best. I study what to wear. I'm up on trends

in music and restaurants, drugs and entertainment. I have all the up-to-date kitchen equipment. I thought if I got hold of all that, then other people wouldn't be mean to me. In fact, maybe I might even have this imperceivable right to be mean to them, just for not knowing or doing the things people who are worthwhile know and do. But, no. Uh-uh. Instead I'm the one who's being juiced out. It's me. Oh God, I'm so wretched and worthless—so swollen in salted, tormenting misery!

MAX: There, there. Maybe you're just—you're probably having your—I mean…Is this your…? Is it time for your…?

L-TIP: *(Cold and fierce.)* What?

MAX: Nothing.

L-TIP: I know what you're suggesting, Max.

MAX: No, no, I'm not.

L-TIP: Okay. Good. Don't. Even if—well, maybe I am. But that's not the point. There's some whole other point.

MAX: I know. I know it's not the point. Hey. Listen. This'll be over. It'll pass. It's temporary.

L-TIP: Right. Like my whole life. It'll be over. It'll pass. While I just stand here, helplessly bleeding out one more egg, a child, a shell, an angel. Oh God. God. I'm having a weep down. *(She starts to cry. Her tears are light blue in color.)*

MAX: L-Tip, I didn't know you felt this way.

L-TIP: Oh, I don't. It's my hormones. They're the ones with feelings. As soon as they open up this spoon store, I'll fix it all out. *(She cries some more.)*

MAX: I can't help it. I love to watch you cry. You're the only one I've ever known who cries blue tears. Remember how I used to pinch and scare you just to see you cry blue tears.

L-TIP: Yeah. Well, too bad it doesn't earn me any K. What time?

MAX: Six minutes. Look, I—Celeb Bites is doing a show on me. Maybe I could arrange for you to do the interview.

L-TIP: Me?

MAX: Yeah.

L-TIP: A job?

MAX: Yeah.

L-TIP: I'll take it. Time?

MAX: *(Showing her his watch.)* Close.

L-TIP: *(Looking at his watch.)* Close.

(As the lights fade, we hear the sound of a clock ticking.)

SCENE IV

The Boardwalk. The sound of a clock ticking continues. Reader is at her box. Her hair and braid are neatly braided with a pink ribbon. She wears a sleeveless blouse. Incredible, long, black hair grows from her armpits. This hair is also neatly braided and tied with pink ribbon. She strokes her lips with the tip of this hair. She is waiting expectantly. The ocean roars. Sea birds squawk. Offshore machinery rumbles in the distance. The sound of a clock ticking starts to fade as Boswell appears. He is walking with a cane. He is distracted yet ebullient. He carries a sheet of his handwriting. He spots Reader and waves the sheet at her.

BOSWELL: Ah ho! You were right. You knew. Pickles. Yes, pickles. It is coming to me for the first time in all this time. A torrential outpouring of creative bliss. I'm calling it, "Death and a Jar of Pickles." Compared to this Boxdom is nothing more than puerile dribble. Why, if I can capture this poster, if it is fully grasped, it may be all we ever need to know. Finished! Done! Complete!!

READER: You haven't said anything about my hair.

BOSWELL: Oh. No. Well, yes, I see. Now, about these pickles. These universal pickles; these monolithic pickles—they're just swimming and soaking in a sea of wretched, godless juices.

READER: Let me see the writing. Where's the writing?

BOSWELL: *(Handing over the pages.)* Yes, of course. Pickle, pickle pickle.

READER: *(Looking over the pages of writing.)* Hmm. Very interesting.

BOSWELL: What?

READER: You're not whole. You're incomplete. Something is missing.

BOSWELL: What? What could be missing? I have my pickles. My poster. When it is complete, I'll have something to display. My masterpiece. I can hold it up to the whole world.

READER: And who will hold you back?

BOSWELL: Everyone. Everyone will be awed and amazed.

READER: Who will hold the real one? The one that feels and stinks and eats and can't sleep and gets so frightened by, by, by, by rainstorms and unpleasant faces and sores that don't heal in the cracks of his hands.

BOSWELL: What do you want from me? You know my condition. It's too late for all that. I have to be reasonable.

READER: Maybe it's time for you to blow your nose on the sleeve of reason. Go past the numbness, tear off the layers of fear and self-loathing, look at the pain, stick your tongue down its black throat. Look into its red, weak, watery eyes. Let your blood howl.

BOSWELL: I don't know what you mean. Such nonsense. Just tell me what to write and it will be written.

READER: Feel my orbs.

BOSWELL: What?

READER: Both of them. Feel both of them.

(Boswell feels her breasts with his hands.)

BOSWELL: *(With his hands on her breasts.)* There. Now please, you must tell me what to write. What do I write?

READER: People.

BOSWELL: Yes?

READER: People come through the trees and look into your eyes. You stop them walking toward you. You stand still and shut your eyes.

BOSWELL: *(Averting his eyes and removing his hands from her breasts.)* I don't know that I do that.

READER: You do.

(Boswell looks at his hands. They are stained with blood and mud and milk.)

READER: What's that on your hands?

BOSWELL: I—don't know.

READER: Look at it.

BOSWELL: It's nothing.

READER: Look.

BOSWELL: It's red and black ink stains.

READER: Where'd it come from?

BOSWELL: From a pen in my pocket. Tell me what to write.

READER: You tell me. Where did it come from? Who does it belong to? It doesn't smell like ink.

BOSWELL: Tell me what to write. Tell me. I'm telling you. If you can you should tell me now. *(He grabs her by the throat.)* Because I cannot go away empty-handed.

READER: Write the name of your beloved.

BOSWELL: I don't have a beloved.

READER: Write it one hundred times.

(He lets her go. She gasps for air.)

READER: Where did it come from? Who does it belong to? It doesn't smell like ink.

BOSWELL: I don't have a beloved.

(Soul music comes up, as the lights fade.)

SCENE V

Boswell's apartment. Later that same day. C-Boy and William are dressed in costumes that are garish in a tawdry makeshift sort of way. William wears a decorated orange splatter suit. They are rehearsing a lip sync routine to a soulful love song filled with joyful longing and a hot beat; i.e., Jackie Wilson's "Lonely Teardrops." William is struggling to keep up with C-Boy who incredibly is a dancing genius. He is capable of all sorts of fantastic feats. His emaciated body twists and turns like rubber. William attempts to spin into his arms and stumbles. C-Boy, the utter perfectionist, shakes his head dismally.

C-BOY: *(No, no, no.)*

WILLIAM: I'll get it.

C-BOY: *(Please observe.) (He demonstrates with a flourish.)*

WILLIAM: Okay. I see. More like this.

(She tries again. C-Boy nods his head in measured approval. He motions to her to try the step with him. They are in mid-spin when Boswell enters. They stop rehearsing immediately. William rushes to click off the music.)

WILLIAM: Boswell, hello. I thought—I'm sorry.

BOSWELL: *(Distracted.)* Yes. Well, I have to— *(He wipes his soiled hands with a rag.)* These modern pens they don't function. They malfunction. Inconvenient all the mess.

WILLIAM: We thought you'd be working on your poster.

BOSWELL: What? No. I can't. It's been—you see there's no one to write down. I have no beloved.

WILLIAM: Well, I'm sorry. We'll get out of your way.

BOSWELL: What are you—your apparel is strange.

WILLIAM: These are our outfits. Tonight we perform in the Spectacular Splat Out Fund Raiser. We're lip syncing to an antique tune. C-Boy, he made up our whole dance.

(C-Boy beams in a strange, sheepish way.)

BOSWELL: Dance? You dance?

WILLIAM: He's very good. He taught me how.

BOSWELL: How what?

WILLIAM: To dance.

BOSWELL: Dance.

WILLIAM: Yes, if you wanted—I mean, we could show you.

BOSWELL: Show me? Why would I? You know I don't—because I simply do not care for entertainment of any sort.

WILLIAM: Yes, well, we should go.

BOSWELL: Alright. Do it. Go ahead. Let me see your dance. I will watch it if I must.

WILLIAM: Okay. Yes. C-Boy, click it.

(C-Boy clicks on the music and they do their dance. The gist of the dance is a crazed C-Boy begging, pleading, cajoling, and romancing William to come back to him. Boswell watches with gripped amazement. He finds himself totally identifying with the demonic C-Boy who is wholly possessed by William and her relentless joy. The song ends. The dancers stop, then slowly, almost sadly, they both look to Boswell for approval. Boswell sits for a moment stupefied.)

BOSWELL: I—I—Stunning. *(He rises to his feet and applauds.)* Stunning. Hear, hear. Remarkable. I—hear, hear.

WILLIAM: *(Numb with shock.)* You liked it?

BOSWELL: Yes.

WILLIAM: Oh, C-Boy, he liked it. He liked it.

(William and C-Boy hug each other joyfully. Boswell stands awkwardly alone.)

WILLIAM: Now we don't have to worry about tonight. Why, if M. Boswell liked it you know everyone else will. Thank you, M. Boswell. Thank you.

(C-Boy salutes Boswell with the Box Salute.)

BOSWELL: I—You're welcome.

WILLIAM: Well, we should go on over. They want us there early.

(C-Boy gestures to their faces.)

WILLIAM: Yes, we have to do our makeup. They're gonna put us in makeup.

(C-Boy and William gather their coats, ears, props, etc. throughout the following. C-Boy communicates to William through pantomime.)

WILLIAM: Now should we wear the rubber noses?

(C-Boy gives a definite "yes.")

WILLIAM: Yeah, I think so, too. They're so zog. Well, 'bye, Boswell, have a good night.

BOSWELL: I—when will you be back?

WILLIAM: Ten is the curfew.

BOSWELL: I—well...Have a good time.

WILLIAM: We will.

BOSWELL: Ah, wait a minute.

WILLIAM: Yes?

BOSWELL: Good luck.

WILLIAM: *(Stunned and honored.)* Thanks. Thanks a lot, M. Boswell. Thank you.

BOSWELL: Yes. Well. 'Bye.

WILLIAM: 'Bye.

(William and C-Boy start to leave.)

BOSWELL: William?

WILLIAM: What?

BOSWELL: Could I come?

WILLIAM: Sure. Of course. Boswell's coming.

BOSWELL: I'll get my coat.

WILLIAM: Oh, he's gonna come see us do our act in person. Boswell's coming. Isn't it wonderful. He's coming. This is so wonderful.

BOSWELL: Well, now let's go. Come on. We don't have all night. Put on your ears. You know how the temperature drops.

(They all three exit in a flurry. The lights start to fade as the Celeb Bites' theme music comes up.)

SCENE VI

Satellite station. The Celeb Bites' theme music plays. L-Tip is interviewing Max on Celeb Bites. Max wears his charm suit and turban. He looks the perfect lost poet. L-Tip wears a dress made of different colored eyeglasses. She has green eyeglasses painted around her eyes. Her persona is that of the highly sexual intellectual. They both wear heavy makeup. A bright pink light burns down on them. The theme music dies down. L-Tip smiles into the camera.

L-TIP: Welcome to Celeb Bites. I'm L-Tip the Hip Lip, your guest host. Tonight we are chewing it up with poet, Maxwell T-Thorp, the man who is going to euth himself for love. Is he a romantic hero or a cowardly imbecile? Let's find out. Hello, Max.

MAX: Hello, L-Tip.

L-TIP: So, tell us, Max, how long do you have?

MAX: It's just a matter of completing the paperwork.

L-TIP: I hear the paperwork's appalling.

MAX: Yes. Dreadful. It could take…who knows?

L-TIP: Well, you fascinate me, M. T-Thorp. Tell us your story. How did you ever reach this point of desperation?

MAX: I, well, I met her when we were very young. We went to school together.

She'd sit at her terminal and make little cooing sounds. At recess one day she shared her soyball sandwich with me. Later we were married. I got a job at the Tank Bureau. I had half a cubicle, access to coffee dot, a key to the M. room, all your basic extra features. Then she divorced me. That's when I discovered, love can kill you.

L-TIP: And yet you sit here looking very zog. Your poems are today's craze. The laser show's in the works. I mean, aren't you being peculiarly short-eyed? Things change very fast in this world. Why, you could find a new love tomorrow. Or perhaps even tonight.

MAX: I don't think so. You see, I'm not one of your twenty-first century use and cruisers who disposes of love like it was last meal's fuel frock.

L-TIP: Yet couldn't it be argued that you are wasting a life that should be cherished by committing this cowardly act of self-aggrandizement?

MAX: I don't see that I'm wasting my life. In fact, just the opposite. Certainly to go on living would be the real coward's play. But I refuse to desecrate my profound love by adhering to the notion that it can be replaced, or forgotten, or lived without. I believe by dying I'm tipping my hat to life and the grand effect it can have on the living.

L-TIP: I'm sorry to say this but listening to you, I don't think you have any idea what real love is. Why, if you understood mature love, you would come to love and accept yourself and not degenerate into this destructive, distorted masochistic indulgence.

MAX: Yes, I'm afraid it's true. I don't know what real or mature love is. It's a mystery to me as I believe it is to most human beings. But the glorious thing is I dove into the ocean anyway, having no idea how to swim, and now I'm going down for the third count and I have no regrets; the water is green and cool and I would rather be here than standing endlessly alone on the parched, dry shore.

L-TIP: I don't understand you. You never even treated her that well. This woman. I—I've done my research. And you pogoed around. You always pogoed around. You forgot her birthday eleven times. You ignored her at parties. You complained about the meals she clicked. You tore the arms off her Chee Chee Kitty.

MAX: All the more reason. All the more reason to salvage the remnants of a love I shattered through reckless abuse.

L-TIP: But there you are again, only thinking of yourself. Why, she wouldn't want—any of this.

MAX: How do you know?

L-TIP: I—she—we've talked.

MAX: Yes. And what does she want?

L-TIP: She doesn't want you to euth yourself. She—She would take you back. If you did not do that.

MAX: But does she...? Is she...? Could she love me still?

L-TIP: I—don't know. Things are so different. Everything.

MAX: I can't go back without it. Always hoping for its return like sawed off legs that will never grow back. Please. Tell me. What?

L-TIP: I—How can I? It's—You'll have to ask her.

MAX: There's nothing to ask.

L-TIP: You're a charlatan. You're just doing this to sell your book. You'll call it off before it's over. *(To the camera.)* M.'s and M.'s that is my prediction.

MAX: I understand your stupidity. You can't help it. You don't know her. The woman, I love. She's like no one else. She cries blue tears.

(They look at each other silently. We hear the sound of distant thunder as the lights fade.)

SCENE VII

Boswell's apartment. Night. Boswell walks with a cane. There is a nearly subliminal sound of distant thunder. C-Boy has been showing Boswell how to click a meal.

BOSWELL: So once more, I walk over there— *(He indicates the micromachine.)* I punch the top button, the red one, the one that comes first. Then I remove my finger and the meals will appear.

(C-Boy nods.)

BOSWELL: I want to get this right.

(C-Boy starts to comb Boswell's hair.)

BOSWELL: I hope she likes rainbow duck. It's a delicacy. Perhaps she doesn't like delicacies. I don't know. How should I know?

(C-Boy stops combing Boswell's hair. He removes a large hairball from the comb and tosses it into the receptacle. Boswell watches this with fine misery. He feels his thinning hair.)

BOSWELL: Oh God. Hair is so much more attractive when it stays on the head. I'd better put on some more Hair Zap. How do my sores look? Are they very ugly? I—I shouldn't be doing this. This is all very silly. I'm going to change my mind in a minute. I'd better come to my senses. I'd better do it fast.

(Boswell exits into the lavatory. C-Boy goes to get his coat and ears. William enters. She wears her splatter suit. She is carrying her helmet and wears a dandy in her hair.)

WILLIAM: C-Boy, hi. I—I'm so glad you're here. Where is he!?
(C-Boy motions to the lavatory.)

WILLIAM: He's clicking dinner for me. Why do you think he's doing that? What do you think it means?

(C-Boy shrugs and heads for the door.)

WILLIAM: Where are you going?

(C-Boy shows her a pass.)

WILLIAM: Go. The recreation machine. Did he buy you that pass?

(C-Boy nods.)

WILLIAM: Go. Go. What does this mean? He wants to see me alone. But why? What's going to happen? Oh, why is he clicking me dinner?

(C-Boy shrugs and exits. William takes off her orange parka and boots. She puts on her white shoes and fools with the dandy in her hair. She is miserable with anticipation. Boswell comes out of the lavatory. He has sprayed black polish on his head. He walks with his cane.)

BOSWELL: I don't know. I don't know. They should uninvent hair. It's nothing but a scourge. *(He realizes he is not talking to C-Boy.)* Oh. Ah...Has C-Boy...? Gone?

WILLIAM: Um.

BOSWELL: Oh. Well. Are you ready for dinner?

WILLIAM: Uh-huh.

(Boswell walks with stiff self-consciousness over to the micromachine. He hesitates a moment, then punches a button. Gravel music plays loudly.)

BOSWELL: I—I—that was the wrong button. A mistake has been made. Wait. Wait.

(Boswell punches several other buttons. The music stops, an alarm goes off. It rings frantically. He keeps pressing buttons. Finally, the alarm shuts off, the micromachine opens up, the dinners come out burnt and charred. Boswell looks at William with blank helplessness.)

BOSWELL: I charred our dinners.

WILLIAM: Oh, well.

BOSWELL: Dinner is charred.

WILLIAM: I have two carrots.

BOSWELL: Carrots. We can't be eating carrots. Not when I'm proposing marriage.

WILLIAM: You're—Who? *(She looks around.)* Me?

BOSWELL: Yep.

WILLIAM: Go.

BOSWELL: Don't answer. Please, don't answer. Not until—There are—I have some reasons. *(He produces a list.)* Number one: If my poster makes a big splash, you could be very rich. Number two: You know my condition; I won't last long; so even if it is a bad marriage, at least it will be short. Number three: You're already living here anyway. Number four: They have those super safe sex kits now. Everyone is using them, even healthy people. They say the results make nature a thing of the past. This would be so much better if I hadn't charred the meals. If the meals were sitting here like I had planned.

(There is the sound of thunder approaching.)

BOSWELL: Oh, my God. A rainstorm. Thunder. I hate those things.

WILLIAM: Boswell—

BOSWELL: Please. You don't have to answer now. Just take your time. Think it over.

WILLIAM: There are things—I could never—Boswell—

BOSWELL: *(Overlapping from "I could….")* Please, I cannot hear an answer now. Not with the storm. Not tonight.

(The sound of thunder grows louder.)

BOSWELL: Oh God, there's thunder. I hate it so much.

WILLIAM: *(Overlapping from "thunder.")* You must listen—I have to—it's wrong—it is—

BOSWELL: *(Overlapping from "have.")* Please—don't. The rain. Don't.

WILLIAM: *(Running on.)* I'm wrong. All wrong! You think I'm nice, but I'm not. I used to kill animals, little animals. I liked to kill them. It made me feel in charge, like I was the boss or a Being, a real high Being. That was a long time ago, but it's still inside me. And I don't know what to do. It will always have been done.

(She stands before him stricken. He longs to comfort her, but is afraid he doesn't know how.)

BOSWELL: Please. It's…Don't. You were young. It's forgotten. Believe me. I swear to you. None of that matters. I want you with me. You are my beloved. Just please now. Please.

(He finally puts his arm around her. The thunder rages. Rain pours down. He holds her tightly. She holds him back.)

BOSWELL: Oh God, the thunder. Are you scared of thunder?

WILLIAM: No. Nothing. Now. I'm not scared of nothing.

(They hold each other as the rain pours down in torrents and the thunder clashes. As the lights fade, beautiful green rain appears on the TVP screen.)

SCENE VIII

The Boardwalk. It is sunset. The sky is orange and green. Waves are crashing. Thunder rumbles. Lightning flashes. The Reader is tearing apart her box. Her shirt is torn, exposing her breasts. Her left breast is caked with mud, her right with blood. Her hair and beard are tangled and bedraggled. Boswell appears. He clings to a sheet of paper.

BOSWELL: Reader! Reader! Where are you? Her name. I have her name. My beloved. Reader! Reader. I—what's happened to you?

READER: I can no longer bear the overwhelming stench of other people's lives. I'm closing up shop.

BOSWELL: Here, let me offer you some K.

(He hands her some money. She takes it.)

BOSWELL: You've helped me so much. You see, I never thought—but sometimes when I'm with her, I forget, I don't remember. There's only us. Would you like to see her name? *(He offers the paper to her.)*

READER: I don't have to. I can smell it. Please. *(She waves the paper away.)* A splatterer from the CTZ. The rancid smell of her stubby hands.

BOSWELL: She works very hard.

READER: Of course. Don't despair. You've done what you have done.

BOSWELL: I—I've never been so happy. We'll start the defrost on her kids, then plan the wedding. She wants an orange dress. If the kids thaw in time, they can be there. I'll buy them orange suits. Later I'll have to teach them all to read and write and clap to music. The alphabet is important. I'll make certain they learn how to cross their *T*'s with vigor and hope. I'm sure it can all be done.

READER: No, I wouldn't worry about the poster.

BOSWELL: The poster. No. I can always mark out some time.

READER: Your sores are red now. Time is ticking.

BOSWELL: *(He looks at his sores; they have turned blood red.)* Well, it was really just some pickles.

READER: Exactly.

BOSWELL: I thought perhaps it could have been good.

READER: Your best. Your signature.

BOSWELL: My signature. But still it's not that important. I mean, after all, she, William, she is the one.

READER: And it would have been such pressure for her being a great man's wife. People might question her. They might not understand your reasons for choosing an unattractive, uneducated, dimwitted splatterer from the CTZ with frozen children that are not even your own. You know; people talk.

BOSWELL: Still, I'm thinking even so, she is the one. Look at the writing. I'm sure it's all there. *(He hands the sheet of paper out to her.)*

READER: You're sure?

BOSWELL: Yes.

READER: You're very sure.

BOSWELL: I—yes.

READER: Then why are you asking me?

BOSWELL: To be...to be certain...I have to be certain.

(The Reader takes the paper from him and looks at it for a long moment.)

READER: M. William Smit. No, she's not the one. You've made a mistake. A mistake has been made.

(She hands the sheet of paper back to Boswell. He takes it in his hand and then walks back to his apartment. He hobbles on his cane in a ghostlike trance. The sunset fades. The sky turns dark.)

SCENE IX

Boswell's apartment. William is wearing a frilly orange dress and has orange dandies in her hair. Boswell enters. His face is white. He looks at the red sores that have appeared on his skin.

WILLIAM: Hello.

BOSWELL: Hello.

WILLIAM: My dress arrived.

BOSWELL: Yes, it's very nice.

WILLIAM: I like it so much. Thank you for giving it to me. It makes me—it's so beautiful.

(The TVP begins to bleep. Boswell clicks it up. An Official appears on the screen. C-Boy is with him.)

BOSWELL: *(To the Official on the screen.)* Yes? Hello.

OFFICIAL: *(On the screen.)* I wanted to inform you that we have retrieved your x-ward, M. C-Boy K-Trill, on his food box pickup. He is officially reinstated as a full-time Gov. ward. You have no further obligations concerning this case.

WILLIAM: Yes. Fine.

OFFICIAL: H.A.N.D.

(Boswell clicks off the TVP screen.)

WILLIAM: They've got C-Boy.

BOSWELL: Yes. I've returned him. *(He goes back to his writing.)*

WILLIAM: But why?

BOSWELL: I can't do everything.

WILLIAM: They're gonna—they'll put him back on the streets.

BOSWELL: He'll have his food box. He'll be no worse off than he was before.

WILLIAM: Please, you can't—we have to think about this.

BOSWELL: When did we start thinking together?

WILLIAM: We don't—I didn't mean—

BOSWELL: You didn't mean what?

WILLIAM: I don't know.

BOSWELL: You don't know what?

WILLIAM: Nothing.

BOSWELL: Yes, well, there it is. Don't you see how impossible this is. You don't know anything. You have no idea how to think. It simply is not something you do on a regular basis. I mean, can you tell me—have you ever wondered—What is your purpose?

WILLIAM: Uh-uh.

BOSWELL: That doesn't surprise me. And yet it seems apparent that, if you are going to be alive, you should know your purpose. But you don't know. You don't even think. See how we are incapable of having any sort of intelligent, meaningful exchange!

WILLIAM: I thought—it seemed—you do love me.

BOSWELL: Did I ever say that? When did I say that? I do not recall saying that.

WILLIAM: You don't have to say.

BOSWELL: Well, if I don't say, if I didn't say, what made you think—excuse me, I forgot, you don't think. So I suppose I have to sit here and explain everything to you. Well, get this flat. Love is a mendacious myth. Everyone is just an egg. A slimy yolk in their own shell. Smash two eggs together, what happens? They break. The result is two chickens are killed, a runny omelet is served, "Good morning, everyone." H.A.N. fucking D.

WILLIAM: You want to call off the marriage?

BOSWELL: I think, perhaps.

WILLIAM: Alright.

BOSWELL: I'm going to devote myself entirely to the pickle.

WILLIAM: I—I.

BOSWELL: What?

WILLIAM: I'll fix you a medical concoction.

BOSWELL: It's not time.

WILLIAM: But, I see—your sores, they're—

BOSWELL: What?

WILLIAM: Red.

BOSWELL: I think you should leave.

WILLIAM: Leave?

BOSWELL: Yes. I don't want you around me while I'm dying. I know how you like to kill and torture dying prey. It's part of your makeup. It's who you are. It makes you feel good. Like you're a Being, a real high Being.

WILLIAM: Oh no, please. Don't. I can't. I'll go. I'll pack. *(She starts to pack.)* I'll go. I—where? If only—I just—I—I wanna go home. I do. But it's—all gone. My home. My family, the silk elm, the red saucer I ate from. And my brother, Andy. How fast he could run across the dirt. How he recited to me such things he would write if ever he could learn to read. I want so much to go see my home. I do. I do. I wish I could dream it all back.

BOSWELL: Yes, yes, you can't go home again. You'd know that if you had an education. But you don't, so you have to learn everything through personal experience. It must be so exhausting. Do you have all of your things?

WILLIAM: Yes.

BOSWELL: Then you should go.

(William picks up all of her belongings and exits.)

BOSWELL: Good then. She's gone. Now I can work. Back to the pickle. My signature.

(Boswell goes back to his writing. As the lights fade, "Celeb Bites" theme music comes up. A huge poster shaped like a pickle comes up on the TVP screen. The poster is covered with a tarp. Various highbrows are eyeing it with anticipation.)

SCENE X

A grassy knoll. Day. L-Tip is interviewing Boswell. A harsh, pink light encir-cles them. L-Tip wears a skintight dress and a peculiar headdress that bob-bles. Boswell has lost most of his hair. He stands with two canes. His sores are black now, but his eyes are still burning. The Celeb Bites' music starts to fade.

L-TIP: Hello, this is L-Tip the Hip Lip and I'm standing here with art philoso-pher, M. Boswell T-Thorp. Any moment now the A.P. Bureau Chiefs will be unveiling M. T-Thorp's new poster, "Death and a Jar of Pickles." Are you nervous, M. T-Thorp?

BOSWELL: Not in the least. In fact, I've never been so relaxed in my entire life.

L-TIP: May I ask, why you have chosen to retreat to this grassy knoll rather than to be present at the Show All Pavilion to see how your poster is publicly received?

BOSWELL: Well, L-Tip, I'll tell you, I love the public. They're all wonderful folks, I'm sure. But I really have no interest in their opinions. I'm secure and fulfilled in whom I am. My poster stands on its own.

L-TIP: Well, M. T-Thorp, you certainly are a man of Himalayan values.

BOSWELL: Yes, well, if you like.

L-TIP: Thank you for talking to us. It's been a true bang-a-roo. And please, H.A.N.D.

BOSWELL: H.A.N.D.?

(The pink circle of light abruptly disappears.)

L-TIP: *(Talking to the crew.)* Okay, fine. Click. Were you able to get in all of my headgear? Sin. Now let's pack up and dust to the Show All.

BOSWELL: *(Coming up to her.)* I thought you were going to ask me for my interpretation of the poster. Why, that interview was vulgarly anorexic and evisceratingly inane!

L-TIP: Please, Boswell, don't start giving me shit. I've just spent the entire morning trying to suck in my stomach.

BOSWELL: You think just because you have your own satellite show—why, I'm getting ready to take this world by storm. When people see these pick-les, nothing will ever be the same. There may well be a referendum to reinstate the office of king.

L-TIP: Well, aren't you just a dose of a toast; zooming down ego highway without any road maps.

BOSWELL: You're just jeally.

L-TIP: I'm jeally! God!

(Max enters; he is horribly distressed.)

MAX: There you are—I—have you heard?

BOSWELL: What?

MAX: Your poster? The unveiling?

BOSWELL: No.

MAX: Don't go down there. It's—they didn't—

BOSWELL: What? It's not good. I can see this isn't good.

(L-Tip clicks in her portable TVP.)

L-TIP: *(Into the TVP remote.)* Stringer—K, are you down there? What's going on? Pan over. *(She watches the action on the tiny TVP screen.)* Oh my God. They're throwing things at your poster.

BOSWELL: Things? What things?

L-TIP: Fruit cores, chairs, mudballs. Look at this, an evil pork is setting it on fire.

BOSWELL: Oh, my God. My poor pickles. Stop them. Won't somebody stop them? Won't the Stick Guards—Won't they stop them?

L-TIP: Looks like the Stick Guards are in on it, too. Why, they're beating on it with spiked mallets.

BOSWELL: My precious poster. My dearest pickles. Why? Oh, why?

MAX: I don't know, I heard they thought it was making fun of our Food Suppliers.

BOSWELL: Our Food Suppliers??!! But I wasn't—I didn't—this was not a joke. This was not in fun. I wanted the people, I wanted them to understand my pickles. Their thoughts, their feelings, their predicament. What it was like for them inside that jar. Oh, why can't they see what I see? If only I had a laser zap. Quick! Someone bring me a laser zap. Bring me a zap.

L-TIP: Stabilize. Stabilize. Remember what you said about your work standing on its own? How you are secure and fulfilled in who you are?

BOSWELL: Lies. All lies. Nothing but lies.

L-TIP: Try to equalize. I've got to go down there. Remember, you're stronger than you think.

BOSWELL: That would be inevitable.

MAX: *(To L-Tip.)* Nice suit.

L-TIP: Drop dead. *(L-Tip hurries off.)*

MAX: Hey, look. I'm sorry, Boz. I'm really sorry. But I suppose if you were, well, grasping at straws, you might see it as something of a compliment that the people would take the time to so brutally and viciously destroy your work.

BOSWELL: Yes, well, why don't we just leave that chaff in the crib.

MAX: Sure, of course. *(A beat.)* Well…isn't it strange.

BOSWELL: What?

MAX: We're both…standing here.

> *(Boswell looks at Max standing on the grassy knoll. He then becomes horribly aware of his own body standing on the surface of the world. Slowly, Boswell starts to breathe very heavily. Max tries to grin, but he seems to lack sincerity. As the lights fade, cheerful piped-in euth music comes up.)*

SCENE XI

> *Euthanasia Gardens. Flowery euth music plays. L-Tip sits on a stone bench. She wears a red coat decorated with hearts, and a red hat with a veil. She carries a TVP remote. William enters dressed in her orange dress that has been dyed red. She wears her W.Y. badge. She also carries a TVP remote.*

WILLIAM: Hi.

L-TIP: William.

WILLIAM: Hi.

L-TIP: It's been…

WILLIAM: Yes. Long.

L-TIP: Where's C-Boy? I heard he's become your ward.

WILLIAM: Yes, he has. He'll be here today. After I come, he's coming. We're trading off staying with my kids. They're in final thaw.

L-TIP: Oh, brill. That's just brill.

WILLIAM: Yes. It's been a very fortunate time for me. I got elected Worker of the Year. Plus we won a bonus vacation to anyplace in the zone that hasn't been splattered.

L-TIP: Oh. Where will you go?

WILLIAM: Anaheim. We've already made reservations to see that famous ceiling they brought over.

L-TIP: What ceiling?

WILLIAM: The one with all sorts of old-fashioned, heavyset people painted on it. I think it's got God in it somewhere and he's going like this— *(William reaches her arm out and extends her index finger.)*

L-TIP: Oh, yes. That's very popular.

WILLIAM: Uh-huh. *(A beat.)* Is he—I mean—Have you seen Boswell?

L-TIP: No. He's not here yet.

WILLIAM: Do you know how he is?

L-TIP: Not good. His sores are black now.

WILLIAM: Oh. I just—I hope I can leave before he comes. I don't ever wanna see him again. Why are we waiting?

L-TIP: The body's being capsulized. It shouldn't be much longer.

WILLIAM: Umm. Would you like to see my kids?

L-TIP: Oh yes.

WILLIAM: I'll click them up.

(William takes her remote TVP and clicks through her number.)

WILLIAM: *(Into the TVP.)* C-Boy, it's me. Look who's here.

(L-Tip waves into William's TVP screen.)

L-TIP: Hi, C-Boy. Jacka, jacka.

WILLIAM: *(Into the TVP.)* C-Boy, show her the kids. Look, there they are.

L-TIP: Oh. Oh. Aren't they shug.

WILLIAM: *(Pointing at the screen.)* That one's Bonnie. And that's Tabell. Look how they can move their hands and toes. In just about a week their lids will start to open.

L-TIP: Sin. Simply, sin.

WILLIAM: *(Into the TVP.)* Thanks, C-Boy. I'll be back as soon as I can. H.A.N.D. *(She clicks off.)*

L-TIP: I—did you know I have a child now?

WILLIAM: No.

L-TIP: Yes, I've been desperate for one for a long time. Here, I'll click her up. *(She clicks through her number.)* Her name's Grace. *(Into her TVP.)* Yes, H.K., please put Grace on the TVP.

WILLIAM: *(Looking at L-Tip's TVP screen.)* Oh, she's very pretty.

L-TIP: Isn't she the cutest and most cuddly. She's the newest thing. They call them Toss 'Em Toddlers. Her natural life span is only three years. Isn't it wonderful. She'll be adorable her whole life. And I won't ever have to worry about those awkward years. Not to mention the high cost of education.

(L-Tip waves good-bye to Grace and clicks her off.)

WILLIAM: Won't it be sad though?

L-TIP: Oh no. It's all completely natural. See, I don't have time for a full-term child. I mean, I'm competing in a world where fantasy puppets set the step. They never take time out for children or family, ultra surgery or even rehab. They're completely consumed with constructing careers. The pressure gets to be devastating. Of course, I'm terrifically unhappy.

Before I started going to my therochief I never even suspected how unhappy I was. Now I'm totally aware of my misery. It's a big improvement. *(Reader appears in a white dress, decorated with pink carnations. She has shaved her beard and her hair is neatly bubbled and coiffed. Her demeanor has completely changed. She is vapid, calm, and glazed.)*

READER: Good morning M.'s. You may come in now, if you like, the capsulation has been completed.

L-TIP: Thanks.

(L-Tip and William head toward the entrance.)

L-TIP: God, don't we look silly. I hate these theme funerals.

(They all three exit. Boswell enters. He walks with two canes. His black sores have spread. He slowly hobbles to the bench and sits down. William reenters. She is wiping away tears. Boswell sees her.)

BOSWELL: Hello.

WILLIAM: Hi.

BOSWELL: Did you go in?

WILLIAM: Yes. Yes. Max. Poor Max. He's so small. They've made him so small.

BOSWELL: They've capsulized him?

WILLIAM: Yes, but he's, well, they've got him smiling. It's this small, little, tiny, little smile.

BOSWELL: Well, they do that, I suppose.

WILLIAM: Uh huh.

BOSWELL: William.

WILLIAM: What?

BOSWELL: I thought I might never see you again.

WILLIAM: Yes, I thought so, too.

BOSWELL: Would you shake my hand?

WILLIAM: Why?

BOSWELL: I don't know. No rock feelings?

WILLIAM: But I do; I have them. I have rock feelings.

BOSWELL: Well, then, I don't know. What is there to do? It's all too late. What is there to do?

WILLIAM: I have to go.

BOSWELL: Yes, well, H.A.N.D.

(William exits. Reader enters. She approaches Boswell.)

READER: Hello. Would you like me to show you to the viewing room? The capsule is on display.

BOSWELL: No. Not just yet.

READER: Take your time.

(Reader strolls around the garden. He watches her.)

BOSWELL: Excuse me. But do I know you?

READER: Me? I don't think so.

BOSWELL: There's something about you. You remind me... Did you ever have a beard?

READER: Yes, I think, perhaps. You see, I was very ill at one point. I've had brain fiber treatments. I'm much better now.

BOSWELL: What was—the problem?

READER: I was malignantly insane. I thought I could read people's lives through their handwriting. I'd take people's K. and spin deluded tales. I made one pathetic man write the word pickle ten thousand times. But I'm much better now.

BOSWELL: Then you—it was all—you never knew...anything?

READER: What could I know? I was crippled with a fevered cranium.

BOSWELL: Oh my God. Oh my God. A mistake has been made.

(L-Tip enters. She is crying blue tears.)

L-TIP: Max. Dear Max. God. How can I live without him? How can I ever live without him? Boswell—

BOSWELL: It's too late!

(Boswell rises to his feet and hobbles in the same direction William departed.)

L-TIP: Yes... But I did...I realize now, I did love him. I loved him all along.

(Boswell stops. He is gasping for air. He points one of his canes in William's direction trembling with determination.)

BOSWELL: It's too late though!

L-TIP: Yes, all along. I loved him all along.

(Boswell lowers his cane.)

READER: I have to believe. I am; I'm much better now.

BOSWELL: William! My beloved! William!

(Boswell moves forward and goes to find William. The lights fade to black-out.)

END OF PLAY

CONTROL FREAKS

FOR HOLLY, HOLLY, HOLLY.
MARRY ME!

Wayne Pere and Carol Kane
in the MET Theater's 1993 production of
Control Freaks.

photo by John Abeyta

ORIGINAL PRODUCTION

Control Freaks was produced by the Met Theatre in Los Angeles, California, in 1993. It was directed by the author and produced by David Beard and Holly Hunter; set design was by Neal Patel; lighting design was by Rand Ryan; costume design was by Ruth Myers and Luke Reiche; sound design/original music was by Joe Cerqua. The cast was as follows:

Sister (Spaghetti/Pinkie) Willard . . . . Holly Hunter
Betty Willard . . . . Carol Kane
Carl Willard . . . . Bill Pullman
Paul Casper . . . . Wayne Pere

World premiere of *Control Freaks* was produced by Center Theater in Chicago, Illinois, in 1992. It was directed by the author; set design was by Rob Hamilton; lighting design was by Chris Phillips; costume design was by Lynn Sandberg; sound design/original music was by Joe Cerqua. The cast was as follows:

Sister (Spaghetti/Pinkie) Willard . . . . Robin Witt
Betty Willard . . . . Marlene DuBois
Carl Willard . . . . Marc Vann
Paul Casper . . . . Champ Clark

THE CAST

SISTER (SPAGHETTI/PINKIE) WILLARD: 30s, has just returned from jury duty
BETTY WILLARD: 40s, Sister's sister-in-law, Carl's wife
CARL WILLARD: 40s, Sister's brother, Betty's husband
PAUL CASPER: 20s–30s, the guest

THE SETTING

The play takes place in Sister's home in Los Angeles. The set is divided into three areas: the kitchen, the yard, Sister's upstairs bedroom. A strange carrot garden in the yard. In Sister's room there is a bed-chair (a chair that is designed to look like a bed), and several cheap wigs on wig stands. There is a large window in her room that overlooks the yard.

The set should be a frightening combination of dream real, fake real, and real. Everything should be kept extremely spare. Basically, if it is not used in the play, don't put it on the set.

THE TIME

Now.

NOTE ABOUT THE CHARACTER SISTER:

Sister has no knowledge of Spaghetti or Pinkie.
Pinkie knows there is Spaghetti.
Spaghetti knows there is Pinkie and Sister.

Carl and Sister's house. Betty, forties, sits at the kitchen table dressed in a sunny, crisp housedress with a full skirt. The table is set for tea for two with china from a toy tea set. Betty stares morosely at the tiny tea setting. It is late afternoon. Sister sits in her bedroom. Her white legs are bare. There is a tattoo on her arm of a face without eyes surrounded by a cracked heart.

SISTER: This is my window. I've been gone for some time. I was on jury duty. We were sequestered. We all stayed together at a convenient motel. We all wore badges. When our case was over, we had to return the badges. We couldn't just keep them like they were a souvenir. The government owns them. They're public property. Still we were able to get quite a bit of wear out of our badges. It was a lengthy deliberation. But, finally, today we sentenced the man in handcuffs. They had him in handcuffs. He had to sit there in front of everyone wearing handcuffs. The rest of us could raise our arms, but he couldn't. He got a lot of time. We decided to throw the book at him. He had come to no good. That's where chance had taken him and it was too late to change his habits. There was no way to break his patterns. He was a bad egg. A rotten apple in a barrel. You might as well spit at him as look at him. I'm sorry to say this man was less than dirt and we had to put him away for good. It was an easy decision. Like choosing chocolate over vanilla.

(Betty suddenly smiles eagerly. Her eyes become bright and cheerful. She rings a little dinner bell.)

BETTY: Teatime! It's teatime! Your tea is served!

SISTER (SPAGHETTI/PINKIE): [SP] Fucking teatime./ [P] Be nice./ [SP] Choke shit. *(Sister comes down the stairs and enters the kitchen.)*

BETTY: Hello! Tea's ready!

SISTER: Oh goody! How pretty! Isn't this adorable! Isn't this cute!

BETTY: You deserve it. You've been working hard.

SISTER: I enjoy hard work. It's good for you. Keeps you honest.

BETTY: Yes, yes. Always have your nose to the grindstone.

SISTER: And what do you do?

BETTY: Me?

SISTER: Uh-huh. For a living?

BETTY: Oh, for money?

SISTER: Yeah.

BETTY: I teach cold reading classes.

SISTER: Cold reading classes?

BETTY: Yes. It's for actors. I train actors. That's how I met Carl.

SISTER: Carl's not an actor.

BETTY: He's got a lot of very good potential. He did a scene from "Major Dad" that absolutely oozed with potential. Do you like lemon or cream?

SISTER: It's tea, right?

BETTY: Yes, tea.

SISTER: I don't put cream in tea. When I think of cream, I think cream is for coffee.

BETTY: Well, how about sugar?

SISTER: Sugar is good. That can go in tea.

BETTY: Lemon and sugar then?

SISTER: Good. Fine. Whatever you say. It's your tea; you made it.

BETTY: Alright. Fine. This is very nice.

SISTER: Yes, having tea and all. Having a spot of tea. Carl tell you anything? He say anything about me?

BETTY: He told me he had a sister.

SISTER: Yes. We're a close-knit family. Carl gets married and goes off sometimes. He'll marry someone for awhile, then he comes back to me and Mother.

BETTY: I was sorry to hear about Mother's accident.

SISTER: It was a cruel blow.

BETTY: Carl says.

SISTER: I was just grateful he was here when it happened.

BETTY: It's good to have a man around the house.

SISTER: Yeah. It's good to have a man around the house.

BETTY: Would you like a Ginger Snap?

SISTER: Do we have any ice cream?

BETTY: Oh, yes.

SISTER: What kind?

BETTY: Chocolate.

SISTER: Good. That's good. We like chocolate ice cream. It's our favorite.

BETTY: I'm afraid—

SISTER: What?

BETTY: There's only enough left for Carl's shake. When he comes home he likes his shake.

SISTER: I know about his shake. I know he likes his shake.

BETTY: Well. I have the Ginger Snaps.

SISTER: These things'll break your teeth. They make houses out of this stuff.

BETTY: I'm sorry about the ice cream.

SISTER: It's not good to be low on ice cream.

BETTY: I'll go to the store.

SISTER: What for?

BETTY: Ice cream.

SISTER: Well, that's not a bad idea. It's not good to be low on ice cream.

BETTY: Is there anything else I should get?

SISTER: The last thing I need is a carton of cigarettes. Camel unfiltered. I don't want them in this house. I don't wanna get cancer of the throat. That is something I could live without.

BETTY: Don't worry, this is a smoke-free house. No smoking is allowed. See, I put up this sampler.

SISTER: Let me see that. You put this up?

BETTY: Yes.

SISTER: You hung it on a nail?

BETTY: Yes.

SISTER: So you put that nail in the wall?

BETTY: To hang the picture.

SISTER: But you don't live here; you don't live here.

BETTY: I'm staying here.

SISTER: Temporarily. Till you get another place. You were evicted, right? You got kicked out on Christmas Day. Carl related it all to me. He picked up you and your Christmas tree and brought you over here. Temporarily.

BETTY: We're married now.

SISTER: What?

BETTY: Carl and me got married in Las Vegas at the Elvis Presley Chapel. It was a spur of the moment decision. Our next plan is to go off on a honeymoon to Maui and drink out of cut-up pieces of fruit.

SISTER: Well, isn't this a nice surprise?

BETTY: Yes, it is.

SISTER: And so sudden. Isn't it sudden? A sudden thing.

BETTY: Carl's the one. He swept me off my feet. "Why put off till tomorrow what you can do today?" he said to me.

SISTER: Yes, that's a good point, a point well taken. But you've caught me off guard. I'm embarrassed. I should have a wedding present for you. I should have brought you a gift.

BETTY: Oh, not to worry. We're going to throw a big reception after the honeymoon, so we'll have a chance to celebrate with all of those we love and treasure.

SISTER: Am I invited to the reception?

BETTY: Well, I'm not sure. It hasn't been discussed. We haven't decided on the invites.

SISTER: Where're my cats? Have you seen my cats?

BETTY: Those two fat cats?

SISTER: Garfield and Plums.

BETTY: Why, those are the fattest cats I've ever seen. They're so fat I entered their picture in a contest.

SISTER: What contest?

BETTY: The fat cat photo contest. I thought they were sure to win first prize, but they lost.

CARL: *(Offstage.)* Hey, Honey! Baby! Sugar Snaps!

BETTY: Oh, there's Carl!

(Carl, forties, enters. He wears a cheap suit and carries a plastic briefcase. He wears black glasses and has on a curly hairpiece.)

CARL: *(Spotting Sister.)* Oh my goodness! Look who's back!

SISTER: Look who's married!

CARL: Pop goes the weasel!

BETTY: I'll fix your shake.

CARL: You know it, Babe. *(To Sister, about Betty.)* Isn't she a winner? Am I a lucky gun?

SISTER: Bang, bang, bang!

CARL: Shoot 'em up! Rawhide! Hey, how was the trial?

SISTER: Oh, he was a bad man. A rotten apple in a barrel. You wouldn't have liked him, Carl. Not one bit. We socked him away for life. I wanted to watch him fry. But they only let you give him life.

CARL: Well, I'm proud of you, Sister. You've done a public service. Good for you, Little Rascal. *(To Betty.)* Did I tell you I had a sister, or what?

BETTY: Oh yes, and now that Sister's back we can cinch the deal.

CARL: Cinch the deal! Alright!

SISTER: What deal?

CARL: Furniture World?

SISTER: Huh?

CARL: I'm opening up a giant furniture market. Don't worry, Little Scampy, you're in. I'm gonna let you work the floor. Here, check out these brochures, these order forms. What do you think? I'm a big fan of this modular bedroom set. It's virtually carefree. It's all been treated with Stain Safe. It's completely soil repellent.

SISTER: But, Carl, I wanted to open up a Frosty Shop. Remember all the frozen delights we invented? We don't know anything about furniture.

CARL: What're you talking? I've been around furniture all my life. What do you think? You need a degree to plop your behind on some foam rubber?!

SISTER: If Mother was here, she'd say this is just another one of your harebrained schemes.

CARL: Mother's not here.

SISTER: No.

(Betty turns on the shake machine. It makes a loud shrieking, monstrous sound that only Sister is aware of. Betty pours the shake into a glass and hands it to Carl.)

BETTY: Here's your shake, honey.

(Carl picks up his shake, takes a small sip, then sets it down.)

BETTY: Don't you like it?

(Carl shrugs noncommittally.)

SISTER: Maybe she didn't make it right. I know how you—

CARL: She made it right. She makes the best shakes I've ever had.

(Carl now makes a big deal out of slurping up his delicious shake as he continues to pout. Sister picks up the brochures and starts looking through them.)

SISTER: *(Reading.)* "Versatile easy chair with sleeper incliner, recliner, and swivel rocker mechanism." That's pretty exciting. "Glue blocks, mortise tenon joints, and the extensive use of screws instead of staples creates a long-lasting, strong construction."

CARL: Can you beat that?

SISTER: Not with a stick.

CARL: So are we all happy with Furniture World?

BETTY AND SISTER: Yes, we are!

CARL: I wanna make both my girls happy. I can't feel good if you're not happy.

BETTY: We're happy, Carl!

SISTER: Happy, happy, happy.

CARL: Well, the deal is set. The deal is made. All the kinks are worked out. What can I tell you? We got the building for a song. I hate to say it, but it was a steal.

BETTY: The owner, he loved you, Carl.

CARL: Paul. Paul Casper. What a swell kid. A real sap but swell.

BETTY: He was impressed with you, Carl. He looked up to you.

CARL: Yeah, yeah. The little puppy's after me to let him be a silent investor in Furniture World. I don't know. Should we let him in? Hey, it's up to you girls.

BETTY: Whatever you think.

CARL: Sister?

SISTER: Do I get a vote?

CARL: You sure do.

SISTER: Alright! Well, then…whatever you think!

CARL: I don't know. I'm not sure. We could use some extra financing. What d'ya say… What d'ya say we have him over tomorrow night. We could fix cocktails.

BETTY: I'll make one of my hors d'oeuvres trays.

SISTER: I'll make Mother's gingerbread men.

BETTY: Perhaps some canapés.

SISTER: The ones with the raisin eyes.

CARL: Hey, whoa! I'm not saying roll out the red carpet! We don't have to anoint him in oil. Let's just get him over for a drink. We'll sign all the ownership papers and then we'll see do we need a silent partner.

BETTY: Mmm, I like that plan. Kiss me, Daddy.

CARL: You got it, Mama.

(They kiss with a disgusting display of vile lust. Sister paces around them.)

SISTER: Aren't you two a pair of lovebirds. Tweet, tweet, tweet! Grrr! Grrrr! *Tweet!!!*

BETTY: You know what, Carl? I think we should find Sister a man. Sister, wouldn't you be happy if we could find you a man?

SISTER: I don't know. There're so few good ones out there. *(To Carl.)* You're the last of the good catches. After you they broke the mold.

BETTY: Still, I think she could use a man. *(To Carl.)* Wouldn't you feel better if Sister had a man?

CARL: *(A beat.)* The right one though. He'd have to be the right one.

SISTER: *(A beat.)* So you think I need a man?

CARL: It might make you happy.

SISTER: Sure. Yeah. Sure, it would. Hey, how about the man who's coming for cocktails? Would he be my type?

BETTY: Oh, no. I doubt it.

SISTER: Well, maybe you have it figured wrong, my type. See 'cause I like different types. I like all types. With me type doesn't matter.

BETTY: So anyone'll do?

SISTER: And type'll do. That's different from anyone. I'm not a pushover. In fact, I'm pretty picky. I choose carefully. I like to look at men through a fine-toothed comb. Who knows? Maybe he's the one I've been waiting for all my life. I wouldn't be at all surprised.

CARL: So maybe you should nab him.

SISTER: Then we could have another wedding. We'd all be one big happy family. Running Furniture World, celebrating birthdays, borrowing cups of sugar, lending each other lawn mowers. It could be a very excellent setup. I'm gonna set my cap for him. Do you think that's a good idea? I should set my cap for him?

CARL: Sure.

SISTER: I'll get dolled-up. I can look good when I try. It just takes some effort. But the results are something to see. People don't recognize me. They think I'm someone else. They think I'm good-looking. "Hey, Sister, that's not you, is it?" "Sure, it's me. I'm wearing mascara!" I doll-up good. I'm a real babe. Shake your boodie.

CARL: Hey, hey! No dirty language. Watch your mouth.

SISTER: Yes, sir, Major Dad! I just got carried away.

CARL: Well, straighten up and fly right.

SISTER: I'm sorry, I just meant—hey, I can look good.

CARL: Yeah, sure. Maybe Betty can help you.

BETTY: Oh, of course I can. We'll do a complete makeover.

CARL: Now why don't you go out in the yard and shovel up that dog mess.

SISTER: Dog mess? We don't have a dog.

CARL: You don't have to tell me. It's some neighborhood dog. I'm gonna have to poison it. There's no other way. Every morning he leaves a big pile of his mess.

SISTER: Well, I'll take care of it. I'll clean it up.

CARL: That's the spirit. It's good to have you home.

SISTER: It's good to be home. *(Sister goes out into the yard. She picks up a shovel.)*

BETTY: Your sister's weird.

CARL: Yeah, I know.

BETTY: She's got a tattoo. It's like she's some sorta kook.

CARL: She won't be around here forever.

BETTY: Yeah?

CARL: Yeah.

(Betty starts to massage Carl's shoulders. Outside Sister discovers the pile of shit behind a bush.)

SISTER: Oh, ho! There you are. Holy smoke. That's a big pile alright.

(Sister scoops up the shit, carries it to a garbage can and dumps it. As Betty and Carl continue their conversation in the kitchen, Sister goes up to her room. Up in her room, she takes off her skirt and shoes and sits in her bedchair wearing her long shirt.)

BETTY: *(Massaging Carl's shoulders.)* After she signs the papers? Then do you think you can tell her to go?

CARL: Maybe. Probably so. Yeah.

BETTY: Guess what panties I'm wearing?

CARL: Let's see, it's Thursday, right?

BETTY: Uh-huh.

CARL: That's ah, that's…I know! "A bowl of cherries, just 4U."

BETTY: Wrong!

CARL: What?

BETTY: Guess again.

(Betty spins around, her skirt flares out. Carl tries to get a peek at her panties.)

CARL: Lollipop Land?

BETTY: *(Laughing as she continues twirling her skirt.)* That's Wednesday!

CARL: Let me see. *(Carl gets down on all fours.)*

BETTY: It's one of your favorites.

CARL: One of my favorites.

(Betty spins off to the bedroom. Carl follows her on all fours.)

CARL: Is it, "Carl's little pussy?'" I like that one. That's a sweet one.

(The lights slowly change as night begins to fall. Sister sits frozen in the bed-chair in her room.)

SISTER (SPAGHETTI/PINKIE): [SP] I'm sitting here wondering what to do—what to do with the *roast beef* on my chest. A pair of eyes in the beef looking through fat and blood…Gristle is an element; it's part of the deal./ *(She breathes heavily, then speaks in a whisper.)* [P] Maybe you should try and move./ [SP] What?/ [P] You've been sitting here a very long time./ [SP] So?/ [P] Maybe it'd be good to move./ [SP] …Go on then. Be my guest. *(Sister gets out of the bed-chair with some effort, then quickly tiptoes over to the window. A sweet expression illuminates her face.)* [P] Hello. This is my window. I'm trying to learn to fly out of it. I asked for a pair of wings for Christmas. I'll take them in any size, any color. Tell Maw I don't give a damn about the color. But I need a pair that works. Wings that don't work are worse than no wings at all./ [SP] Is that you, Pinkie?/ [P] Yeah. Is that you, Spaghetti?/ [SP] It's me.

(Carl enters the kitchen wearing pajama bottoms. Sister freezes.)

SISTER: *(As Sister.)* Footsteps.

(Carl picks up a big soggy sponge and drains water over his face and neck.)

SISTER: It's him. He's down there.

(Sister takes off her underpants and comes down the stairs carrying them. She enters the kitchen, Carl looks up at her.)

CARL: Sister?

SISTER: Yeah. I forgot to wash out my underwear.

CARL: Oh.

SISTER: Why are you still up?

CARL: Can't sleep.

SISTER: Oh.

CARL: I keep thinking this time everything's gotta work out. All the pieces have gotta get in place and stay there. I've had trouble before. But no more. It's too late to fail again. This has got to be my ticket. A cat only has nine lives. It's closing in on me. I'm forty-plus. I look good for my age. No one knows I've had sutures sewn in my head to keep this mop in place. I can dive in a swimming pool. I don't but I could. I don't know. I just feel like I deserve better. I deserve more. When do I get my piece of the pie? I don't want dog scraps. Where's my roast beef?

SISTER: *(After a beat.)* Don't worry, Carl. I'll help you get your roast beef.

CARL: *(Near tears.)* You will?

SISTER: Sure.

CARL: That's my girl. There's no one I can love any more than you.

SISTER: Yes, and there's no one I can love any more than you.

CARL: I know that. In my heart I know that.

SISTER: Carl. I got something for you. *(Sister gets a bowl.)*

CARL: What? I don't deserve anything. I don't deserve a thing. I never have. *(Sister presents the bowl to Carl.)*

SISTER: M&M's. All the red ones. I saved all the red ones for you.

CARL: Well, look at that. That's very thoughtful. *(A beat.)* Would you... Would you feed them to me?

SISTER: *(A beat.)* Sure, Carl.

(Sister picks up a handful of the red M&M's. She feeds them to Carl one by one. Carl eats them slowly at first, then he eats them faster and faster. Finally, he is licking them out of the palm of her hand. Betty enters in a negligee.)

BETTY: Carl.

CARL: I couldn't sleep. I was hungry. She fixed me some M&M's.

BETTY: How sweet of her. Do you want me to fix you a shake?

CARL: Yes, I do.

BETTY: I will then. What's this in the sink?

(Betty picks up Sister's soaking wet underpants.)

SISTER: Those are mine. I'll take them. I have to hang them out to dry. *(Sister takes the underpants, twists and shakes them, then goes to the backyard.)*

BETTY: Did you see that? She shook water at me. I don't like this; she gives me the creeps. Washing her personal items in our kitchen sink. Look at that ring. Where's my Ajax? *(Betty starts cleaning the kitchen sink.)*

(In the yard Sister hangs her underpants out to dry, then goes upstairs to her bedroom.)

BETTY: This has got to be spotless. We want our porcelain to sparkle. Everything has got to stay sanitized! *(Pleading to Carl.)* Won't you please help me?!

CARL: Sure, Baby, sure. I'll help you. I'll protect you. I'm your man. Didn't I save you once already?

BETTY: Yeah. Me and my Christmas tree.

CARL: You and your Christmas tree, that's right.

BETTY: It's just—everything was going just right and then she had to come into the picture.

CARL: Look, as soon as she signs the papers—

BETTY: Tomorrow night, right?

CARL: Yeah. Paul Casper's coming at six P.M. He'll be here with the papers.

BETTY: Good.

CARL: Who knows—maybe that sap'll take her off our hands. He's not married or encumbered. Maybe he'll want her.

BETTY: *(Shaking her head.)* That guy's bad news. He's got problems. Severe problems.

CARL: Like what?

BETTY: Nothing. Just some things I observed while you were off checking the plumbing in the ladies.

CARL: What things?

BETTY: I don't want you getting mad at me. None of it is my fault.

CARL: Hey, don't you know, I know nothing could ever be your fault?

BETTY: *(A beat.)* Well, when we were standing there in the warehouse, he started looking at me.

CARL: Yeah? He looked at you? Well, you're good to look at. I guess he couldn't help himself. That's something I can understand.

BETTY: He took off his jacket and stretched his arms above his head. There were big sweat marks underneath his arms.

CARL: Kid's got no manners. Maybe I should teach him some manners.

BETTY: He said I got him hot. Looking at me got him hot. He said would I—

CARL: Yeah?

BETTY: "Suck him dry."

CARL: Oh no.

BETTY: "Suck me dry. Make me cry like a baby. Like a little baby. I wanna come through your nose."

CARL: This—What? This is… My God. I'm sick. I'm sick. *(Carl is secretly turned on.)* I'll kill him. I—I'll kill him.

BETTY: Carl, no.

CARL: I will. I'll smash—I'll rip—I'll murder. That's right, I'll murder him.

BETTY: Murder? You would murder him for me?

CARL: Yes.

BETTY: Oh, God. Oh, Carl. When?

CARL: I don't know. Soon.

BETTY: Tomorrow night?

CARL: Right. Yes. That'll be the time. That's when.

BETTY: Do you think it'll be before or after hors d'oeuvres?

CARL: I don't know.

BETTY: I'm wondering for shopping purposes.

CARL: I don't know. Whatever seems right.

BETTY: I'll cook in case.

CARL: God. This was gonna be good. Things were gonna be different. We were making improvements. Now I have to murder this—this slime. Oh God. It just makes me sick.

BETTY: Oh, it makes me sick too. It does. It does. Maybe you shouldn't do it.

CARL: What? I should just go on and go ahead with the deal? Include him in as a silent partner?

BETTY: Yeah.

CARL: But he insulted you.

BETTY: It wasn't the worst I ever—

CARL: Worse what, you ever what? What?

BETTY: *(A whisper.)* Swallowed.

CARL: God. You… You did it then?

BETTY: For you. I did it for you. So you could be somebody.

CARL: God—this—God—no. This—really, Betty. This is not how I get to be somebody. Wrong. We are thinking wrong here and now I have to commit murder. Otherwise, I have no dignity. No human dignity. No right to walk upright. I'd have to regress to all fours.

BETTY: But he was going to be our main investor.

CARL: I know that. And it's too bad but he dies. As soon as he signs the bill of sale, he's gone.

BETTY: You do love me.

CARL: Yes.

BETTY: Show me how.

CARL: No. I can't. I have to kill him first. Then you'll be pure again and you'll respect me all the more because I took care of you. I took a stand. A respectable stand.

BETTY: Oh, Carl, you're such a good strong man.

CARL: Yeah? Well, how 'bout you fix me that shake now. You know just how I like it.

(Betty turns on the shake machine. Sounds of loud, violent lovemaking mixed with the sick sounds of deranged people laughing and screaming on a roller coaster come from the machine. Sister sits up in the bed-chair, waken from a terrible dream.)

SISTER (SISTER/SPAGHETTI/PINKIE): [SIS] Where's my face? Where's my face? What have they done with my face? I can't stand around here without a face that is not going to work, everything must work, let it work out. Please, I am begging you. Drench, drench. "Can't you straighten up and fly right?!" Fly—fly—/

(Sister races to the window. The noise from the shake machine stops.)

SISTER (SISTER/SPAGHETTI/PINKIE): [SP] I fell out a window. I fell out a window. I wanted to fall and crack open my skull./ [P] What would be inside? Oh, such surprises: tangerines, necklaces that sparkle, gold teeth, fine ribbon, chocolate wrapped in red foil. All my brains are treasures. How wonderful what I see. I could weep with joy. Rainbow tears drift from the window. It's an outrage. Who will catch the tears? No one is below; I am crying colored tears and no one is below.

(The lights dim to black, then slowly brighten to a pink-gold sunrise. We hear the sound of birds chirping. Carl enters the kitchen from his bedroom, then moves out into the yard. He wears his pajama bottoms. Sister sleeps at the window. Carl looks up at her, sees she is sleeping then squats behind a bush and takes a big shit in the yard. He gets up and exits to his bedroom. Sister sniffs and sniffs again.)

SISTER (SISTER/SPAGHETTI/PINKIE): [P] I smell something. Something bad./ [SP] You don't./ [P] I can't help it, I do. I have to tell the truth. To thine own self be true./ [SP] I don't think so./ [P] I do./ [SP] Yeah? Well, you've never once gotten up and braved the light of day without lying your whole heart out. You tell yourself, I'm not gonna die; what I do is important; my life is good; I'm gonna have a nice day. Ah, ah, ah! That's better. Now I can rise to my feet soaked in the come of canards and meet the day. Hello, day! Tweet, tweet. The birdies are chirping./ [P] Ooh, aren't those baby birdies sweet?!/ [SP] I'd like to snap their scrawny necks.

(Sister puts on her skirt and shoes. She takes off the wig she is wearing and puts on a different one. We see she is nearly bald with horrible little bloody tufts sticking out all over her head.)

(Betty enters the kitchen humming. She is dressed in the same outfit she wore

yesterday. She pours a liquid mixture into a frying pan. Carl enters wearing the same suit he wore in the first scene.)

CARL: Good morning, Honey.

BETTY: Good morning, Sweetie.

CARL: What's for breakfast?

BETTY: Bubbles.

CARL: Mmm, my favorite.

BETTY: Goodie. Oh, Carl?

CARL: Yeah?

BETTY: I'm thinking we shouldn't mention anything to Sister about...

CARL: What?

BETTY: Our plans for the guest.

CARL: No, no. Absolutely. Let's keep that under our hats.

BETTY: Right. Just act natural.

CARL: Yeah. Like any other day.

(Sister comes down the stairs.)

SISTER: Good morning, world!

CARL: Good morning, Sister.

BETTY: Nice day. Carl, are you ready for your bubbles?

CARL: You bet.

(Betty blows bubbles from the liquid in the frying pan. She blows the bubbles over to Carl who pokes at them with his fork and gobbles them up.)

CARL: Mmm. Scrumptious. So light. They just melt in my mouth.

SISTER: I thought you never ate breakfast.

CARL: I'm a changed man.

SISTER: Mother would never believe this. Carly eating a big wholesome breakfast. Breakfast was not his bag.

CARL: *(Wiping his lips.)* Goodness! I'm stuffed!

BETTY: Breakfast is the most important meal of the day. It's full of nutrients. Now, everyone, I'm making out a shopping list. Does anyone need anything from the market?

SISTER: Yes, I do. I'm making gingerbread men to serve our guest this evening. They were Mother's specialty.

BETTY: Oh. Well, I'm sure our guest will be delighted. What ingredients do you need?

SISTER: Let's see...Gingerbread mix. Oh, and raisins. Don't forget the raisins. Mother always used the raisins for their eyes. *(To Carl.)* Remember how she'd let us help her put them in? *(Pretending to put raisins in the eyes of gingerbread men.)* Bing. Bing.

CARL: She didn't like it if you ate the raisins.

SISTER: No, but if one fell on the floor, you could have it.

CARL: It had to be an accident. I mean you couldn't just start throwing raisins on the floor. It had to be an accident. Then you could eat it. Other than that, you'd have to wait till the men were cooked and then you could eat out their raisin eyes.

BETTY: I never thought much of raisins. I have no real use for them.

SISTER: Good! More raisins for us!

BETTY: Well, I'm off to the market. I'll be back shortly.

SISTER: Oh, and maybe you should pick up some red glitter. After we sign the papers it'd be fun to throw up some big handfuls of glitter. *(She mimes throwing up big handfuls of glitter and watching it fall.)* Yo! Yo! Whoosh!

BETTY: I—well—excuse me—But I have an opinion here. Carl?

CARL: Yes, Betty, what's your opinion?

BETTY: Glitter makes too big a mess. It's sort of pretty for one second, then there's this big mess.

SISTER: I'll clean it up.

BETTY: That's impossible. You can never clean up all the glitter. You'll always be finding it in shoes and corners for years and years to come. It's a great big mess. I vote no on the glitter.

SISTER: I vote *yes.*

BETTY: Carl?

CARL: *(A beat.)* I think maybe we should…table the issue.

BETTY: *(A beat.)* I don't understand. I thought you wanted a lovely home? This can never be a lovely home with cheap, filthy glitter sticking up under our sink, gummed all up our air vents.

CARL: Alright. No glitter. It's too big a mess. We can't have it.

SISTER: I want glitter!

CARL: I said, "No!" Look, we have to have rules. Sometimes it's very good to have boundaries. Free rein'll freeze you. Ya gotta put a man on a path to make him happy.

BETTY: That is so true. That is a truth. You know what, Carl? If you ever get tired of the furniture business, you should become a philosopher. You could write a hit book in a minute.

(Carl blushes. Betty pecks him on the cheek, then hands Sister a basket.)

BETTY: Oh, Sister, would you go out in the garden this morning and pick some fresh vegetables? We'll have a garden salad with dinner. It's full of nutrients. *(Betty exits humming.)*

SISTER: Where're my cats? I haven't seen my cats.

CARL: She's allergic to cats. I put them in a cage. They're out in the backyard.

SISTER: You don't put cats in cages. Cages are for chickens or rabbits or hamsters. They don't even make cat cages.

CARL: You're getting an attitude. Don't get an attitude. *(A beat.)* I gotta go get some poison. Tonight I'm gonna get rid of that neighborhood dog.

(Carl goes into the yard. Sister follows him outside carrying the basket.)

SISTER: I don't think she's gonna fit in around here. She doesn't even like raisins.

CARL: Hey, maybe you're still young or something. Maybe you've never stopped to think about *my* needs. But I do have a few. Aren't I allowed to have just a few?

(Sister kneels on the ground and starts pulling up vegetables.)

CARL: Try to understand. I need a homemaker. Someone to care for me. To make things cozy. She feeds me meals; she waxes the floor. She wears a different colored negligee each night of the week. She sews dainty little writing on her panties. It reads, "Carl's girl," or "Carl's little pussy." I think that stuff is cute. Nobody's ever done that sort of thing for me.

SISTER: *(Pulling up vegetables.)* So you've found yourself a mate. I'm very happy for you. I just hope it doesn't end in cheap divorce or desertion like your last three marriages.

CARL: *(A beat.)* You know what's going on with you? I'm starting to get it now. It's starting to make itself clear. You're jealous.

SISTER: What?

CARL: I think you're just plain jealous.

SISTER: Don't say that.

CARL: Jealous 'cause you can't get a man. You can't get a man.

SISTER: Hey, look, I don't care. You wanna fuck her? Stick these carrots up every place in her; make her scream like a pig? Fine! *(She breaks carrots in two and throws them at him.)* Fine! Save the carrots! I'll cook them up for dinner and serve them with butter. I'll eat a big serving of them! I'll ask for seconds! That's how jealous I am, you rotten fucking failure!!!

CARL: *(A beat.)* Pick up those carrots. Pick them up. All of them. Now.

(She slowly crawls on her knees and starts picking up broken carrots.)

SISTER: I'm sorry, Carl. I didn't mean to—I'm sorry—

CARL: Don't talk. I oughtta rip your head off your shoulders. Did you get all the carrots?

(She nods her head, her fists full of broken carrots.)

CARL: I don't think you did.

(Carl picks up a dirty, broken carrot, takes it to her, and jams it in her

mouth. *Carl walks out of the yard, leaving Sister kneeling in the dirt. Sister crawls to the basket and drops the carrots into the basket.)*

SISTER (SPAGHETTI/PINKIE): [SP] I gotta be careful. I gotta watch my mouth. Speaking in evil./ *(She slaps herself.)* [P] Don't hit me!/ [SP] Shut up! I will if I want to!/ *(She slaps herself and pulls at her hair.)* [P] Ow! Ow! Ow! Stop it! You're hurting me./ [SP] Then, shut up. *(She stops beating herself and sighs with exhaustion—as Sister.)* Oh goodness. Goodness. *(Tiptoeing around the yard.)* I don't know who I am anymore. There's this real sense I am lost. I have gotten lost. The path has disappeared and the berries have been eaten by the wren. I'm out here all alone and I can't even call because I don't know what name to call. Who would come and get me? What if I called for them and I called and then I was forsaken.

(The shrieking sound of cats howling blares across the sky.)

SISTER: *(As Sister.)* My cats! Where are you? I hear you. Garfield? Plums? *(Sister discovers her two fat cats crammed in a tiny cage hidden between the bushes.)* Oh, there you are! Why, they've caged you up. Put you in a cage. Not to worry. Cages can be good. You have bars. Something to hold on to. Solid. You're not lost. You're there in the cage. People can watch you. But they can't touch. They may throw peanuts. Peanuts can hurt. But they can't kill. If you're in the cage. Good kitties. Good kitties. *(Sister returns the cats and goes to check her soggy underpants.)* Still wet. Dripping wet. I can't wear pants that are this wet. Dry, will you. *(Sister heads up to her room through the outdoor stairway.)* I gotta doll-up. I'm setting my cap for the guest. Carl'll be proud of me. He'll see I'm really good-looking. He'll see I can get a man. *(Sister enters her bedroom, then exits into her bathroom.)* *(Betty enters the kitchen from the carport door, carrying a sack of groceries. She starts taking the groceries out of the sack. The "groceries" are all identical cans of string beans. She puts the cans in various places as though each can were a different item. Paul Casper, twenties–thirties, enters. He is thin and wiry with a broken nose. He wears a silver necklace and a dagger earring.)*

PAUL: Hello, Mrs. Willard.

BETTY: What do you want?

PAUL: …More.

BETTY: Get out of here.

PAUL: I thought you invited me.

BETTY: Later. That's for later. You're supposed to come here later.

PAUL: I wanna come now.

BETTY: No. Go away. Later you can come back by. We're having cocktails and hors d'oeuvres. But I have to prepare all that. I have to do the preparation.

PAUL: Let me help.

BETTY: It's woman's work. You'd be in the way.

PAUL: That's where I wanna be—in your way.

BETTY: I don't think Carl would like this. You talking to me this way.

PAUL: I don't think Carl would like how you talked to me on top of the coffee table.

BETTY: I don't remember saying anything.

PAUL: You don't? That's funny.

BETTY: I'd like for you to leave.

PAUL: You told me you wanted to suck me dry. You said you wanted to make me cry like a little baby. You said you wanted me to come through your nose.

BETTY: ...I didn't mean it.

PAUL: What? You didn't mean what?

BETTY: Anything I said or did.

PAUL: It felt like you meant it. It felt exactly like you meant it. It felt like you lost control.

BETTY: No. I was acting. It was all an act.

PAUL: I don't believe you.

BETTY: I just did it so you'd give Carl a good price on the building.

PAUL: Yeah?

BETTY: Yeah.

PAUL: I don't believe you.

BETTY: Why not? It worked, didn't it? You're selling the place to him for peanuts.

PAUL: Yeah. That's true. I am. But that's 'cause I want to get rid of it. I want someone to take it off my hands.

BETTY: Why's that?

PAUL: I got the word. Some ponies I owe are gonna explode it on Sunday.

BETTY: So you're selling Carl a building that's gonna be blown up?

PAUL: Kaboom.

BETTY: Why are you telling me this?

PAUL: 'Cause I don't want you to be there. I want you to be with me.

BETTY: I just told you everything I said or did was for Carl.

PAUL: And I think I mentioned, I don't believe you.

BETTY: I love Carl. Carl loves me. We have a lovely home.

PAUL: Uh-huh.

BETTY: You don't believe me, but Carl would do anything for me.

PAUL: You're nothing but an ornament to Carl. He only wants the deodorized airbrushed version of you. I want all of you. Every sweet dirty part.

Naked under fluorescent lights. I crave all your wrinkles and bags and ugly lies. I never ever want to fuck you in the moonlight.

BETTY: *(A beat.)* Carl's going to murder you. Tonight when you come over. He's making plans to kill you.

PAUL: Why?

BETTY: You insulted me.

PAUL: Did you tell him I did?

BETTY: Yes.

PAUL: Why did you tell him that?

BETTY: I don't know. I wanted to see—I wanted to know—I wanted proof— he loved me.

PAUL: He doesn't love you. He's too stupid to love you. He doesn't even know you were a whore and burnt apartment buildings for money and drowned your son in a bucket.

BETTY: *(Weakly, staggered.)* How do you know that was me?

PAUL: I'm looking at your face.

BETTY: *(A beat.)* I never should have married Carl. He's not for me. I think I was desperate. It was Christmas Eve. I was being evicted. I tried to get the money. That night I went to the Pleasure Chest. I bought some rubber gloves and condoms. I jerked two guys off in the parking lot. Neither of them paid me. I went back to my apartment and sat down in the corner of the green couch wearing my coat. I sat there the longest time in my coat. The sun came up. I wanted to cook eggs. I wanted eggs and hot coffee. But I just sat there and then night fell. The following morning I was still there in the coat. The doorbell rang; it was Carl coming by for his cold reading class. I told him things weren't so good. I told him I was in a bad way. He took me out to McDonald's and he bought me an Egg McMuffin. It was congealed and cold. I ate it. Then I fucked him. We went back to the apartment. It was padlocked. My things had been put out in the yard. I got some stuff: clothes, a hair dryer, the Christmas tree, and then I moved in here and tried to make it work.

PAUL: Let's kill Carl.

BETTY: Really?

PAUL: I think so.

BETTY: Can't we just run away?

PAUL: Don't you want his money?

BETTY: He doesn't have any money. His mother left it all to his screwed-up sister.

PAUL: But he's buying my building.

BETTY: Only with her signature.

PAUL: Hmm.

BETTY: After he pays you for the building, we'll have half the money.

PAUL: Right. But wouldn't it be better if we had all the money? Maybe I could marry the sister and then kill her.

BETTY: I wouldn't mind seeing her dead. As a matter of fact, she's setting her cap for you.

PAUL: Yeah?

BETTY: She's trying to find a man.

PAUL: Great. Make me look good to her. Build me up. Can you do that, baby?

BETTY: Yeah. I can do that.

(Carl enters the yard. He carries a brown sack. He is singing "When Johnny Comes Marching Home Again.")

BETTY: There's Carl—You gotta go.

PAUL: Hey, whatta ya say we kill him just once for good measure?

BETTY: Yeah, maybe, yeah.

PAUL: Give me some of you. I want some of you before I go.

(Betty sticks her hand up between her legs. She gasps, then holds her wet fingers out to Paul. He grabs her hand and smears her scent across his lips and nose. Carl enters just as Paul exits.)

CARL: I got the poison.

BETTY: Poison?

CARL: I thought it'd be a good way to go. You know, with our guest.

BETTY: Oh yes. But, well, I—I'm having second thoughts.

CARL: Sure you are. You're a woman. This is man's work. Relax, let me take charge.

BETTY: But, I mean, it's just...I don't...Isn't Sister setting her cap for this guy?

CARL: *(Ominously.)* Sister better watch her step if she knows what's good for her. If she doesn't straighten up and fly right, she could be next. *(Taking a can of poison from the sack.)* I got plenty of pest control. For anyone who gets pesty.

(The lights dim down below and go up on Sister's room. Sister enters from her bathroom. She has on a blonde wig with ringlets. She wears a bra and petticoat, high heels and dangling earrings. She carries an evening dress with a full net skirt. She holds the dress up to her body and parades around the room.)

SISTER (SPAGHETTI/PINKIE): [SIS] How to get a man! How to catch a man. How to reel one in. That is the question./ [P] Well, it certainly helps being a virgin./ [SP] A virgin? Are you a virgin?/ [P] I think I'm a virgin./ [SP] I'm not so sure./ [P] Oh really?/ [SP] I have my doubts./ [P] I hope you're right./ [SP] I thought you liked being a virgin./ [P] There's always this fear./ [SP] Fear?/ [P] Of the unknown. *(Pulling at her bangs.)* [P] I don't like these bangs./ [SP] No.

(Sister rips off her bangs. She tosses them out the window just as Betty enters her room after a perfunctory knock.)

BETTY: Hello.

SISTER: Hi.

BETTY: I—thought you might want some help.

SISTER: Help?

BETTY: I thought maybe I could give you some tips on how to set your cap for our guest.

SISTER: Tips? I need tips?

BETTY: Maybe. I don't know. Do you date around much?

SISTER: I like to keep love at bay.

BETTY: Why's that?

SISTER: You know what they say: Only love can break your heart.

BETTY: Did someone break your heart?

SISTER: Once. But I got this tattoo to forget him by.

BETTY: What is it?

SISTER: A face with no eyes surrounded by a cracked heart.

BETTY: Did it hurt?

SISTER: No. It felt good. What tips do you know?

BETTY: *(A beat.)* First thing is don't be overeager. Never say nice things to him. Curb that impulse. Tell him he makes your skin crawl. Tell him to stay away. Tell him the mere sight of him makes you wanna carve out your eyes. You know, play hard to get.

SISTER: Right. Play hard to get. They give that advice in magazines.

BETTY: Yeah, exactly. So what're ya gonna say if he proposes?

SISTER: Proposes? You mean marriage?

BETTY: Yeah.

SISTER: I'll say sure! Thanks! I do! I do! Now kiss the bride! *(She makes smacking sounds with her lips.)*

BETTY: Wait a minute. Think about it. You're not playing hard to get.

SISTER: But he wants to marry me. He wants me to be his bride!

BETTY: Oh no, not really. He's testing you. He wants to find out if you're easy. If you're a slut, a tramp, a whore. No nice girl ever says yes to a first-time marriage proposal.

SISTER: Gosh, I don't know. I think about it and it'd be hard to keep saying, "No." I mean I never ever remember even once saying, "No," and I'm speaking of my whole life.

BETTY: Well, go ahead then, be my guest. He'll end up tossing you away like a piece of unfinished toast.

SISTER: Toast?

BETTY: Yeah.

SISTER: Well, I hope he doesn't do that. I'm not toast. I'm better than toast.

BETTY: Then play hard to get. No matter what he says, say, "No." Always "No." Keep telling him "No, no, no!"

SISTER: "No." I'll tell him "No." Now I better check on my gingerbread men.

BETTY: I'll take them out for you. You fix your earrings. You've got them on backwards.

SISTER: Oh!

(Betty exits down into her bedroom. Sister turns to Spaghetti/Pinkie.)

SISTER: [P] So there, you see, all you have to do is say the magic word— "No"—and he won't think you're less than toast./ [SP] But I am less than toast./ [P] Ssh, they don't have to know./ [SP] Oh, they'll know. They'll spot it right off. You'll never pass the mustard./ [P] I won't?/ [SP] No way. Come on, let's get while the getting's good./ [P] Where?/ [SP] Out the window. *(Sister goes to the window and hangs the pink dress outside.)* [SP] Now jump. Go on, jump./ [P] Wait, I need my wings. Without wings I will die./ [SP] Yes, but before you'll be sailing through the air like glitter./ [P] But that'll go so fast and then I'll be smashed./ [SP] Not while you're in the air. In the air every second is forever. Now fly. Just fly. Fly, fly, fly! *(Sister sails her dress out the window. Return to Sister.)*

(Paul appears in the yard. He sees the falling dress and catches it in his arms.)

PAUL: Woh! Woh! *(Speaking to the dress.)* How do you do? So nice to meet you. Shall we dance? *(Paul waltzes the dress around the yard, singing a song.)* Mmm. The way you move. I feel like I've known you all my life. Will you marry me?

SISTER: *(Yelling down from her window.)* Hey, that's my one fancy dress and I don't know if I can let you marry it.

PAUL: Why, hello there.

SISTER: Hi.

PAUL: Did you really think I wanted to marry this dress?

SISTER: I don't know. You asked it.

PAUL: I was being playful.

SISTER: Oh. Playful.

PAUL: Do you know who I really want to marry?

(Sister shakes her head.)

PAUL: The girl who fits into this dress. That's the girl for me.

SISTER: Well, I—I mean, it's my dress.

PAUL: Yes. I believe you. I have no doubt. Would you do me a favor and come step into your gown?

SISTER: Alright. *(Sister comes down the outdoor stairway.)*

PAUL: What's your name?

SISTER: Sister Willard.

PAUL: Nice to meet you, Sister. I'm Paul Casper.

SISTER: You're the guest.

PAUL: Yes.

> *(Paul helps Sister into her dress. It is a perfect fit.)*

PAUL: Beautiful. Just beautiful.

> *(Sister turns around.)*

PAUL: Breathlessly beautiful. *(Dropping to his knees.)* Sister Willard, will you please marry me?

SISTER: I—I—I—I— *(Sister timidly shakes her head back and forth.)*

PAUL: What?

SISTER: *(Shaking her head.)* Uh-uh.

PAUL: Was that yes?

SISTER: *(A whisper.)* No.

PAUL: No?

SISTER: No.

PAUL: *(Approaching her.)* But I—I love you, Sister Willard. I love you more than words can say.

SISTER: No. Stay away.

PAUL: I can't. I could never stay away. Not from your lips, your hair, your tattoo.

SISTER: I said, "No." No. The mere sight of you makes me want to scoop out my eyeballs.

PAUL: For God's sake. I'll—I'll have plastic surgery. I'll change my face, my voice, my sex! Anything! Anything for you.

SISTER: No.

PAUL: I won't take no for an answer.

SISTER: No, no, no, no, no.

PAUL: Yes.

SISTER: No!

PAUL: Oooh. I really like it when you tell me no. It's starting to get me hot. Tell me no some more. Please, tell me some more.

SISTER: No.

PAUL: Yes.

SISTER: No, no, no! Ten thousand times no!

PAUL: Yes, yes—I want it.

SISTER: No, no, no—

PAUL: Yes!

SISTER: No. Oooh. *(Sister starts having spontaneous orgasms all across the yard.)*

PAUL: Come on, baby.

SISTER: Ooh! Ooh!

PAUL: More, I want more!

SISTER: No! No! A zillion times, no!

PAUL: Yes! Oh, yes!

SISTER: Ooh! Ooh!

PAUL: Take it.

SISTER: No, no, no, no.

PAUL: Yes, yes.

SISTER: Oooh! OOOh! OOOOOH! OOOOOOOHH! *(Sister collapses to the ground exhausted and panting.)*

(Paul produces a giant engagement ring.)

PAUL: I'm gonna ask you just one more time. Sister Willard, will you marry me?

SISTER: I—I—I— *(Convulsing with orgasms all alone on the ground.)* OOh! OOH! OOOHH!

PAUL: You will?

SISTER: *(Weakly.)* Yes.

(Paul puts the ring on her finger. Betty enters the kitchen from her bedroom. She wears a frilly apron over her dress. Carl enters.)

BETTY: It's party time! *(Betty takes a plate of canapés out of the refrigerator.)*

CARL: Yes. It'll all go off without a hitch. Smooth as glass. There's no need for concern of any sort.

BETTY: I'll take out the hors d'oeuvres.

CARL: Yes, I'll turn on the Malibu lights.

(Betty and Carl enter the yard and discover Sister and Paul lying on the lawn side by side.)

BETTY: Well, look who's here.

CARL: What's going on?

SISTER: *(Showing her ring.)* We're engaged, Carl. We're getting married. I got a man.

CARL: What do you mean? You don't even know this punk.

PAUL: I'm afraid it was love at first sight. At least for me. Sister had some initial hesitation, but I finally was able to win her over.

SISTER: It wasn't easy. Was it, Paul?

PAUL: Not in the least.

SISTER: I must have told him "No" over a zillion times.

PAUL: But when she at last said "Yes," I sensed she meant it.

SISTER: Aren't you happy, Carl? Aren't you happy for me?

CARL: *(To Paul.)* Get outta here.

PAUL: What?

CARL: I said get outta here before I break your face.

BETTY: Carl—

PAUL: Look, Carl, don't be a hothead. Relax.

CARL: You relax this— *(Carl hits Paul.)*

BETTY AND SISTER: Carl!

PAUL: Hey, man?! What's your beef?

CARL: What's my beef? I don't have any beef. All I get are dog scraps!
(Carl swings at Paul again. Paul comes back at Carl. They tear into each other. Paul quickly gets the upper hand and starts pummeling Carl. The women come in and break them up.)

BETTY: Will you knock it off. Stop it. Come on!

SISTER: *(Overlapping.)* Don't! Stop! Don't! You're hurting him! Stop, please. You don't have to kill him!

PAUL: He's stupid, your brother!

SISTER: He just lost control or something. Usually he's really nice. He's a nice guy.

BETTY: *(To Carl.)* Carl! Hey, hey! Carl, what're you doing? You're supposed to kill him in an orderly fashion after the papers are signed.

CARL: Right. Right. I lost my head.

BETTY: Woh! That was a good one! Let's give him a hand! *(She starts clapping.)* My star pupil! Acting is believing! I'm telling you, this man could be one of the great screen actors of our generation. He claims he's too old to break into the biz. He sees his age as a limitation. But I tell him, "Hollywood loves newcomers. They snarf them up. Go ahead. Do yourself a favor. Be the flavor of the month." But he says, "Nay, I'll stick to furniture." But he has it. He has got it. The potential. Major potential. In all my years as a cold reading coach, I've never seen such a bundle of it.

SISTER: *(To Carl.)* You mean you weren't really mad?

CARL: No. What? Hey! I was acting. This is great. Someone's finally taking my little sister off my hands. After all these years, she's finally found a man. Me and Mother never thought it was possible. *(A beat.)* So! How 'bout we go on and sign those papers, then eat some of Betty's hors d'oeuvres and have a little toast.

PAUL: *(Producing the papers.)* Yes! Those papers. I have them. They're right here. Ta-da! *(Fumbling for a pen.)* Now where's a—
(Betty and Carl both produce pens.)

BETTY AND CARL: Here, here.

PAUL: Got one, thanks. *(Paul quickly signs the papers, then hands them to Carl.)* There you go.

CARL: Now, Sister, I believe we need your John Hancock. *(Carl hands Sister the papers and a pen.)* Right on the dotted line.

SISTER: What am I signing?

CARL: What do you mean "What am I signing?" You're signing a paper I'm telling you to sign.
(Sister reads over the contract.)

CARL: What's this? Malcolm Forbes, Jr. we got here? Go on already. Sign it.

SISTER: ...No.

CARL: What?

SISTER: If I'm marrying Paul, why should I buy his building? I mean shouldn't we just share and share alike?
(Everyone laughs politely at her.)

CARL: No, no, no. Excuse me, Paul. She doesn't have a head for business. Let me explain. I'll make it extremely simple. You have to sign the paper so I can open up Furniture World.

SISTER: *(A beat.)* But I wanna spend the money Mother left me to open up a Frosty Shop. I want to experiment with all the frozen delights.

CARL: Hey, what're you doing here? You want me to knock your head off your shoulders?

SISTER: No.

CARL: Then sign the paper.

SISTER: *(Reckless and sexy.)* No, no, no, no, no, no, no! God, that's fun! Now I believe I'll go bring out the gingerbread men for our guest. They're my specialty! *(Sister exits into the kitchen.)*

CARL: Did you see that? Did you see that? How am I supposed to handle that and not break open her face?

BETTY: Your sister's weird.
(In the kitchen Sister opens the oven and discovers the gingerbread men are burnt. She quickly pulls the tray of men out of the oven, burns her hand, and drops the tray onto the floor. All the burnt men shatter.)

SISTER: Ooh! They're all burnt! Oh no! Oh no! They're all broken. My little men! *(She kneels down among the black broken gingerbread men and tries to piece them back together.)* Broken! Burnt, black, and charred. All in pieces with melted eyes.

(Outside everyone has heard Sister's wailing. Carl shakes his head.)

CARL: I don't know what's going on here. Maybe she's got the PMS disease. Women. Can they make you sick or what?

(Betty begins passing out hors d'oeuvres.)

BETTY: Hors d'oeuvres?

CARL: I mean what makes them so special? All that equipment they're always lugging around. Making such a big deal out of having babies. Bearing brats. Think about it. Dogs, cats, mules, cows—you don't see them getting morning sickness. Why's that? Answer's simple. It's something "women" make up 'cause they're just too prissy to live.

BETTY: *(To Carl.)* Try a tuna spread, honey.

CARL: No—I—I think it's time for a toast. I think we all could use a little toast. *(Carl goes into the kitchen. As soon as he is out of sight, Paul and Betty leap on each other. They roll out of sight behind trees and bushes. In the kitchen Carl discovers Sister kneeling among the gingerbread men trying to piece the charred crumbs together.)*

SISTER: I can't make them fit. Nothing will fit. It's all pieces. Not one man survived.

CARL: Throw that away. Put it in the garbage.

SISTER: Away. I'll throw them away. Away. Like unfinished toast.

(Sister throws the burnt men into the garbage. Throughout the following, Carl sets a tray with four glasses on the kitchen table.)

SISTER: Carl.

CARL: What?

SISTER: Why aren't you hitting me?

CARL: I'm taking into consideration your extenuating circumstances.

SISTER: What circumstances?

CARL: You have woman problems. But I'm going to fix you a nice drink. After you drink it, you'll feel a whole lot better. Now go wash off those burnt crumbs. Make yourself decent.

SISTER: Decent. Right. Decent. *(Sister goes up to her room and exits into the bathroom.)*

(Carl opens up a bottle of blue wine and starts pouring blue wine into glasses. Outside Betty and Paul reappear extremely disheveled. They quickly try to regain control.)

PAUL: God, I'm addicted to you before we even start.

BETTY: Are we gonna kill Carl?

PAUL: What do you think?

BETTY: Kill him. I hate him.

PAUL: Alright. I'll have to make it look good though, so Sister won't get suspicious. So she'll still marry me.

BETTY: I don't want you marrying her. Let's run away.

PAUL: We need money. After they blow up my building, I got nothing.

BETTY: I can always turn some tricks.

PAUL: Face it, those days are gone.

BETTY: What do you mean they're gone? I thought you wanted to fuck me under fluorescents?

PAUL: Yeah, but baby, I'm in love with you. I'm not fucking your body. I'm fucking your soul.

BETTY: I think my soul's been fucked enough.

PAUL: Hey, you know what I'm saying. I only have eyes for you.

BETTY: Yeah?

PAUL: Yeah. When I think of you I get butterflies in my stomach, those old-fashioned kind. The tiny yellow and white kind. The kind that tickle. Remember them?

BETTY: Yeah. Maybe.

PAUL: So how's Carl planning to kill me?

BETTY: Poison. But don't worry. Don't sweat. I got it figured. I'm going in and doing the old switch-a-roo with the glasses number. That'll put a fly in his ointment.

PAUL: Aren't you the cagey one.

BETTY: Grrr.

(Paul drops to his knees in front of Betty. He starts slowly kissing and licking her from her ankles to her thighs. Sister enters her bedroom from the bathroom. She waves three burning cigarettes.)

SISTER (PINKIE/SPAGHETTI): [P] Has someone been smoking up here? Remember this is a smoke-free house. No smoking allowed. *(Sister opens a drawer that is overflowing with cigarette stubs. She sticks the cigarettes into the mound of gray ashes.)* Good. Good. Now you're good except for the cookies./ [SP] Ssh. They don't have to know the cookies crumbled. Keep it under your hair. *(She feels up under her wig—as Sister.)* Ooh! Umph! These ringlets aren't you. They're not close. Not by a good measure. *(Sister takes off her wig and looks for another one.)* Let's see… There must be another one—a someone here—who could be you. Come out, come out, wherever you are… *(Sister hears soft moans coming from the yard below. She moves to the window and looks down.)*

(In the yard, Paul is still sucking on Betty. Her moans intensify, then they subside. Betty and Paul break away from each other. Betty straightens her apron and moves into the kitchen. Sister stands still for a moment staring down at Paul, then exits into her bathroom. Betty enters the kitchen. Carl has the blue wine poured.)

BETTY: You need any help?

(Carl takes a poison pellet from the box.)

CARL: This one's for our guest. *(Carl ritualistically drops the pellet into a glass. The blue wine fizzles and green vapors appear.)* And this one's for our little Sister. *(Carl drops a second pellet.)*

BETTY: Carl—

CARL: She deserves it.

BETTY: Alright. I—I'll bring out the tray. It'll look more natural—a woman bringing out a tray.

CARL: Yes. We'll—we'll do this just this once. Then we'll have a lovely home. *(Betty nods. Carl goes into the yard.)*

CARL: *(To Paul.)* Betty's coming with the drinks. Everything's under control. *(Carl goes and turns on the Malibu lights. The sun is starting to get red in the sky. In the kitchen, Betty takes two more pellets from the box of poison. She drops one into a glass.)*

BETTY: To Carl, from Carl's little pussy. *(She drops a second pellet into the wine bottle.)* And don't forget Sister's little pussies. *(Betty picks up the tray with four glasses and the wine bottle, then goes out into the yard.)*
(Sister comes down the outside staircase wearing a tinsel wig. She looks shaken and shattered.)

CARL: Ah, the wine.

PAUL: How nice.

(Betty sets down the tray and very carefully starts handing out glasses of wine.)

CARL: It's blue wine from the Napa Valley. You can drink it and not get drunk.

PAUL: Does it have alcohol?

CARL: Two hundred proof.

PAUL: Why don't you get drunk?

CARL: It's a metabolic wonder.

BETTY: Cheers, everyone!

CARL: To Furniture World!

(Everyone clinks glasses.)

ALL: Cheers./ Cheers./ Cheers./ Cheers./

(A beat. Sister, Betty and Carl drink their wine. Paul fakes a stumble and his wine goes flying.)

PAUL: Oops! Gosh! Lost my balance. 'Least I saved the glass. *(A difficult pause.)* Now when shall we have the wedding?

SISTER: You still want the wedding?

PAUL: What? Of course I do. Don't toy with me. Here, let's have a toast to our eternal union. *(Paul pours everyone more wine.)*

CARL: Ah, yes! To the wedding couple.

BETTY: To love throughout the ages.

CARL: To people who need people.

BETTY: Cheers!

(They all toast. Carl, Sister, and Paul drink their drinks. Betty brings hers to her lips then stops.)

BETTY: I think, if no one minds, I'll feed my wine to Sister's darling little kitties. After all, they should be a part of the celebration.

(Betty gives her wine to the cats in the cage. Paul looks at her suspiciously.)

PAUL: Betty—

BETTY: What? Yes?

(Carl and Sister begin to groan and reel around the yard.)

SISTER: I don't feel so good.

CARL: Oh my goodness. Woh, my gut. I feel kinda like I've been poisoned. Betty?

PAUL: *(Starting to feel strange.)* You did something…

BETTY: Sister, you'd better check on your cats. They don't look so good.

SISTER: My cats? My cats—Garfield and Plums. *(Sister runs to the cat cage.)* Oh no. Oh no.

PAUL: *(Getting sicker by the minute.)* You double-crossing bitch. What's wrong with you?

BETTY: I guess I lost my balance. Oops.

SISTER: My cats are dead! *(Sister holds up two fat, furry, horrible-looking fake dead cats.)*

(Carl staggers over to Betty and shoves her to the ground.)

CARL: I trusted you.

PAUL: *(Producing a gun.)* Does anybody mind if I shoot her?

CARL: Be my guest.

BETTY: No—

(Paul shoots Betty several times, emptying his gun into various portions of her body. She dies lavishly.)

BETTY: Aah! Shit. Oh shit.

CARL: Shut up. You deserve it. *(Carl goes into the kitchen and starts pouring the contents of various strange bottles into a big pot on the stove.)*
(Betty lies bleeding to death in the yard. Sister is cramped with pain.)

SISTER: You shot her.

PAUL: Sure. She killed your cats. I won't allow anyone to ever kill your cats again.

SISTER: You won't?

PAUL: *(As he falls to the ground.)* No. I'll take special good care of you as long as I live. For the rest of my life; until I'm dead and gone; till my very last breath is drawn.

SISTER: Then you forgive me?

PAUL: Oh yes.

SISTER: I'm innocent.

PAUL: Completely.

SISTER: And we're in love?

PAUL: Yes, love, yes.

SISTER: Then I don't care that we're dying. I don't care. It's like living to me. It's like being born fresh from the ground.
(In the kitchen, Carl has prepared an antidote to the poison. He drinks a healthy dose of the potion and is quickly revived.)

CARL: Ahh, yes! *(He brings the pot outside, stirring it with a strange object.)* Sister—
(Sister pulls herself to her feet.)

SISTER: Carl, I'm innocent. All is forgiven. Finally, he loves me and all is forgiven. Let's celebrate! Let's celebrate! *(Sister lurches up the outside staircase, alternately dancing and cramping in pain.)*
(Carl looks at Paul.)

CARL: *(To Paul.)* I have the antidote.

PAUL: For the poison?

CARL: But you have to pay.
(Sister reels to her window. She throws out handfuls of red glitter. She is laughing and coughing and gasping for air, as she watches the glitter fall.)

SISTER: Innocence is proclaimed! The verdict is not guilty! And someone could love me after all. After all...

CARL: Hey! Hey, Sister. You're wrong. You're very wrong.

SISTER: No, no, a thousand times...

CARL: He doesn't love you. He's nothing more than an opportunist. He's just using you to get your money. Your inheritance.

SISTER: *(Overlapping.)* No, please, don't let me know. Just keep it a secret. I can die very soon.

CARL: Tell her, Paul.

PAUL: What?

CARL: How you feel about her. Exactly how you feel about her.

SISTER: Please, let it be a secret. A secret. I'll be good. Sshh! Sshh!

PAUL: I don't love you. You're pathetic. I just wanted your money. I was using you the whole time. You're nothing to me. Nothing to me but unfinished toast.

CARL: *(To Sister.)* I think it was time you heard the truth.

PAUL: *(About the antidote.)* I need that now.

CARL: I know you do, Paul. But I want you to crawl for it. Can you do that? Can you crawl for it? Let's see your crawl. Get down on your knees. Now crawl. *(Carl extends a lifelike rubber vibrator out to Paul.)*
(Paul starts crawling to Carl, as Carl stirs the potion with the vibrator.)

CARL: Watch this, Sister. Watch this puppy crawl.

SISTER: I knew it all along. I saw them kissing in the garden. They were kissing in the garden. Sucking fruits. Suck, suck, slurp, slurp.
(Paul has crawled up to Carl. Carl takes the vibrator out of the pot and lets Paul suck the potion off the rubber cock. Sister falls and lurches down the stairway as she delivers the rest of her speech.)

SISTER: Mashing fruits in each other's faces, red with juices, swollen with heavy bruises. Why do I forget I've forgotten what I see? All along, all along I don't remember I forgot...

CARL: *(To Paul.)* Good dog. He's a good dog. *(Carl takes the vibrator out of Paul's mouth and kicks Paul to the ground.)* Sister, what do you think? Should I kill him or let him go?

SISTER: *(Weakly.)* ...Whatever you think.

CARL: *(To Paul.)* Get outta here. You deserve to live.
(Paul leaves the yard in a sick sweat. Sister lies dying at the foot of the outdoor stairway. Carl takes the pot over to her. He scoops up handfuls of the potion for her to drink.)

CARL: There, there. I'll take care of you, Little Scampy. Just like I always have. I'm the only one who ever looked out for you. I'm the only one who ever will. There. Is that better now? Are you better?

SISTER: Yes. I—better.

CARL: Good. Then could you go make me a shake? I need my shake.

SISTER: Yeah. Sure, sure. I know you like your shake. *(She gets up and starts for the kitchen.)*

CARL: Wait. Before you go, I want you to put on those underpants.

SISTER: They're still wet.

CARL: Put them on anyway. It's not decent for you to go around without anything on underneath. It could get you in big trouble.

(Sister puts on the wet underpants.)

CARL: Ha, ha, ha, ha!

SISTER: What?

CARL: Nothing. I just liked seeing that slime crawl to me. It was nice. I had him under control.

(Sister goes into the kitchen to make Carl his shake.)

SISTER (SPAGHETTI/PINKIE): [P] I'm thinking I'm remembering forgetting./ [SP] Ssh. Bury the hatchet./ [P] I did. I buried it. It's breathing though. It's buried and breathing./ [SP] Ssh. Don't speak. Speaking is evil./ [P] I know nothing to speak of, but this I can say—there are scars on my tonsils from secret screaming./ [SP] Sssh.

(Sister turns on the shake machine. Rumbling sounds, as though the earth was breaking open, tinkling glass about to shatter, cracking wood, a faraway shriek. Sister turns off the machine. She pours the shake into a glass. She puts several pellets of poison into the glass, then picks up a giant butcher knife and walks outside carrying the shake and concealing the knife.)

SISTER (SPAGHETTI/PINKIE): Here's your shake.

CARL: Thanks, Little Rascal. *(Carl drinks his shake.)*

SISTER: Carl, I wanna ask you something. And I need you to speak the truth.

CARL: You can always believe me.

SISTER: But what if what you say isn't true?

CARL: That's when you have to take the leap of faith. That's something they teach you in church.

(Sister brings out the knife and gingerly threatens him with it.)

SISTER: You hurt me, didn't you?

CARL: No. When?

SISTER: I don't know when, but you did it.

CARL: *(About the knife.)* Put that down.

SISTER: I don't think so.

CARL: *(His stomach starts to cramp.)* Ooh.

SISTER: What's the matter? Tummyache?

CARL: Yes—I—did you…? I need the—

(Carl reaches for the pot containing the antidote. Sister kicks the pot over. The potion spills out across the yard.)

SISTER: Get away from that!

CARL: Hey! Look. What do you want?

SISTER: Tell me about it.

CARL: What?

SISTER: When you hurt me. When I was little. *(Threatening him with the knife.)* Tell me.

CARL: I—I guess. Once I...

SISTER: What? I want to know.

CARL: It was when you were sleeping.

SISTER: I was sleeping?

CARL: Yes, I—I sodomized you once when you were sleeping.

SISTER: I didn't wake up? That seems like something if someone were doing it to you—you would wake up.

CARL: I was very gentle. I went slow. You slept like a baby.

SISTER: I didn't stir?

CARL: You didn't stir.

SISTER: And that was the only time.

CARL: Virtually.

SISTER: What do you mean?

CARL: Occasionally, I'd come in your room in the morning and I'd let you suck me. You'd swallow every drop like feeding milk to a hungry baby.

SISTER: But I must have—was I asleep?

CARL: You were drowsy.

SISTER: Drowsy. I was drowsy. And that was all?

CARL: Virtually. Except for when I'd pick you up from school and take you out in my pickup truck and fuck you good.

SISTER: But every day you came for me. Every day you picked me up from school.

CARL: Virtually.

SISTER: And even still.

CARL: Yes, still, yes.

SISTER: This is very bad.

CARL: Yes.

(Sister waves the knife across her body.)

SISTER: I've been touched by evil. All over. Every place.

CARL: Forgive me. I wanted to show you the ropes. I thought that's what I was doing—showing you the ropes.

SISTER: I hate you! I hate you! I need to kill you!

CARL: Please, don't. Forgive me. Please, forgive me.

(Sister stalks Carl. He lurches away from her and trips and falls into his own shit.)

CARL: Oh, God! God! Shit! Don't kill me! Please, Sister, I'll do anything! Don't kill me!

SISTER: I have to kill you. I have to. Because I have to kill you!

(Carl tries to get away from her. He throws himself into the bushes. She lunges in the bushes after him and stabs him over and over and over again.)

CARL:	SISTER:
No! No! Forgive me!	You're a bad egg, a rotten
Help me. Forgive me!	apple in a barrel! I'm
	sorry to say this man was
	less than dirt and we had
	to put him away for good.

SISTER (PINKIE/SPAGHETTI): [P] I didn't mean it./ [SP] Yes, you did./ [P] Help me./ [SP] We have to leave. *(Sister takes off her dress and shoes.)* We're leaving this garden of sorrow. This dump yard of despair./ [P] How will we go?/ [SP] We'll fly./ [P] My wings aren't ready yet. They're on order, but they haven't arrived./ [SP] We'll go without wings. We've done it before./ [P] When?
(A flying harness is lowered from the grid. Sister climbs into the flying contraption.)

SISTER (PINKIE/SPAGHETTI): [SP] There was a time once long ago and pain was like glass stuck inside, but it didn't hurt—no hurt—because we were not home. We were flying./ [P] Yes. I remember. Yes. Dash away, dash away. That's what they tell to the reindeer. A whisper to the deer. Remember the story? It was in the story. The pages of old. Dash away./ [SP] Yes./ *(She flies out over the audience.)* [P] Oh, we're flying! Look, we're off toward home. And I can grasp stars with my hands and shells with my toes—pink shells, angel kisses. *(She suddenly stops flying as she spots the deserted dress below.)* Oh no. Oh, wait. There's someone, she's down there. Who's down there?/ [SP] It's Sister. You remember Sister./ [P] A long time ago there was a Sister./ [SP] And now she knows./ [P] Knows what?/ [SP] Everything./ [P] I remember everything. We must go back for her./ [SP] We can't. We're escaping. Now fly! Please, fly!/ [P] But she's down there! She's down there!/ [SP] We'll die. It will kill us. Oh. Oh. Oh. Oh./ [P] Oh. No. Please come! *(She flies down, grabs the dress, then sweeps back up, sailing with the dress in her arms.)* I remember you. I remember you. You had short yellow hair and you pressed flowers with rocks and you dreamed one day you would become an astronaut, but things were bad and for a long time you were afraid. I remember you. Very well. I remember you. *(She dances across the firmament with her dress.)*
(Lights fade to blackout.)

END OF PLAY

REVELERS

FOR DALE, DAN, COLLEEN, CINDI,
CENTER THEATER, CHICAGO,
AND THE CHEAP CHAMPAGNE

John Heard and Deirdre O'Connell
in New York Stage and Film Company's 1994 production of
Revelers.

photo by Dixie Sheridan

ORIGINAL PRODUCTION

Revelers was produced by New York Stage and Film Company in Poughkeepsie, New York, in 1994. It was produced by Peter J. Manning. It was directed by Leonard Foglia; set design was by Michael McGarty; lighting design was by Don Holder; costume design was by Tom Broecker; sound design was by Darren Clark. The cast was as follows:

Caroleena Lark	Amelia Campbell
Bob Gray	Michael Warren Powell
Kate Spoon Mulligan	Deborah Rush
Jasper Dale	Dennis O'Hare
Eddy Canary	John Heard
Victor Lloyd	Deirdre O'Connell
Timothy Harold	Kevin Sussman

Revelers was produced by Center Theater in Chicago, Illinois, in 1996. It was directed by Dan LaMorte; set design was by Joseph Wade; lighting design was by Jeffrey C. Bruckerhoff; costume design was by Lynn Sandberg; sound design/original music was by Joe Cerque. The cast was as follows:

Caroleena Lark	Robin Witt
Bob Gray	Mark Vann
Kate Spoon Mulligan	Peggy Goss
Jasper Dale	Dale Calandra
Eddy Canary	Robert Maffia
Victor Lloyd	Monica McCarthy
Timothy Harold	Kevin Mullaney

THE CAST

CAROLEENA LARK: 20s, Jill of all trades at Red Lantern Theater (RLT)
BOB GRAY: 40s, brother of the deceased
KATE SPOON MULLIGAN: 40s, housewife, former acting student
JASPER DALE: 40s, artistic director of Red Lantern Theater (RLT)
EDDY CANARY: 40s, a poet/bum
VICTOR LLOYD: 40s, a successful actress in L.A.
TIMOTHY HAROLD: 20s, a successful filmmaker

THE SETTING

The play takes place in and around Victor Lloyd's cottage in northern Wisconsin, on the shore of Lake Michigan.

THE TIME

Spring.

ACT I
PROLOGUE

Spotlight comes up on Victor. She is speaking into a video camera.

VICTOR: *(Into camera.)* Hi. Hi. Hello, everyone. Hello, dears. I can't tell you how sorry I am that I am going to miss Dash's memorial. His great finale. But I know he, of all people, would understand "The show (in my case, the film) must go on."

Please know, dear friends, that although my flesh is absent, my soul is present.

Enjoy your stay at my lake cottage. My assistant Bert will get you the keys. It's a shame Dash never had time to visit while he was alive. But now he can rest there in peace forever by the lake under the enchanted trees.

I miss you all so much! Next season I must come back to Chicago and do a show for The Red Lantern. As you know, I've always longed to do Blanche in *Streetcar*. Dash was the first one who ever told me, "Vickie, you were born to play Dubois!" How he believed in me...

Oh dear, I'm going to break down if I continue. Please. I'm so sorry I won't be with you. I'll send flowers. I love you all. *(Blowing a kiss.)* Your Vickie.
(Blackout. Music up.)

SCENE I

Victor Lloyd's lake cottage—the living room. There are three entrances and exits: the front door, to the kitchen, and up the birch-tree staircase. Prominent in the room is a life-size cutout replica of Dash Grey, a dashing man in his forties with blazing eyes, sensual sneering lips, and a thin pale wolflike face. He is gesturing triumphantly with a red umbrella. Various stage props surround the figure including: a long blond wig, a red veil, congo drums, hideous masks with the eyes stabbed out, a life-size teddy bear. There is an ancient tree that grows through the room, giving the feel of enchantment. Caroleena Lark, twenties, a young woman wearing bright green shoes, stands behind a video camera with Bob Gray, forties, a man dressed in brown polyester. They watch Victor's tape.

CAROLEENA: Can you do something more like that?

BOB: No.

CAROLEENA: Here is the problem, Bob, you are an amateur. You are not comfortable in front of a camera. I think you need direction. That's when I tell you what to do and you do it. Okay. Move over by Dash. Closer, Bob. Unfold your arms. Bob. Good. Now put one arm around him. Put your arm around Dash.

> *(Bob complies.)*

CAROLEENA: Now smile but with sadness.

BOB: I—can't do this. *(Bob moves away from the cutout.)*

CAROLEENA: *(Urging him back.)* Fine then. It was just a suggestion. I was trying to give you some direction. Go on back over there and talk about him. Please, Bob, we have a time constraint. *(She turns on the video camera.)*

> *(Bob moves beside the figure of Dash.)*

CAROLEENA: Rolling. We're rolling.

BOB: Danny—

CAROLEENA: Dash.

BOB: Dash. He was my brother. But he died. When he was born his name was Daniel Frank Gray. We called him Danny but you people call him Dash.

CAROLEENA: *(In a whisper.)* Tell about where you grew up.

BOB: We grew up in Casper, Wyoming. We had a mother and—a father. We both went to school: grade school, junior high, and high school. I got married. Danny never did.

CAROLEENA: You've got to do better than that.

> *(Kate Spoon, forties, a small, energetic woman, enters carrying a piece of toast on a plate. She wears a bright sweater decorated with rhinestone cats.)*

KATE SPOON: I've made cinnamon toast.

CAROLEENA: I'm in charge here and you've got to do better than that. Now isn't there something you remember from childhood? Some memory you could share?

BOB: One time Danny put glass in my bed. I slept on the top bunk and he put broken glass all in my bed.

KATE SPOON: I like that story. It's very poignant. But try to expand your vocal range. Your voice is extremely monotonous.

CAROLEENA: What else can you remember? Can you remember anything else?

BOB: No.

CAROLEENA: Dash says he put on plays every summer. What were those like?

BOB: I don't know. I never went. I didn't go.

KATE SPOON: Not very supportive.

CAROLEENA: Why didn't you go?

BOB: I never did. Because I didn't. *(Bob shrugs.)*

KATE SPOON: Let him tell the one about the glass in the bed.

CAROLEENA: Could you tell it in a way that would show Dash in a flattering light?

(Bob nods apprehensively.)

CAROLEENA: Okay. Action. *(She turns on the video camera.)*

BOB: Well, I came in from taking a bath in the tub. I was all clean and I got in my pajamas and I jumped up on the bed and there was all this broken glass from Coke and Seven-Up and Orange Crush bottles and I cut myself up real bad. I still have some scars.

KATE SPOON: He has the most liltless voice.

BOB: It's the way I talk. *(Bob walks away from the cutout of Dash, disheartened and hurt.)*

KATE SPOON: I'm sorry, it's just unusual, that's all. You have a unique vocal range.

CAROLEENA: Listen, Bob, I assured Jasper I could do an excellent job on your memorial tape with Dash. Please, I'm on thin ice around here and it's vital that I do a very good job.

BOB: *(Mouthing.)* I'm not talking.

CAROLEENA: What?

BOB: *(Mouthing.)* I'm not talking.

CAROLEENA: I just want to say, I know what's going on around here and it's sabotage.

KATE SPOON: Who're you talking to? Are you talking to me? Don't involve me.

(Jasper Dale, forties, enters wearing baggy pants, a torn sweater, and rubber thongs. He has long, stringy, black hair and his intense face is blemished with four or five unsightly warts.)

JASPER: *(Running his fingers through his long, greasy hair.)* He's here. I found him. Caroleena, you were right. I never knew you had such power. But, this Eddy Canary, to see him in your mind's eye.

CAROLEENA: *Sss! Sss! Sss!*

KATE SPOON: *(Overlapping.)* He's here? Eddy Canary's here?

JASPER: Outside.

CAROLEENA: I was right. I knew I'd be right.

KATE SPOON: Is he coming in?

JASPER: He's not well—motion sickness—the car.

KATE SPOON: *(Looking out the window.)* There he is right there, getting sick in the drive.

CAROLEENA: *(To Jasper.)* I told you. Didn't I tell you? I'm a very good psychic.

JASPER: *(Twirling his greasy hair around an index finger.)* You're spooky. Really, it's spooky. He was right there in the plaza feeding bread crumbs to the pigeons with a red carnation pinned to his jacket. I got chills all over.

CAROLEENA: Just like I said. I said it'd be red.

JASPER: You're spooky. I mean it was really…He looked at me like I was something expected.

KATE SPOON: *(Who has been primping.)* Do you think he'll remember me? It's been so many years. He hardly knew me in the first place. I'm no one he should know.

(Eddy Canary enters. He is pale with thinning hair that is matted to his head with sweat. He grins a charming death grin; a red carnation is pinned to his coat.)

JASPER: Eddy. Come in. Are you feeling alright?

EDDY: Excellent. Yes.

JASPER: Well, ah—

(Eddy spots the cutout of Dash.)

EDDY: Aah!

JASPER: Yes, Dash. There's Dash.

EDDY: Looking good.

JASPER: He wanted to be here. He requested it.

EDDY: Understandably, absolutely, his last hurrah.

JASPER: Yes, I'm afraid. I'm afraid that's so. Ah, this is Dash's brother Bob.

EDDY: Bob.

JASPER: And this is Kate Spoon.

KATE SPOON: I don't suppose you remember me? I was in Dash's class years ago. I did a scene from *Trojan Women* and Dash threw an apple core at me. Later at the Pub you said both of us had suffered and because of that, no matter what—wherever we went—whatever paths we took we would always be "kindred." Then we clinked glasses.

EDDY: Dash threw an apple core at you!

KATE SPOON: It knocked me in the chest, then Dash stood up, pointed at me with his red umbrella and yelled, "Where's your truth, you rolling cow?" I left the theatre after that. I married a man I never loved and my whole life changed. I don't suppose you remember when we made that toast?

EDDY: Vividly. Yes. Oh yes.

KATE SPOON: You're being polite. I can tell you're being polite. In fact, we've hardly met.

CAROLEENA: I'm Caroleena Lark. I'm the one who found you. I mean I saw you feeding the pigeons in my mind's eye and I saw what time and where and the red carnation.

EDDY: Yes.

CAROLEENA: I'm a very good psychic.

EDDY: Remarkable.

CAROLEENA: I'm spooky.

KATE SPOON: Are you hungry? I could—

EDDY: Starved.

KATE SPOON: Well, I'll—here you must eat. There's prosciutto. I remember how much you liked prosciutto.

EDDY: (Overcome with nausea.) Fine. I—air. (Eddy exits out the front door.)

KATE SPOON: (After an awkward beat.) Jasper, what do you want? Some salami, some chicken salad? A slice of brisket?

JASPER: I can't eat anything. I can't eat a thing.

KATE SPOON: A bowl of raspberry sorbet?

JASPER: I'm not eating anything.

KATE SPOON: I'll bring macaroons, the ones with cherries. (She exits.)

JASPER: Fine, but I'm not eating, I'm not eating, I'm not eating.

BOB: I'd like something to eat.

JASPER: Well, go get it! Serve yourself. I'm not waiting tables this week.
  (Bob exits to the kitchen.)

JASPER: He's nothing like Dash. They're nothing like brothers.

CAROLEENA: I know, it's like me. I'm the only one in my family who's been a success.

JASPER: Well, I must say, you did surprise me. You are, in fact, a very good psychic. Against all odds we've actually found Eddy Canary and gotten him here. Except for Victor Lloyd, Dash's circle is complete!

CAROLEENA: Victor Lloyd and Earl Bell.

JASPER: Earl's not important. Who was he? What was he? Dash's minion of the month.

CAROLEENA: Earl the squirrel. Earl the squirrel. Chip, chip, chip.

JASPER: Everything's going just as Dash would have wished except that Vickie's off doing that cartoon whatever. Playing something with a tail.

CAROLEENA: Herlagator.

JASPER: Really, it's awful.

CAROLEENA: If anyone can pull off Herlagator, Victor Lloyd can. She's so beautiful.

JASPER: Believe me, Vickie looks far better in the movies than she does in real life. Out there they can make any dog shine.

CAROLEENA: But don't you think she's a great actress? Remember in "Sea of Onyx" when she said, "I return your pearls."

JASPER: Please, she's a half-baked affair. A facile technician who lacks…Hmm, how shall I say it kindly? Who lacks all divine soulfulness. Dash and I always had to beat it out of her. It was exhausting, but in the end she generally was presentable. Forgetting, of course, her Lady Macbeth—a performance so unspeakably sickening that I breathed a sigh of relief when the Jeff Committee failed to file criminal complaint.

CAROLEENA: Hmm…Yes. I see what you're saying. Sometimes she could have, well, you know, more…more heart.

JASPER: Don't be an imbecile. Victor Lloyd has a mammoth heart, like a throbbing third breast. Remember that monstrous basket of peonies she sent me for the opening of *EARTH!* And for Dash! *(He indicates a gigantic basket of dead flowers.)* She's always sending flowers. She's a very loyal friend.

CAROLEENA: Uh-huh, right, I know. You're always saying how she's saying she wants to come back and do a giant benefit for the theatre.

JASPER: I gave her her start in the theatre. We have an immutable bond.

CAROLEENA: Great. That's really great 'cause we gotta get some money bad. The papers keep reporting that we have to close our doors.

JASPER: The Red Lantern is not closing. That's not an option. I promised Dash we would continue. I swore to him. That, this memorial, and giving up Winstons. He was holding these three fingers and I swore.

CAROLEENA: Oh, Jasper! Yes. Yes. 'Cause I don't know what I'd do without the Red Lantern Theatre. I don't know what I'd do.

JASPER: Something. You'd do something.

CAROLEENA: No, I wouldn't.

JASPER: Yes, you would. Stop pretending to be so helpless when you've got all this weird power. *(Zigging his arms through the air like lightning bolts.)* Zzzz! Zzz! Zzz!

CAROLEENA: Only for you. I only have power for you. Sss. Sss. Sss. *(She pats her chest lovingly with the palm of her hand.)*

JASPER: Please.

CAROLEENA: I'm sorry.

JASPER: You have to stop having those feelings for me.

CAROLEENA: I know. I can't.

JASPER: Then keep them to yourself because they're sick.

CAROLEENA: I know. It's just…I'm sick. I'm sick.

JASPER: I've told you and told you that nothing about you appeals to me. You're not my type. It's suffocating.

CAROLEENA: I know. I'm sorry. I'll stop. Just please don't let me go. Don't let me go.

JASPER: I said I wouldn't.

(Kate Spoon enters with a tray.)

KATE SPOON: Here's the snack. Where's Eddy?

CAROLEENA: Outside. I—I'll… *(Caroleena exits out the front door.)*

KATE SPOON: Have you told her she's being let go?

JASPER: It's better if I wait till after the service.

KATE SPOON: Well, she's very edgy. I think she suspects.

JASPER: Yes, I'm sure. She's a very good psychic.

KATE SPOON: Spooky.

JASPER: I'm thinking we should, I don't know, demote her. Relieve her of some responsibilities.

KATE SPOON: A demotion would humiliate her. It'd be too cruel. We have to let her go.

JASPER: Well, but really. It's so…I mean what if she…what if she…

KATE SPOON: I'm afraid that's life.

JASPER: Oh well. April is the cruelest month.

KATE SPOON: April? They're all cruel. So what about Eddy Canary? Where has he been all these years?

JASPER: I didn't ask.

KATE SPOON: I read somewhere he was institutionalized in an insane asylum in Oslo for pulling out all of his teeth with a pair of pliers.

(Eddy and Caroleena enter.)

EDDY: It's lovely out there. The blue spruce.

KATE SPOON: Yes, we're having dinner in the Chinese pagoda at sunset.

CAROLEENA: We're eating all of Dash's favorite foods.

KATE SPOON: Oysters, caviar, sun-dried tomatoes, goat cheese…

CAROLEENA: We're videotaping all the food; everyone's dressing up.

KATE SPOON: Eddy, I've made you a light snack. What beverage do you prefer? I remember you liked bourbon. I mean, when we made our toast, it was with bourbon.

EDDY: Water's fine.

KATE SPOON: Caroleena.

CAROLEENA: *(To Eddy.)* Perrier or Evian?

EDDY: Either's fine.

CAROLEENA: Well, Perrier comes in green bottles.

EDDY: Fine.

> *(Caroleena goes to the bar to get Eddy's drink. Eddy starts to eat. He seems to be enjoying it.)*

KATE SPOON: *(To Eddy.)* So…have you written anything new?

> *(Eddy shakes his head, smiling with dread, then resumes eating.)*

KATE SPOON: I read an item not long ago—well, actually, it was fairly long ago, five maybe ten years—that you were working on a great new novel while residing in Scandinavia. Norway, I believe it was…Oslo.

EDDY: Yes, that book; I don't mean to boast, but it was, I think, my epiphany.

KATE SPOON: Oh, we must see it!

EDDY: I'm afraid on a black dark night I burnt it all to ash.

KATE SPOON: You didn't! Please! What a tragedy.

EDDY: Yes. Well, no. I'm lying. All these years I've written nothing at all. Forgive me, I was wanting you to have a favorable opinion of me.

KATE SPOON: But why? I'm no one; I'm nobody.

EDDY: Yes, well, but I just thought it would be more pleasant.

JASPER: Pleasant? Pleasant? I don't believe Eddy Canary—I mean in *Cannibal Road* no one had concern for pleasant! It was all just Grrrrr—pure palpable Grrrr! A ravishing orgy of Grrrrr!

EDDY: That must have been back when I had my teeth.

JASPER: *(Running his hands through his hair and sucking it.)* Yes, well—I know people change, they can't always…It was just an observation. Something stupid to say.

KATE SPOON: Jasper, why do you suck on your hair? What must it taste like?

JASPER: Straw. Like greasy straw.

> *(He nays like a horse. Caroleena brings Eddy a bottle of Perrier.)*

KATE SPOON: Anyway, Eddy, I do hope you'll write a new great book so you can adapt it into a play and do it at our theatre.

CAROLEENA: What theatre's that? What theatre's that?

> *(Jasper recklessly starts eating macaroons.)*

JASPER: Yes, yes, like *Cannibal Road,* that play, that production. What a milestone. It made our name. Garnered us a reputation. I'll never forget your portrayal of Kyle Blue.

KATE SPOON: I've never seen anyone as sexy as you were back then.

JASPER: Every night Vickie and I would watch your final shaving scene from the wings. How you'd stare at your face while slitting your own throat.

EDDY: I did that well.

CAROLEENA: What theatre do you belong to, Kate Spoon?

KATE SPOON: I've made an investment in the Red Lantern.

CAROLEENA: What does that mean?

JASPER: *(Shrugging it off.)* She gave money.

CAROLEENA: Oh.

KATE SPOON: He was sexy though. I mean back then, wasn't he a very sexy man?

(Jasper sucks his hair and shrugs.)

KATE SPOON: *(To Eddy.)* I'll never understand why you gave up acting after just one play.

EDDY: I preferred real bourbon to tea.

KATE SPOON: Well, if you want to oversimplify…

EDDY: If at all possible.

(Bob enters from the kitchen.)

BOB: I had a salami sandwich and some Swiss cheese on bread with mayonnaise, a Cherry Coke, potato chips and eleven Oreos. *(A beat.)* Who do I pay?

JASPER: What?

BOB: I want to contribute my share.

JASPER: Pay Kate Spoon.

CAROLEENA: I brought things too.

KATE SPOON: Let him eat for free. Eddy Canary's eating for free.

BOB: I want to pay. Here's three dollars.

(Bob gives the money to Caroleena who has extended her hand. Bob exits out the front door.)

KATE SPOON: *(Remarking after Bob.)* You shouldn't have stuffed yourself. Dinner's not far off and everyone's stuffing themselves. *(To Jasper.)* Look at you. I thought you weren't hungry.

JASPER: I'm not.

KATE SPOON: Then why are you eating macaroons?

JASPER: Eating is not always indicative of hunger—oh ye of the literal, linear mind.

(Caroleena laughs.)

KATE SPOON: I know you think I'm not artistic. I don't go around barefoot slurping my hair, and you assume I'm not artistic but I am. In my heart I know I am.

JASPER: I wasn't suggesting—all I meant was—although I'm eating macaroons, all the same, I'm not hungry.

KATE SPOON: It doesn't matter. No one has ever believed in me. I'm used to it by now. I've always had to rely on my own inner strength.

JASPER: I—really—whatever.

KATE SPOON: Yes, it's silly. Anyway it's time to start the final dinner preparations. We can't miss the sunset; it's Dash's last. *(Kate Spoon exits to the kitchen.)*

CAROLEENA: She wasn't supposed to be here. She wasn't supposed to come. All of us here, Dash wanted us here. Us and Victor Lloyd, but not her. She drove all the way from St. Louis to visit his hospital room and he told me to tell her he was feeding.

JASPER: We'll edit her out. Why do you think I keep telling her to stand on the outskirts?

CAROLEENA: She shouldn't be here at all.

JASPER: Fine. Why don't you go tell her to leave? Go on, Caroleena. Tell her she's not welcome. Tell her to get out.

CAROLEENA: Okay, okay. I'm sorry. I just—what she said to you about eating macaroons…

KATE SPOON: *(Offstage.)* Caroleena, could you come videotape me preparing the hors d'oeuvres?

CAROLEENA: Alright. Coming! *(To Jasper.)* I'm sorry, okay? I'm sorry. Ssss. *(Caroleena exits.)*

EDDY: Where's Vickie?

JASPER: She's not coming?

EDDY: Isn't this her cottage?

JASPER: Yes. Dash always wanted to see it. Victor sent us pictures, but she's always so busy and he never got up. So he asked to have his ashes scattered up here around the lake.

EDDY: I have to say, and this is probably a lie, but I was hoping to see her. To see Victor, Vickie, Vick.

JASPER: Here's a picture.

EDDY: Yes, they've changed her nose.

JASPER: Her profile is destroyed.

EDDY: I'd like a drink.

JASPER: Help yourself.

EDDY: Have you got a cigarette?

JASPER: I quit. I'm on nicotine gum. It's hideous.

(Bob enters from the front door carrying a box.)

BOB: I found this lizard in the pagoda. It looks hurt. It might be dead.

(Eddy looks at the lizard. He pokes it with his finger.)

EDDY: I think it's dead.

BOB: You sure?

JASPER: Here, let me see that. *(Jasper takes the box and vigorously shakes it back and forth.)* Yes, it's dead.

SCENE II

Victor Lloyd, forties, a willowy woman with sunglasses and unkempt hair piled under a purple hat, enters through the front door. She lugs a shoulder bag and staggers with exhaustion. She is startled to find her front door is unlocked and even more unnerved by the odd assortment of stage props gathered in her living room.

VICTOR: No. Oh please. Really… *(She reacts to an artificial donkey's head with personal horror and mortification.)* God.
(Caroleena enters through the front door, oblivious to Victor. Caroleena is dressed in a yellow evening gown. She wears a hair extension decorated with stars. Tears are welling in her eyes. She clutches her chest gasping for breath.)

CAROLEENA: It's not fair. It's not fair. I was on Dash's list! My name was on it; hers was not. Now she puts everyone's name on his cake except for mine. My name should be on his cake. I wanted to be on his cake! *(Caroleena spots Victor.)* Oh, no. You're…Hi.

VICTOR: Hi.

CAROLEENA: They said you weren't coming.

VICTOR: *(Ever hopeful.)* Wasn't this last week?

CAROLEENA: No, now. He wanted to be strewn in April.

VICTOR: April? When's April?

CAROLEENA: Tomorrow it starts.

VICTOR: I'm confused. I thought…Last week I sent flowers.

CAROLEENA: Yes, they're big. They died. Here. *(Caroleena points to the massive arrangement of brown, dead flowers.)*

VICTOR: Oh.

CAROLEENA: I—I'm sorry. I'm very…It's awful how you saw me crying on a first impression.

VICTOR: Well, it doesn't matter. Believe me, I don't care.

CAROLEENA: You do have a large heart. Very big. I'm Caroleena Lark. I work at RLT. I have a formidable acting gift and hope someday to work on the stage, but for now I'm a Jill of all trades. I build sets, hang lights, do maintenance, box office, props, concessions, lobby displays. I'm indispensable to the operation.

(Kate Spoon enters with Eddy Canary. They are carrying the cutout of Dash. Kate is dressed in an evening gown.)

KATE SPOON: *(To Eddy, about the cutout.)* Careful, careful. Easy now. *(Spotting Caroleena.)* Caroleena, I did not deliberately exclude you from Dash's cake. It was an honest mistake. I simply forgot about you completely. *(She sees Victor.)* Oh goodness. Victor Lloyd, you're here. She's here! Why, look how you look. Just like a person. Your home is wonderful, the perfect setting, I adore the simplicity. Anyway, you don't remember me. I'm Kate Spoon. I took classes from Dash with you many years ago. Dash threw an apple core at me. Isn't this amazing. Now everyone's here from the original cast of *Cannibal Road.*

VICTOR: What? Not Eddy Canary?

KATE SPOON: But this is Eddy Canary.

(Kate Spoon points to Eddy who is busy at the bar.)

VICTOR: Really?

KATE SPOON: Of course. Eddy, tell her it's you. I'll get Jasper.

CAROLEENA: Let me get Jasper. I saw her first.

KATE SPOON: Jasper!

CAROLEENA: I came upon her!

(Kate Spoon and Caroleena race out the front door. Victor looks at Eddy who is sipping a drink.)

VICTOR: I thought you were dead. Weren't you shot by a stray bullet and nobody identified the body for several months?

EDDY: Not really.

VICTOR: Happened in Baltimore.

EDDY: Another guy, perhaps.

VICTOR: Someone who wasn't you?

EDDY: Would be my guess.

VICTOR: So where's the woman with the silver hair and artificial leg? What was her name?

EDDY: Her name.

VICTOR: Say her name.

EDDY: My wife's name.

VICTOR: Yes.

EDDY: Jenny Brown.

VICTOR: Yes.

EDDY: Long gone, Jenny Brown.

VICTOR: A trail paved with skulls.

EDDY: Exactly. And you?

VICTOR: Me?

EDDY: How are you?

VICTOR: I? Me? Read all about it.

EDDY: Right. Yes. You've had two divorces and a pug named Pip. You collect hats and advise people to drink great quantities of spring water.

VICTOR: You look completely different.

EDDY: You look the same.

VICTOR: Ish. I mean, my nose.

EDDY: Well, that.

VICTOR: At least you're alive.

EDDY: Ish.

VICTOR: I thought you were dead.

EDDY: We've said all that.

VICTOR: Right. *(A beat.)* How're we doing?

EDDY: Awful?

VICTOR: Umm. Yes, I know.

EDDY: Ha! Humph.

VICTOR: What? What are you thinking?

EDDY: Well, nothing. Ha! Just, I mean, well, as bad as this is—it's very good.

VICTOR: You think?

EDDY: Umm.

> *(Kate Spoon swings open the front door and enters the room. Jasper enters and points at Victor with Dash's red umbrella. Caroleena is at Jasper's heels running the video camera. Jasper is dressed in red.)*

JASPER: *(To Victor.)* You're here!

VICTOR: Jasper!

JASPER: I knew you wouldn't miss this.

VICTOR: No, never. No.

> *(Victor and Jasper embrace.)*

JASPER: Dash's circle is complete. As I promised him. As I promised. *(To Caroleena.)* Here, get us with Dash.

> *(Victor and Jasper stand before the cardboard cutout of Dash.)*

JASPER: *(To "Dash.")* She's come. Your protégé has returned. *(Jasper picks up a red silk veil and drapes it around Victor.)* From your Lady Macbeth. A masterful triumph!

VICTOR: Please, I was so young.

JASPER: Genius knows no age.

(Bob enters carrying a smushed cake. His shirt is covered with red icing and chocolate cake.)

BOB: I was carrying in the cake and I fell.

KATE SPOON: Did you destroy the cake?!

BOB: I dropped it.

(The phone rings. Victor goes to answer it.)

KATE SPOON: Who told you you could carry it?

BOB: I was trying to help. You said it looked like rain.

KATE SPOON: I never said you could carry it!

VICTOR: *(Overlapping into the phone.)* Hello… Yes, Timothy, I'm very upset, very unhinged… What?… Look, you little shit, I'm finished! I'm hanging up my tail—go hire a Gila monster! *(Victor slams down the phone.)*

JASPER: Very good. *(To Caroleena who is still running the camera.)* Did you get that?

CAROLEENA: Uh-huh.

KATE SPOON: *(To Victor.)* Who was it?

VICTOR: Timothy Harold.

JASPER: *(With ultimate disdain.)* The cartoonist.

VICTOR: Umm.

KATE SPOON: Timothy Harold?! *The* Timothy Harold?!

VICTOR: *(To Jasper.)* Look at your warts. They're growing spiral hairs.

KATE SPOON: He was on this phone.

JASPER: *(With insouciance.)* I have an ugly face.

VICTOR: It's perfect.

JASPER: Please, I'm ugly. It's an inherited trait. You should see my mother.

BOB: I don't know what to do. I forgot to pack another shirt.

TIMOTHY: *(Offstage.)* Hello.

KATE SPOON: Who's that?

JASPER: It better not be Earl Bell. It better not be Earl Bell.

TIMOTHY: *(Offstage.)* Hello! Hello! Victor, please. I know you're in there! I followed you in my car.

(The phone begins to ring.)

VICTOR: It's Timothy.

KATE SPOON: But he just phoned—

TIMOTHY: *(Offstage.)* Please, Victor, I know you're upset. But I want to address your grievances. Take affirmative steps.

(Kate Spoon rushes to the door and opens it. Timothy Harold, twenties, enters holding a cellular phone. He looks like a misplaced schoolboy with his

heaps of brown hair, wire-rimmed glasses and flushed pink cheeks. He cuts off the phone; the ringing stops.)

KATE SPOON: It's Timothy Harold! It's him. He's so young.

TIMOTHY: Hello.

KATE SPOON: I love all your work. *Little Miss Priss* and *Cat O' Nine* are animation masterpieces.

BOB: I saw those with my kids.

TIMOTHY: Oh goody. Yea! Goody-good. *(To Victor.)* I hope you don't mind, I followed you from Toronto.

VICTOR: I see. Umm, well. These are my theatre friends.

TIMOTHY: How do you do? How do you do? How're you? Victor, could I talk to you about the film a moment?

VICTOR: I'm very shaken, very unhinged.

TIMOTHY: Let me assure you, the entire special effects team has been noosed. They'll never work again. I plan to bring criminal charges. At the end of the day they'll all be reduced to pulp. Zap.

JASPER: *(Indicates the cutout of Dash.)* Please, we're here to mourn the loss of a dear friend, not to be plagued with your cartoon notables.

TIMOTHY: What?

JASPER: Dash Grey. Great innovative genius of the Chicago theatre world. *(Bob exits to the kitchen.)*

TIMOTHY: *(To Victor.)* I'm so sorry. I thought you left because of the gator mishap.

VICTOR: I hate that fucking gator.

TIMOTHY: Well, I'm having the giant gator completely dismantled. I've issued orders to incinerate its remains.

VICTOR: I was practically decapitated and burnt to a crisp all at once when that monster blew up.

TIMOTHY: It was a close one. I admit it. I apologize. I apologize.

VICTOR: I'm very shaken. Very unhinged. I don't even know what...I mean, Dash is dead. Eddy's not. That monster exploded. Oh, what does it mean? What? What? I don't know. Tell me, does anyone know?!

EDDY: No, but isn't that part of the fun?

VICTOR: I hate you.

EDDY: *(With grand hope.)* Still?

VICTOR: Yes. God, yes! Standing there like a decayed regret. Ah! Ah! *(Victor hurls herself at Eddy. Jasper holds her back.)*

EDDY: Adrenaline!

VICTOR: God, those eyes! Ah! Ah!

EDDY: Ah, adrenaline!

VICTOR: I can't be around the thought of you! Ah! Ah! Ah!

EDDY: Ah! Ah! Ah!

JASPER: Please, Vickie, Eddy, Eddy, Vickie. Dash wanted this to be celebra-
tory. He asked us to revel in his honor. "A colorful circus for a departed
ringmaster."

VICTOR: I have to go outside. *(To Jasper.)* Would you come?
(Jasper nods.)

VICTOR: I'll take off my shoes. It'll be like summer.

TIMOTHY: I—I'll wait. I'll make some phone calls.
(Victor and Jasper exit.)

KATE SPOON: *(To Timothy.)* How old are you?

TIMOTHY: Twenty-four. How old are you?

KATE SPOON: Oh, well! Top secret! Top secret! Ssh! Ssh!
(Bob enters rubbing a big wet stain on his shirt with a damp towel.)

BOB: It wasn't Dash's favorite meal that we had. Dash's favorite meal was ham
and applesauce, not what we had.

CAROLEENA: It was too. He made up the list. It was his own list.

BOB: Well, maybe his favorite dish changed. We didn't keep up much. It
could have changed and I didn't know.

CAROLEENA: I have a shirt you could buy.

BOB: Huh?

CAROLEENA: I sell mood T-shirts. It's a sideline. I have some in my suitcase.

BOB: How much?

CAROLEENA: Fifteen.

BOB: Are they nice?

CAROLEENA: I'll show you.
(Bob and Caroleena exit left.)

KATE SPOON: *(To Eddy.)* Now what shall I have, Mr. Canary? What would I
like?

EDDY: Bourbon?

KATE SPOON: You do remember.

EDDY: Vividly.

KATE SPOON: Oh, I knew you would, I knew you would.

EDDY: *(To Timothy.)* Would you like a drink?

TIMOTHY: No, I don't.

EDDY: He doesn't.

KATE SPOON: He's too young. We'd have to card him. We'd have to ask him for his driver's license to prove he was twenty-one because he looks so young.

(Timothy sighs deeply with despair. Kate Spoon turns to him.)

KATE SPOON: Why, what's wrong? Are you crying?

TIMOTHY: I'm not. No. My eyes are weak. I—I—

KATE SPOON: What?

TIMOTHY: It's nothing. My eyes have always been weak. They've always been very sensitive to the light.

SCENE III

Later that same night in Victor's living room. Timothy paces back and forth talking on his cellular phone.

TIMOTHY: *(Into phone.)* Sorry, sorry, so sorry. Look, M.J., I'm not going to deal with any more of that red oily goo and cyanide, onward to radio control…Zoom Zump! I've already conceded the tongue of flames. The swivel tail is a character trademark, without it Tailzig has no through-line…Fine, then fine, we'll tread water for a week. We can shoot all the closeups of Victor screaming…What? Victor? She's fine, basically…No, I don't think it's going to be any problem whatsoever…Well, you know agents…Absolutely, that's way out of line; but, factually speaking, the monster did explode…Yes, of course. Zump, zump. I'm aware of the official version…Christine Berry?! Absolutely not. Absolutely not. Victor's my ideal vision of Herlagator…I don't agree. She's very convincing as the reptile…Yes, they are problematic, but we can always animate her legs in post p. Exactly. It's our movie. Now get back to it, M.J. Bang! Zap! Zump!… *(Timothy hangs up and immediately starts working on his laptop computer.)*

(Kate Spoon and Eddy enter from the kitchen. Kate Spoon carries a pad and pencil. Eddy makes for the bar.)

KATE SPOON: Oh, it's Timothy Harold hard at work on his cartoon creations. We're not disturbing you, I hope. Eddy must have some quiet so he can write a poem for the service tomorrow.

EDDY: I—Please, there's nothing I have to write.

KATE SPOON: But you must. Just a short poem, a line, a word, any thought, any pearl. Here, dictate to me; I'll be your muse.

EDDY: First a drink.

KATE SPOON: It might loosen you up.

EDDY: Might. Yes.

KATE SPOON: Take your time. We've got till dawn, the night is an infant that has yet to crawl.

EDDY: Kate Spoon, I...You're very kind, but I work best in solitude.

KATE SPOON: But I don't like to leave you. Suppose you can't think of anything? What if nothing comes to you, and you're afflicted with a writers' block?

EDDY: Very thoughtful of you. Still I'll do better if you go. Believe me, deep in my heart I am an isolationist.

KATE SPOON: Well then, I'll wander down to the pagoda and rehearse Hecuba's lament. I believe it will play passionately under shimmering light of moon. Ah, I feel so wonderful tonight. Write well, fellow artists. Adieu. *(Kate Spoon waves to them and exits out the front door.)*

EDDY: God, people's waves...

TIMOTHY: What?

EDDY: They're unbearable. It's the faith that impales me.

TIMOTHY: Interesting remark. Interesting quip. You're a writer?

EDDY: I wrote one book.

TIMOTHY: What book?

EDDY: *Cannibal Road.*

TIMOTHY: Would it make a good movie?

EDDY: That I don't know.

TIMOTHY: I'd like to have a look at it. Could you get me a copy?

EDDY: I'm not sure there is one.

TIMOTHY: Oh.

EDDY: Um.

TIMOTHY: So what have you done since you stopped writing?

EDDY: Good question. Provocative. I'll have to give that one some thought.

TIMOTHY: Oh. Well, how do you know Victor?

EDDY: We met years ago at an outdoor fruit stand. She was stealing a peach.

TIMOTHY: I noticed earlier...she seemed to be...upset with you.

EDDY: Yes.

TIMOTHY: What was—do you mind my asking?—that about?

EDDY: That? Well, I think, and yet it's more complex naturally. But we were, Victor and I, at one point together and there was, I would say, a love. My wife found out and ran off to the Yucatan. I followed her because she only had one leg. Unfortunately, when I found her, the other leg was gone as well. After some time, she died unpleasantly. The thing I most remember from the whole experience is, even without her legs, I never really could love her the way I loved Victor… And you?

TIMOTHY: Me? No, no. Ping. Dong. I'm much too busy for love. Ping. Zap.
(Jasper and Victor enter. Victor wears a lyrical lavender gown and is barefoot. Jasper carries two shades of nail polish.)

VICTOR: I want one foot fuchsia and one foot crimson. I'm not the same. I can't be. I'm different all over.

JASPER: *(To Victor.)* Where?

VICTOR: Up there. The tree.

JASPER: My lady.

TIMOTHY: Hello, Victor.

VICTOR: Talk to my agent.

JASPER: I'm going to paint her nails.
(Jasper and Victor climb into the tower.)

EDDY: *(To Timothy about Victor.)* You can't have her.

TIMOTHY: What?

EDDY: You can't have her. You don't deserve her.

TIMOTHY: You're goofy.

EDDY: Good God. He called me goofy…I won't be subjected to such hapless endearments in my frail, teetering state. Get him out of here! Remove him at once!

JASPER: Eddy, what's wrong with you?

EDDY: I've lived a futile life; my nerves are shattered.

VICTOR: Poor Eddy. He seems to have overshot the Palace of Wisdom.

EDDY: It's true I am no longer fit for human consumption.

JASPER: *(About Eddy.)* Still I could find him attractive. I mean if I were still finding people attractive.

VICTOR: Dear Jasper.

JASPER: It frightens me how I don't need love.

VICTOR: Whatever happened between you and Dash? You were the perfect ones.

JASPER: It was all stupid, stupid, stupid, stupid.

VICTOR: Of course, but what?

JASPER: A very simple act. I feed my dog Snags a piece of linguine from the table. In a Rasputanesque rage, Dash cleared the table shattering my grandmother's wedding china. He said he was living in domestic hell, but I think it was something deeper. You don't leave a love of fifteen years over a flung piece of pasta. All the same, I got rid of my dog Snags.

VICTOR: Poor Snags.

JASPER: All for nought. I never was able to reinstate myself with Dash. He even stopped casting me—he claimed my extreme charisma unbalanced productions.

VICTOR: Umm.

JASPER: Eventually, I was able to badger him into producing the world premiere of *EARTH!*

VICTOR: Your musical version of *THE GOOD EARTH.*

JASPER: Right. I wrote the libretto, the lyrics, and music—directed and starred in the role of Wang Lung.

VICTOR: Yes, it was a smash hit. I remember sending flowers.

JASPER: Actually, it was quite a formidable disaster. I'm only speaking financially and critically, of course.

VICTOR: Oh well.

JASPER: Exactly. I told Dash, Oh well, I tried and I failed. My creation was received with unmitigated horror. I stuck my neck out—the axe fell swift. But, in the end, in spite of everything, I consider it a salute to my integrity. Integrity. Now there's a word some of us in this room might find hauntingly unfamiliar.

VICTOR: What?! Are you speaking of me?! You're not speaking of me?!

JASPER: No! Not you! He. The cartoonist. The one who derives all his work from the funny papers. A product's worth nothing to him unless it can be distributed mass bulk—homogenized with MSG.

TIMOTHY: I…excuse me. Should I take offense?

EDDY: Yes.

TIMOTHY: I—Victor, doesn't the man in the red suit understand my films gross millions?

JASPER: There! He admits it! His generic infantile sensibilities have garnered him an empire. I, on the other hand, still keep myself afloat in a job where I must wear a paper hat.

VICTOR: You don't still work at Chicken Bob's?!

JASPER: Only when I want to eat.

VICTOR: God, it's not fair! You're so talented, so gifted, and you've worked so hard. You've given your heart and guts and soul to the theatre. Oh, it's not fair. It's just…What can I say, the world's not fair!

JASPER: I'm not asking for awards or banquets. I only want it acknowledged that I'm a world-class actor.

VICTOR: Someday.

JASPER: Yes, someday. Who knows? The pendulum might swing the other direction and I could become as rich and famous as you.

VICTOR: Oh, please, you wouldn't want my life. Look at my life. I have no family, no friends, no children, no mate. At present I'm performing opposite fire-breathing fiberglass…It's all so endlessly empty.

JASPER: And I always thought…

VICTOR: No, no. I'm miserable, too.

JASPER: Poor Vickie.

VICTOR: Poor Jasper.

JASPER: Poor Vickie.

VICTOR: Poor Jasper.

EDDY: *(To Timothy.)* Do you want to shoot them or should I?

TIMOTHY: I don't think that man is in step with our world today.

(Bob enters wearing a mood T-shirt that is dark brown.)

BOB: Is there a TV anywhere?

JASPER: TV, what an imbecile.

VICTOR: No, I'm sorry. There's not.

(Caroleena enters from the kitchen smelling her hands.)

CAROLEENA: Smell my hands.

(She waves her hands up to Jasper, then goes to Eddy who smells her hands, then goes to Timothy who does not.)

CAROLEENA: Smell them. Smell my hands.

TIMOTHY: What?

CAROLEENA: I've been eating tangerines. My hands, they smell like oranges and lemons and pink fruit.

JASPER: *(To Victor.)* She's like this, Caroleena. She was an abused child.

CAROLEENA: *(To Bob.)* Look at you! Your mood T-shirt's turned brown. When I gave him the shirt, it was a light neutral beige, now it's mud brown.

BOB: Maybe I started to sweat.

CAROLEENA: Brown indicates depression. You must be depressed.

BOB: No.

CAROLEENA: It could be subliminal. Do you think it's subliminal?

BOB: No.

CAROLEENA: Hmm. Let me see your palm. I'll unravel things. I'm a very good psychic. It's one of my many indispensable talents. (She takes his hand and smells it.) Mmmm.

BOB: What?

CAROLEENA: Cashews, almonds, macadamia…

BOB: I—I ate five handfuls of mixed nuts. How much for a handful?

CAROLEENA: Mmm. Fifty cents. But wait. Bob, wait. I'm getting something. It's coming to me. It's coming to me. Two. You're going to have two children.

BOB: Right, I have two kids already.

CAROLEENA: You have a very long lingering lifeline.

BOB: I do?

CAROLEENA: And great sensitivity. The cones on your fingertips reveal extreme vulnerability, acute intuition, and a keen sense of observation.

BOB: Uh huh.

CAROLEENA: Ah, here's a marriage fold. You will be married.

BOB: How... How many times?

CAROLEENA: Once.

(Bob pulls his hand away.)

BOB: Oh.

CAROLEENA: What's wrong?

BOB: My wife left me. I travel a lot.

CAROLEENA: You work for U.P.S. Deliver boxes.

BOB: Yeah. Will she come back? *(Holding out his hand to her.)*

(Caroleena ponders his hand.)

CAROLEENA: No.

(Bob withdraws his hand.)

CAROLEENA: Why'd she leave?

BOB: She said I was inarticulate and couldn't express my feelings. Her and the kids moved in with this guy. He's a bricklayer. He's got a nice place. He built it.

CAROLEENA: I guess it's hard.

BOB: Very sturdy.

CAROLEENA: Your shirt's turning black.

BOB: What does that mean?

CAROLEENA: You don't have to pay for the mixed nuts. I purchased them and you don't have to pay. They're expensive, mixed nuts. Much more so than just all peanuts.

BOB: I bet black's not good. Maybe I'm sweating. Maybe it's my sweat.

(Kate Spoon enters through the front door with cymbals in her hands. She crashes them together.)

KATE SPOON: Oh no, no! Tear the shorn head, rip nails through the folded cheeks. *(Kate Spoon crashes the cymbals once again for dramatic emphasis.)* Hecuba is resurrected. Fire from ashes! Dash to Dash! *(Indicating the cutout of Dash.)* When he sees me tomorrow he will throw rose petals from heaven.

CAROLEENA: I don't think so.

KATE SPOON: She doubts. She doubts. What do you think, Jasper?

JASPER: *(About Victor.)* Her nails look wonderful. Let's have champagne. *(Jasper descends from the tree to seek champagne.)*

KATE SPOON: I think I've proved it. I think I've shown. You're never too old to make dreams come true. If you just keep wishing and working, anything is possible.

CAROLEENA: You could never be a brain surgeon.

KATE SPOON: I most certainly could, if I wanted to be and set my mind to it and worked very, very hard.

CAROLEENA: They won't take you in medical school after the age of thirty-five.

KATE SPOON: I never heard that.

CAROLEENA: It's true.

JASPER: Caroleena, get everyone a glass.

CAROLEENA: And it's too late for you to be a prima ballerina or a concert pianist or the King of Norway or even a jockey.

KATE SPOON: Those are extreme examples.

CAROLEENA: I'm just saying, "The world is no longer your oyster."

KATE SPOON: Nor is it yours.

CAROLEENA: What? What do you mean, "Nor is it mine?" What does she mean?

KATE SPOON: Tell her, Jasper.

JASPER: What?

KATE SPOON: She already knows. I can tell by her radar eyes. She's just being spooky, pretending not to know.

CAROLEENA: Not to know what? Not to know what? Oh, I'm going crazy here; I'm going crazy. But first, before I go crazy, tell me, someone. Tell me, please, how-many-glasses-do-we-need for-champagne?

TIMOTHY: Seven.

JASPER: *(Popping open champagne.)* Cheers, everyone! To Dash!

KATE SPOON: We don't have glasses.

(Caroleena starts passing out glasses.)

VICTOR: I don't want a glass. I can't drink that cheap champagne.

TIMOTHY: I've got some Cristal in my car. I'll get it. *(Timothy exits.)*

KATE SPOON: *(To Jasper.)* Start pouring.

(Jasper starts pouring.)

BOB: Did you ever notice when you go inside a grocery store it gets colder?

EDDY: Yes, I have. I've noticed that.

BOB: I think it's because they have to keep the produce cold, and then they've got the freezer section and that's really cold. I try to remember, but I usually don't, to bring a sweater.

(Jasper fills Caroleena's glass with champagne.)

CAROLEENA: You're letting me go.

JASPER: *(To Kate Spoon.)* You told her.

KATE SPOON: It's her. I never did.

CAROLEENA: It was a mistake. You told me to mop the floors and I forgot, but I thought I had time in act one and I could finish it all up before intermission. But that little man left early; he didn't finish the act; I think maybe he didn't like your play. I don't know why; I thought it was good, I thought it held merit.

JASPER: You don't mop the lobby after the audience has arrived, any idiot knows.

KATE SPOON: It's not good policy. It gives a bad impression.

JASPER: That rotten little man is making legal threats. Our insurance, of course, has not been paid.

CAROLEENA: You said you'd overlook it. You said this time you'd overlook it.

KATE SPOON: It was a board decision.

CAROLEENA: What board?

KATE SPOON: We have a new board.

CAROLEENA: But I can't live without it. I can't live without the Red Lantern Theatre. Please. I can't live without it.

(Timothy enters through the front door with a bottle of Cristal.)

TIMOTHY: Here's the Cristal!

(Caroleena runs out the front door.)

TIMOTHY: Where's she going?

JASPER: To kill herself, I surmise.

TIMOTHY: What's wrong?

JASPER: Cancel my life. Just cancel the rest of my life. God. What's this? Now my gum is stuck in my hair. *(To Dash's cutout.)* All for you, Mr. Grey. And what, what, what have you ever given me? Excuse me, I'm going off to get drunk on the cheap shit. *(Jasper grabs the cheap champagne and exits to the kitchen.)*

KATE SPOON: It's unfortunate to end the evening on such a note. But there are times when we are not reasonable. *(To Eddy.)* Have you written your piece?

EDDY: Except for the finishing touches.

KATE SPOON: Well, I'll leave you to it.

(She starts turning off the lights. Bob exits up the stairs.)

KATE SPOON: It's time for bed, everyone. The service is at dawn. That's…I won't even tell you how soon. Bedtime. Morpheus calls. Oh well, dawdle if you must; but tomorrow, and tomorrow and tomorrow will be here soon. *(Kate Spoon exits.)*

TIMOTHY: *(Handing Victor a glass of champagne.)* Champagne. The Cristal.

VICTOR: Thanks.

TIMOTHY: I don't want you to worry. M.J.'s negotiating with your agent. Everything will be settled. It will all work out.

VICTOR: M.J.'s threatening to replace me with Christine Berry.

TIMOTHY: No. That's all a bluff.

VICTOR: It seems my legs are stoutish. Not actually, of course, just on film.

TIMOTHY: Please don't take any of that personally. It's how M.J. negotiates. Don't worry, I'll clear all this up. Trust me, Vickie. I'll take care of things. More wine?

VICTOR: No.

TIMOTHY: It's your favorite.

VICTOR: Go away.

TIMOTHY: Don't treat me like this. Please, I can't bear it. I'm so foolish the way I feel. Did none of it mean anything to you? Was I only a one-time fling?

(Eddy reacts.)

VICTOR: Please, go away.

TIMOTHY: You're everything I ever wanted. I'll do anything.

VICTOR: Go. Can you go? You're acting like a child.

TIMOTHY: Yes, I know…I'm so silly. So goofy. I don't know how to act. I don't know how I should be. Ping… Zap… Loopy…thump thump thump. Ping! *(Timothy exits out the front door.)*

VICTOR: What a complete fuckwit.

EDDY: Not so much a fuckwit that you didn't…

VICTOR: Yes?

EDDY: I would not presume to imagine. And yet…I do.

VICTOR: I hate you.

EDDY: Still?

VICTOR: Yes. Still. Still, oh, Eddy, Eddy, Ed, why did you ever come here?

EDDY: To see you, to see you, to see you. I think that's why. There was a mention—I heard your name and I remembered…I remembered loving you. Strange ache, like cutting a red pear with a sharp blade: hurt, bite, juice.

VICTOR: What do you want from me?

EDDY: What can I have?

(Bob enters from left, heading for the kitchen.)

BOB: I've come back for a snack. I've come back for a snack.

(Bob exits to the kitchen. A pause. Victor speaks softly.)

VICTOR: Have you finished your writing?

EDDY: Yes.

VICTOR: May I see?

EDDY: Yes.

VICTOR: *(She picks up the blank paper.)* Um. Do you know why?

EDDY: I think so.

VICTOR: Can you say?

EDDY: I'm afraid if I write, it won't be any good.

VICTOR: Is that why you pulled out all of your teeth?

EDDY: I don't know. It may have been. There were other factors. That I can't say. *(He takes her hand, then pulls her toward the door.)*

VICTOR: What, Eddy, please?

EDDY: Victor.

VICTOR: Where are we… Where are we going?

EDDY: That we don't know.

(They exit out the front door. Bob enters from the kitchen munching a large brownie.)

BOB: I got a fudge square. I got a fudge square. *(He realizes he is alone, then notes his shirt.)* Oh. Look, I've turned blue. What does it mean if I'm blue? *(About the brownie.)* Mmm, these are good. My favorite. *(To the cutout of Dash.)* I wonder what your favorite was. When we were kids, it was chocolate pie with meringue. No, that was my favorite and Dad's favorite. I guess I don't remember yours. *(Bob sits eating his brownie.)* *(The lights fade to black.)*

END OF ACT I

ACT II
SCENE I

Victor's woods around the lake. A small stage has been erected. The cutout of Dash has been placed upon it. A large fantasy tree grows near the stage. A tightrope wire runs from a tree branch to a metal pole. Makeshift seating, including wooden stools, a tree stump, a plush ottoman, and a wicker bench create the audience area. Dawn is breaking. Kate Spoon is on stage practicing different poses to end her speech. She wears a Greek robe and sandals. Timothy sits in the audience working on his computer with the cellular phone and video camera near to him.

KATE SPOON: Which pose for the end? Which do you think? Watch me, Timothy. *(She does three poses.)* Timothy, look up! Look at me! *(She starts the poses again.)*

(Jasper enters. He wears a yellow tuxedo and colorful shoes.)

JASPER: Where is everyone? I was looking and I couldn't find my shoes and no one is here. People are missing.

KATE SPOON: You're covered in dust balls. What's all this lint and hair? You're sticky.

JASPER: I was crawling on the floor. I told you I couldn't find my shoes. Look at this, dawn is breaking. Everyone's missing.

KATE SPOON: I sent Bob; he's out searching.

JASPER: I mean they'd better get here. Good God, look at these beasts! *(He starts stomping spiders that are crawling on the stage.)*

KATE SPOON: Timothy's going to videotape the service for us.

JASPER: But does he have the slightest idea how to work a camera? This video's for our archives; it's vital because it's Dash's last—his only—

KATE SPOON: Yes, of course. He's a professional.

TIMOTHY: I don't understand this? I've shot three feature films. They've all grossed millions; I don't understand.

KATE SPOON: Yes, yes, we know.

JASPER: Fine, then, fine. I'm sure you're very capable. Excuse me, please. It's just no one is here; the sun is rising; Dash wanted dawn, the dawn light. *(He spots another bug and stomps it.)* Horrors!

KATE SPOON: I'm so unphotogenic. I don't take a good picture. I always photograph like an older person. Like I'm not young anymore.

JASPER: *(Stomping spiders.)* Victor has a very serious spider problem.

TIMOTHY: Brown Recluse, I believe.

JASPER: It's definitely a siege.

KATE SPOON: Will you stop! Will you stop killing them?! Really, stop!

JASPER: Why should I?

KATE SPOON: We are all God's creatures.

JASPER: That I don't doubt. *(He slowly squashes a spider to death.)*

KATE SPOON: Well, you certainly are no St. Francis of Assisi. No, you are no St. Francis of Assisi. Goodness, I am always saying things that are so funny. If I would just spend fifteen minutes a day writing down the funny things I say, I'd have a book of a hundred funny things in a very short time.

(Jasper responds by stomping more spiders. Victor appears from under the platform. She wears her clothes from the night before. She is covered with vines and leaves.)

VICTOR: Will you stop that fucking stomping?! Jesus, are you trying to split my skull?!

JASPER: What are you...Where's Eddy?

VICTOR: I need coffee. I must have caffeine.

KATE SPOON: Here, I have a thermos and croissants. *(Kate Spoon rushes to her picnic basket.)*

JASPER: *(To Victor.)* I hope you realize you have a very serious spider problem.

TIMOTHY: Why were you sleeping under the...with all those leaves?

VICTOR: I can't—you have a pimple on your nose. Go away.

KATE SPOON: Do you take milk?

VICTOR: Black.

TIMOTHY: I'm sorry about last night. I'm sorry about last night. I'm sorry about last night.

KATE SPOON: *(Passing out strawberries.)* Strawberries, strawberries, strawberries, strawberries, strawberries.

VICTOR: This is very surreal.

(Jasper discovers Eddy under the stage. Eddy crawls out in shameful disrepair. He's bruised and bloodied and covered with filth.)

JASPER: There he is. Eddy. Jesus, shit.

TIMOTHY: *(To Victor.)* He was down there with you? He was down there?

KATE SPOON: Look at you! Oh, look at you! Why have you been out here rolling in the dirt?

EDDY: Ah, dirt, dirt, dirt! Dirt is a masterpiece!

KATE SPOON: This is not good. I suspect he's been drinking. He needs to wash completely. There could have been rats under there, rodents!

(Eddy removes a bottle of vodka from his pocket and takes a slug.)

JASPER: There's no time for all this hygienic concern. The sun! The sun!

EDDY: *(Spotting Victor.)* Victor, Vickie, Vick. Grr. Grr.

VICTOR: You're too much for me. Stay away. You frighten me. You're not young, you're not young, you're not young anymore.

EDDY: I—I'm not surprised. Still I did roll across hills for you. I fell out of trees.

VICTOR: You fell out of trees because you were drunk.

EDDY: Forgive me. I want to live life as if there is no tomorrow.

VICTOR: But there is, you see.

EDDY: Strange that, yes. I had a dream about you last night. It was so clear I wrote it down. It expressed things I did not know.

VICTOR: Where is it? Let me see.

TIMOTHY: Please, don't. It's only a dream. Dreams aren't real. I'm making you an offer.

EDDY: *(Searching for the paper.)* I scribbled it down on a paper bag.

VICTOR: Where, where is it?

EDDY: It's here. Somewhere. It's all about you.

BOB: *(Enters in a greenish-yellow shirt.)* Help! Hello! Help! Please. I found…

KATE SPOON: What?

BOB: Where's…I don't see her. The girl, Caroleena. She's not here. She's not here.

JASPER: No one's seen her since she left last night. She's off somewhere having a sulk.

BOB: I think…Oh no. Oh, oh, oh, oh, oh.

JASPER: What?!

BOB: I think she…I think she's dead.

JASPER: This is a very bad joke.

BOB: I found this letter. It's all about, "how it is now time to die."

JASPER: Where'd you find that?

BOB: In the kitchen. Crumpled in a ball on the kitchen floor.

JASPER: *(Taking the note.)* I wrote this. This is mine. For God's sake, you shouldn't be snooping through crumpled pieces of paper, I don't think really.

KATE SPOON: Jasper, how could you do such a thing?

VICTOR: Yes? God. How?

JASPER: What? It's nothing. I write these all the time. I wrote several last night. It's how I deal with depression. Doesn't everyone do it? I thought everyone did it?
(A marked silence.)

VICTOR: May I see?

JASPER: It's not one of my better efforts.

KATE SPOON: May I read it next?

JASPER: No, only her.

VICTOR: This is very pessimistic.

KATE SPOON: I don't understand why you would write such a thing. It borders on morbid behavior.

VICTOR: You want to be sprinkled up here with Dash.

JASPER: I thought he wouldn't mind.

KATE SPOON: You never know. Dash was very unpredictable, hurling apple cores left and right.

VICTOR: Well, it's all beside the point. Jasper's not dying or anything of the sort for several thousand years. I'm sure Dash would agree.

(Suddenly, a host of pink petals drifts down from the tree, sailing through the air like snowflakes.)

JASPER: Why, look!

VICTOR: My God. It's a sign.

JASPER: A sign from Dash.

EDDY: Petals.

KATE SPOON: What? No. It's not really…it was just some petals—the wind.

TIMOTHY: *(Factually.)* There is no wind.

EDDY: Falling.

JASPER: No, it was a sign. It was Dash. I can feel…

VICTOR: Dash.

JASPER: *(To the heavens.)* Dash, are you…? Is it you? Is it really you?!

VICTOR: Dash?

(A sea of petals cascades from the sky.)

JASPER: My God. It is. It's really…

EDDY: Blossoms.

VICTOR: Marvelous.

BOB: Wow!

JASPER: It's you! It's you! Dash, my Dash!

TIMOTHY: No, it's the girl in the green shoes. She's up there in the tree.

JASPER: What? Shoes—what? Fucking Caroleena.

(Caroleena swings down from the tree. She is dressed in a pink acrobat's costume.)

CAROLEENA: April Fools! It was me! April Fools!

VICTOR: Fooled! We were all fooled!

EDDY: Bravo! Bravo! Take a bow.

BOB: I thought…I didn't know. Gosh.

(*Caroleena takes several bows.*)

JASPER: I have one thing to say to you. This is passive aggressive. Passive fucking aggressive. God, look at the light. The sun. The sun. This is—we've wasted… No further diversions will be tolerated! We must begin!

KATE SPOON: I'll pass out the programs.

VICTOR: Has M.J. spoken to my agent?

TIMOTHY: First thing this morning he's calling her. It will all be settled.

(*Kate Spoon is passing out programs.*)

VICTOR: What's this?

KATE SPOON: A portrait of Dash as Banquo's ghost.

VICTOR: *(To Eddy.)* What is she? The Johnny Appleseed of bad taste?

EDDY: Grr. Grr.

JASPER: Bob, Bob, Bob, it's really not complicated. You just start the tape when I point at you. You just press a button. It's very simple.

CAROLEENA: *(About Bob.)* You've turned yellow-green. That means you're nauseous.

BOB: I thought you were—I thought you had gone.

KATE SPOON: *(To Timothy.)* Use all of your skills to give it some real umph! And remember, make me look like a movie star.

(*Jasper bangs the cymbals once more.*)

JASPER: *(To the cutout of Dash.)* Ladies and gentlemen, Dash Grey, a legend!

(*He applauds; the others rise to their feet and cheer.*)

JASPER: But say no more, for the man would not wish it. His wishes were, and I quote… *(He reads from a piece of paper.)* "At my final celebration, dear friends, I implore you to eschew all sad speeches, clever anecdotes, and dreary eulogies. Instead, I crave a colorful circus for a departed ringmaster. Act, dance, sing, swing on ropes, play your pipes but, above everything, I beseech you to revel for me. Revel for me with all your hearts, so that I might sleep in peace knowing my troubled life has ended with a song." *(Jasper gently folds the speech up and speaks to his audience.)* Thus let us begin with a tune. A tune Victor and I performed many moons ago from my very first musical, *Cookie's Cooked.* In retrospect, I realize this is not my most sophisticated, nor is it my most accomplished work. Yet I know it held a special place in Dash's heart, for I dedicated it to him all those many years ago when we were young and full of hope and did not know what times our lives would hold.

VICTOR: I remember—I remember Dash once saying to me—"Music is often the one thing that makes life bearable."

JASPER: Yes, oh yes, I can imagine him having that sentiment. And now I give you the song "Cookie" from the musical, *Cookie's Cooked. (Jasper motions to Bob.)* Maestro.

(Bob turns on the tape. In the song and dance act that follows, Jasper remembers, with fascist precision, each and every word and movement. While Victor, who appears never to have heard the song in her life, improvises brazenly and charmingly mugs and shimmies her way through the number.)

JASPER AND VICTOR:

Oh, Cookie, my baking powder
My sugar lump
My little honey
My little stump.

I like to sift your flour
Love t'shake ya by the hour
When I twirl my spoon in your bowl…!

Sugar roll, sugar roll, sugar roll.
Raisins! Nuts! Butter! Cherries!
Cherries, cherries, cherries!
Cookie, you're for me! Cookie, you're for me! Cookie, you're for me!
(Applause. They bow. Victor takes a solo bow. Applause rises. Jasper grins at Victor with masked rage.)

KATE SPOON: I'm next, but one moment. I must do some preparation.

VICTOR: Wasn't that fun! Such fun, that old song. *(Elated.)* God, and I thought I'd forgotten it.

JASPER: You seemed…I mean, there were lapses.

VICTOR: Only you would have noticed. I thought I covered the glitches brilliantly. I'm an inspired improviser.

JASPER: I just thought you would have remembered more of the actual…well, what we actually did in the act. I mean we performed it for ten solid months, eight shows a week. I don't understand how you could have forgotten so much.

VICTOR: Maybe you should have done it on your own, like you planned.

JASPER: No, I wanted you. I asked you last night to do it with me. It's better with both of us.

VICTOR: But you weren't pleased. I forgot things.

JASPER: You were spectacular. I couldn't have asked for more. You'll always be my favorite partner. Really, you are Cookie.

KATE SPOON: Psst. We may begin.

JASPER: Yes, well, next honoring Dash is Ms. Kate Spoon Mulligan. She will be doing a speech of Hecuba's from Euripides' immortal *Trojan Women*. *(Jasper steps aside as Kate Spoon tragically hobbles down to stage center on a gnarled walking stick and begins her speech.)*

KATE SPOON: *(As Hecuba.)*

"And I, my aged strength crutched for support on staves,
whom shall I serve?
I shall be slave to Odysseus, lord of Ithaka!
Oh no, no!
Tear the shorn head,
rip nails through the folded cheeks.
Must I?
To be given as slave to serve that vile, that slippery man,
right's enemy, brute murderous beast,
that mouth of lies and treachery, that makes void
faith in things promised
and that which was beloved turns to hate. Oh, mourn,
daughters of Ilion, weep as one for me.
I am gone, doomed, undone,
O wretched, given
the worst lot of all."

(Near the end of Kate Spoon's speech, Jasper takes out an apple and winds his arm around like a pitcher on the mound. But at the last moment, instead of hurling the apple at her, he viciously bites into it. Kate Spoon bows majestically. There is a swell of relief followed by applause.)

JASPER: Thank you, thank you, thank you, Kate Spoon.

(Eddy gets up from his seat and teeters toward the stage. Kate Spoon takes a seat next to Victor in the audience.)

KATE SPOON: Well, I got through it. I got through it…I thought there were moments.

VICTOR: Several.

JASPER: Next I present a writer Dash revered beyond all others for his untamed passion, searing wit, and blinding insight. Please welcome Eddy Canary, genius at large.

(Eddy haltingly ascends the platform; Jasper descends into the audience.)

KATE SPOON: This is so exciting; he's going to read something new. A new poem he's written for the occasion. I was his muse.

(Eddy walks to the center of the stage. He stands still a moment, then collapses.)

VICTOR: Eddy?

JASPER: Are you alright?

EDDY: Oh yes, yes. I'm fine.

KATE SPOON: What's the matter? Did you trip?

EDDY: No, I was just standing here; I was standing here and I collapsed. You know, it happens now and again. I'm afraid the infrastructure's disintegrating. Rather rapidly, it seems.

KATE SPOON: Would you like me to read your poem for you?

EDDY: No. No, thank you. You see, I've got it all up here. *(He taps his mind with his index finger.)* Up here in these soggy cells. I—I just need a moment.

KATE SPOON: Well, it's a good thing we're videotaping. He hasn't even written it down.

VICTOR: No.

JASPER: I hope I don't break down when I hear this. He's such a powerful writer.

EDDY: *(He clears his throat.)* Dash. I'm sorry you are dead. *(Eddy pauses a moment, then walks off stage and takes a swig from his bottle.)*

CAROLEENA: Has he finished?

BOB: I don't know.

KATE SPOON: Is that all?

JASPER: Unless he continues.

VICTOR: Were you moved?

JASPER: Only at the very end.

KATE SPOON: I think he's drinking too much. I was very disappointed in that poem. It's such a tragedy. Eddy, why don't you stop drinking so you can write another work of genius? Why don't you stop destroying yourself and save your life?

EDDY: Because, because, because, because, because, because, because.

(Caroleena blows a red toy trumpet.)

CAROLEENA: I'm ready, please.

JASPER: Yes. And now Caroleena Lark will perform an act.

CAROLEENA: As a final tribute to my great mentor, Mr. Dash Grey, I would like to perform a circus feat. Dash, as you know, I have never walked on a tightrope before, but I have always dreamt I could. So today, with your help from the stars, I will do it. I will be my dream. *(Caroleena blows once more on the horn. She then puts down the horn, picks up a red umbrella, flips it open, and starts off across the trembling wire.)*

KATE SPOON: She's going to fall.

JASPER: And break her neck.

(Caroleena begins to wobble.)

VICTOR: Oh dear.

BOB: Oh boy.

CAROLEENA: I—I…Help! *(Caroleena falls, terribly ungracefully. She bounces around helter-skelter on the safety harness, making growling noises. Caroleena is transformed into the embodiment of Dash, taking on his voice and mannerisms.)*

TIMOTHY: Ping! Zap!

EDDY: An acrobatic mishap.

JASPER: Big surprise. Really, how idiotic. She's never…I mean, you don't just walk out on a wire without years of training.

TIMOTHY: That was some pratfall you took. Are you okay?

CAROLEENA: *(As Dash.)* Of course I'm okay, you cartoon cretin. *(Taking in the gawking crowd.)* Jesus, such a bunch of mortal maggots. *(To Kate Spoon.)* Get out of my way. Move, you sow! Move!

KATE SPOON: What are you…? Really! Such sour grapes!

BOB: Are you going back up?

JASPER: Caroleena, get down! That's enough. Idiot. She's an idiot.
(Caroleena/Dash climbs back up and walks across the wire with agile expertise. She twirls the red umbrella and bows with sweeping flourish.)

VICTOR: Yes! Oh yes! Yes!

EDDY: Such a dainty clown!

KATE SPOON: Miraculous.

JASPER: Very good! Very good. I must say.

CAROLEENA: *(As Dash.)* Oh, must you. Wart hog!

JASPER: What? Get down from there so I can strangle you. Right now, Caroleena. Your turn's up!

CAROLEENA: *(As Dash.)* I'm not Caroleena. *(She snaps the umbrella shut.)*

KATE SPOON: What a stupid girl!

CAROLEENA: *(Pointing the umbrella at Kate Spoon, as Dash.)* Excuse me, what is she doing here? She was not on my list. *(To Jasper.)* Get her out of here, you fucking little piss fuck! *(Picking up a rubber ball.)* Get her out or I'm going to pelt her with these balls. I've done it before—remember apple core?!

(Dash/Caroleena taunts Kate Spoon weakly with a ball as her Dash energy peters out.)

KATE SPOON: My God, she's pretending to be Dash. This is in such bad taste. Such bad taste!

JASPER: Do you realize what you're actually doing here? You're ruining Dash's memorial, after I've bent over backwards to follow all of his instructions. To make everything exactly the way he wanted.

CAROLEENA: *(As Dash, his energy re-emerging.)* Where's Earl Bell?

JASPER: What?

CAROLEENA: *(As Dash, gaining strength.)* Where's Earl Bell? You remember him? My lover and companion for the last five years. He was the first. The very first on my list. Why isn't he here?

JASPER: Don't do this. This is not...

CAROLEENA: *(As Dash.)* You didn't even ask him to come. You didn't even let him know.

JASPER: I thought it would upset him; I thought it would be too hard.

CAROLEENA: *(As Dash.)* Liar. You just wanted to exclude Earl so you could take the crown!

KATE SPOON: Caroleena, really, this is a sacrilege!

CAROLEENA: *(As Dash, to Jasper, weaker and weaker.)* I hope you realize how you've degraded your art, and even existence, all for filthy dirty ducats chiseled from that rolling cow.

KATE SPOON: It's not true. I'm not just at RLT because of my contribution. You saw today, in my speech, I have talent. Didn't you see it, Jasper? Didn't you see I have a gift?

JASPER: Yes. It's...yes.

CAROLEENA: *(As Dash—collapsing.)* Where is your truth?!

(The sky crackles with blinding white lightning. Everyone ducks.)

KATE SPOON: Aah!

VICTOR: Oh my God!

JASPER: Jesus, shit, shit, shit.

CAROLEENA: *(Revived as Dash, to Jasper.)* That's right! Cower, crawl, slither. RLT would not now be financially crippled if you had not whined and thrown tantrums and twisted my emaciated arm until I finally allowed you to do that overpriced dead elephant of a musical, *Earth!*

JASPER: Please, I know there were problems.

CAROLEENA: *(As Dash.)* It was abominable, no one came, critics hated it, Asians picketed, costumes and set pieces were forcibly repossessed due to your mad extravagance. And then, to keep the fiasco festering, on closing night you drink three pints of green chartreuse, and make poisonous phone calls to all of our VIP subscribers.

JASPER: Oh, fine, fine, wipe the floor with me. Don't you know I'd go out and beat my head in with a rock, if I thought it would do any good at all.

VICTOR: Jasper, what in the world?! Why, I didn't know the theatre was having financial difficulties.

CAROLEENA: *(As Dash, gaining strength to confront Victor.)* How would you know? We never see you or hear from you. You disdain our existence. Seven times you've sworn to return and play Blanche in *Streetcar.* Seven times you've left us with false advertisement and useless fliers.

VICTOR: I've always intended to come; it's just there've been circumstances.

CAROLEENA: *(As Dash.)* Face it, Vickie, you're a shitty friend.

VICTOR: How can you say that? I'm a very good, very thoughtful friend. I'm always sending flowers. Huge bouquets!

CAROLEENA: *(As Dash.)* Your assistant, Bert, sends the flowers. He even writes the notes. He even wrote the note telling me it was not convenient for me to come up here and visit you on what was to be my last bout of decent health. And I never saw you again.

VICTOR: Yes. I remember I didn't want to be distracted at that time, and…I never saw you again, that's true. Oh, I'm such an empty, horrible person and I don't understand how it happened. I started out—I had this dream—I followed it, my dream, and now it's mine. But all the same I'm so unhappy. I don't know why I'm so unhappy. I don't think it should be this way. Oh, Jasper. I have to come back to you and the Red Lantern. I'll sell my estate in Pacific Palisades, invest the money in the theatre, move back to Chicago, find my center, do the classics!

CAROLEENA: *(As Dash, rising from a stupor.)* Nothing Shakespearean, if you please! Remember your noxious L. Macbeth!

JASPER: Shut up! Hush! *(To Victor.)* Your Lady Macbeth was glorious. Why, I can see you right now doing the Oresteia trilogy. Walking barefoot across a set of black steel.

KATE SPOON: Yes, I—I love Greek tragedy. I can never get enough. It's ancient, it's universal, the roles are meaty. Electra!

JASPER: *(A beat.)* I don't really need her now, do I? *(To Victor.)* With your name and talent and generous contribution, why would I need her?

KATE SPOON: But I thought…You said my speech—I proved in my speech I have talent.

JASPER: Do you want to know what I really thought of your speech? *(He pro-*

duces the apple core.) Here's what I really thought of your speech! Here's my review! *(He hurls the apple core at her.)*

KATE SPOON: Oh God! Oh God! My husband Otto was right! No one likes me unless I'm giving them his money. I'm just an ugly, stupid woman filled with vain, pathetic, pathetic dreams! *(She exits.)*

JASPER: I should not have thrown that apple core at her. A baser instinct. A primal urge. Oh, why is it?! Why is it?! Now that I've hurt her badly, I feel bad.

CAROLEENA: *(As Dash.)* Eddy!

EDDY: Yes, Dash?

CAROLEENA: *(As Dash.)* Perhaps you should. Now.

EDDY: Ah, so it is. Victor, Vickie, Vic…My red pear. Be with me. I want to write poems about you. There are so many, all in my head.

VICTOR: I'm sorry, Eddy, you're impossible.

EDDY: Ish.

TIMOTHY: I have your agent on the line. Victor, please. Sally wants to talk to you.

VICTOR: Tell Sally, tell her…

EDDY: I'll send my fingers to you one by one in the mail.

VICTOR: I don't want them. Why would I want them? This is so like you. You never knew what to give me. You never knew what I'd like.

EDDY: You liked the glass elephant I gave you. The one you hurled at me when I left.

VICTOR: Yes, that was the only good thing I ever got.

TIMOTHY: Sally is begging to speak to you. She just wants a moment.

VICTOR: Umm. I…umm.

TIMOTHY: Just a brief word. A professional courtesy; a personal kindness.

CAROLEENA: *(As Dash. She viciously swings the red umbrella at Timothy. He drops the phone and falls to his knees.)* Leave her alone, you fucking Philistine! Ah! Ah! Ah!

JASPER: *(Overlapping.)* Yes, Dash! Yes! Hear, hear!

VICTOR: *(Overlapping.)* Dash, don't kill him! Please, he's very young. Dash!

TIMOTHY: I don't understand this. Why is everyone pretending the girl in the green shoes is actually the deceased? *(To Bob.)* I mean you don't think that that is actually your brother?

BOB: No.

TIMOTHY: See there. He'd recognize his own brother.

CAROLEENA: *(As Dash.)* I don't think so. He never actually knew me at all.

BOB: I know I would recognize my brother.

CAROLEENA: *(As Dash.)* Funny you spent all those years pretending not to. So disgusted that I was your brother, Casper's sissy ghost. That's why I put the glass in your bed, to hurt you for being so ashamed of me.

BOB: But you didn't.

CAROLEENA: *(As Dash.)* No, I admit it. I was young and didn't know how bad glass hurt. I do now and I'm sorry.

BOB: But it was me. I put the glass in Dash's bed. Like she says, everyone thought he was a sissy and I wanted to show them I felt so too. I lied to you when we were making that tape yesterday.

JASPER: *(A beat.)* Yes. I've seen those scars on Dash. I know them.

BOB: It cut him up bad.

CAROLEENA: April Fools. April Fools.

JASPER: Aah! Aah! I'm having a stroke. I'm having a stroke. But first I have to kill her. *(He starts climbing the tree to get to Caroleena.)*

TIMOTHY: Sally, are you there? I can't...Hello?! Hello? Zed. Zoo! *(Timothy slings down his cellular phone that has gone dead and exits in pursuit of another line.)*

JASPER: God, give me the strength to grab her by her throat and strangle her until she dies...turns mauve and dies.

BOB: Is it over now? Has the memorial stopped? When do I do my piece?

VICTOR: Fooled. We were fooled. What does this mean? What does any of it mean?

EDDY: That we don't know. Victor, Vickie, Vick. What can I give you? What do you want?

VICTOR: What do I want?

EDDY: Um?

VICTOR: Did you really...did you actually...did you write it?

EDDY: Did I write it?

VICTOR: The dream?

EDDY: Ah, the dream.

VICTOR: Yes.

EDDY: The dream about how I feel? My feelings for you?

VICTOR: Did you write it in writing?

EDDY: Yes.

VICTOR: Let me see.

EDDY: I—yes. Here.

(Eddy hands her a crumpled piece of paper. She takes it and begins to read it. A moment of painful silence.)

EDDY: *(To Bob.)* Bob, please, I'm longing for a cigarette.

BOB: Go get a pack of cigarettes?

EDDY: Please.

BOB: What brand?

EDDY: Winstons. Please.

(Bob exits. Victor finishes reading Eddy's dream.)

VICTOR: You dreamed of me.

EDDY: Yes.

VICTOR: Riding naked on a horse. I was painted green and I cut off your head with a meat axe. Headless, smeared with blood you ran after me; you caught me; I looked at you. Stars bloomed from your neck; the stars had eyes. It's awful; it's awful. I love you. There's no living without you.

EDDY: And yet.

VICTOR: What? Eddy? Ed?

EDDY: Um? Yes?

VICTOR: Tell me. What? Please.

EDDY: It won't... No teeth. It will not. Where are the Winstons?

(They stand together under the hot, harsh morning sun. Lights fade to black.)

SCENE II

Same setting. Early sunset. Jasper faces upstage scrubbing lipstick off of the cutout of Dash. Bob sits on the edge of the stage counting his money and adding up his expenses. His T-shirt is brown.

BOB: I had seventy dollars. I brought seventy dollars with me. Two twenties and three tens. Or maybe it was three twenties and one ten, but I think it was the former. Caroleena picked me up and she asked me for money for gas. I gave her a ten. Or maybe it was two fives. I should have kept better track. I need to watch my pennies. I'm going to have to write an I.O.U. I've eaten too much.

(Victor enters. She has cleaned up and changed clothes. She is dressed casually—L.A. elegant.)

VICTOR: Jasper.

(Jasper turns. We see he has a long scratch across his face.)

JASPER: There you are.

VICTOR: What happened to you?

JASPER: Caroleena let a tree branch hit me in the face when I was chasing after her.

VICTOR: Did you ever catch her?

JASPER: *(Going back to scrubbing.)* Not yet but she won't escape. I've got the keys to her car. Where's Eddy? We're supposed to be spreading ashes at sunset.

VICTOR: Well, I don't know really. What happened to Dash?

JASPER: Vandalism. Someone wrote *Fuck You* in lipstick right across his face.

VICTOR: My God, who would do a thing like that?

JASPER: Whom do you think? Kate Spoon, of course. She's seeking revenge after being usurped from the inner circle of RLT. People's motives are so transparent.

VICTOR: Umm.

JASPER: God, what a relief to be rid of that one. Such an unoriginal mind, *Fuck You?!* Really! Now, dear, I'm thinking it's imperative that we throw a spectacularly glamorous gala to celebrate your return to RLT. We may even want to consider performing a number or two from *Cookie's Cooked.*

TIMOTHY: *(Offstage.)* Victor!

VICTOR: Hello! We're here!

(Timothy enters, bright-eyed.)

TIMOTHY: Vickie, I was looking for Bob. Bob, could I talk to you for a moment?

BOB: I'm going to have to write an I.O.U. For some food. Who should I write it out to?

TIMOTHY: Listen, I have something to discuss with you. Come with me. I can improve your life.

(Bob and Timothy exit. Jasper watches them go. He does a parody of Timothy's walk. Victor laughs. Egged on, Jasper parodies Bob. Jasper picks up the pad Bob left on the stage and reads from it.)

JASPER: Look at this! He's kept track of everything he's eaten! "Five table-spoonfuls of grape jelly, eighteen slices of bologna, one layer cake." I presume the one he so unwillingly smothered.

VICTOR: Please stop, stop!

JASPER: My God, this man, his mind is like jello pie with several slices missing.

VICTOR: *(Laughing.)* I swear, Jasper. Only you—only you can really make me laugh. You know it's not going to work out for me to come back to the theatre after all.

JASPER: What?

VICTOR: Timothy's met all of my demands. I have to finish the film. No, really; otherwise, they might sue. I spoke to my agent. My hands are tied.

JASPER: But after—after, you could come after.

VICTOR: Maybe. For a show. I could come and do a show. I've always dreamt of doing Blanche in *Streetcar.*

JASPER: I feel...I mean I don't understand what's going on?! Because you stood here only hours ago, proclaiming how unhappy you were, how your life had no relevance, how you'd become a horrible, empty person and you wanted to change everything, find your center, do the classics.

VICTOR: Maybe we should go on and scatter the ashes.

JASPER: Excuse me? What? Am I...Am I speaking to you in invisible ink?

VICTOR: Jasper, don't make me...I'm trying to spare your feelings.

JASPER: My feelings?! Please! Please, please, please.

VICTOR: Look, dearest. I know RLT means everything to you. But in the greater scheme of things, it's just not relevant. I mean, do you really think I'd be willing to give up everything and move back to Chicago just to be some grand guppy in a glob of spit?!

JASPER: Oh well. Oh well.

VICTOR: See there. See? Now you've made me hurt your feelings. I should have just lied to you. Every time I'm remotely honest someone always gets upset.

JASPER: Let's just scatter these ashes and get the fuck out of here. Eddy! Bob! Eddy! Where's Eddy?

VICTOR: I don't think he's likely to reappear.

JASPER: Oh no? Why not? He seemed to be trailing you like shit on a shoe.

VICTOR: I put an end to all that. I used the ultimate weapon to drive him away. I told him I loved him. He shrank. Eddy Canary, what a sad, sad case.

JASPER: He's not the only sad—I mean he certainly is not the only...

VICTOR: What? He's not what? Did you lose your train of thought?

JASPER: No. I just decided not to proceed with it. You should be grateful.

VICTOR: Timothy Harold asked me to marry him.

JASPER: Little Lord Fauntleroy?

VICTOR: I've accepted for the moment.

JASPER: Great. Really good. Now you'll have a husband and a child. Two birds, one stone. I'll send you a rap tape by Jammy Jam Jelly for your wedding gift. Oh, and you'd better start saving your money for his college education, not to mention your own plastic surgery!

VICTOR: You shit! You asshole! Go drop dead in a sack!

(Victor exits. Jasper yells after her.)

JASPER: Your Lady Macbeth sucked! It gagged! It sucked!!! Oh God. Oh God. What am I gonna do? I've got to calm down. I know, I know. Suicide notes; death missives; extinction epistles. *(He picks up the pencil and pad Bob left on the stage. He climbs up the tree.)* Perhaps, I'll hang myself in her tree. How would she like that? I'll cut open my veins and bleed all over the foliage. I'll set fire to all of her woods and burn to death in the red hell inferno. *(Jasper disappears into the foliage of the tree.)*

(The stage is quiet for a moment. Eddy enters. He spots Kate Spoon's picnic basket and goes for it.)

CAROLEENA: *(Offstage.)* Is it clear?

EDDY: Clear.

(Caroleena enters. She is a bit scruffy from her romp in the woods.)

EDDY: *(Offering her some food.)* Some crumbs?

CAROLEENA: I'm starved. *(She runs over to get a stale croissant.)*

EDDY: Butter?

CAROLEENA: Yes. Are the berries okay?

EDDY: *(Tasting.)* Tart but highly edible.

CAROLEENA: You must be an expert.

EDDY: What?

CAROLEENA: On rotting food.

EDDY: Well…

CAROLEENA: I mean from being a bum.

EDDY: Umm, well. I have developed an acute sense of the rotten.

CAROLEENA: Have you been one of our homeless for a very long time?

EDDY: It seems to me that I have.

CAROLEENA: Imagine, they all thought I envisioned you through clairvoyance. Wait a minute. Wait a minute. It's coming to me. It's coming to me. He'll be wearing a red… Yes, it's a red carnation. And wings. I see wings…

EDDY: Pigeon wings.

(They laugh gaily.)

CAROLEENA: We fooled them.

EDDY: Yes.

CAROLEENA: On that day—that day I came upon you standing in front of the Surplus Food Warehouse wearing no shoes, holding up that sign…

EDDY: *Shakespeare For Spare Change.*

CAROLEENA: Yes. And you recited to me about the cracked cheeks.

EDDY: King Lear.

CAROLEENA: And I thought if I could make them think I was a very good psychic. If I could make them think I was, then they would not let me go. But...

EDDY: Yes?

CAROLEENA: Now I'm let go.

EDDY: Ah, so it is.

CAROLEENA: Poof.

(Eddy takes out a pack of cigarettes.)

EDDY: Cigarette?

CAROLEENA: Cigarettes? Where'd you get the cigarettes?

EDDY: Bob went for them when Victor and I had a talk.

CAROLEENA: You talked.

EDDY: Um.

CAROLEENA: What did you say?

EDDY: Have you got a match?

CAROLEENA: I have a lighter. I always carry one. I have so many. My father collected them from all over the world. After he shot himself in Mexico, they sent them all to me in a shoe box. This one's from...Casper.

EDDY: *(He lights his cigarette. As he lights his cigarette, he manages to set his clothes on fire.)* What's this? I've ignited myself. Oh, really. *(He beats out the flames and discovers a piece of paper.)* God. Here it is.

CAROLEENA: What?

EDDY: The dream I had last night.

CAROLEENA: What does it say?

EDDY: *(He folds up the paper.)* I realize everything. I see everything. But I don't do anything about it. I'm weak, weak, weak.

CAROLEENA: Do you love her?

EDDY: *(Meaning yes.)* Umm.

CAROLEENA: Are you going to be with her?

EDDY: *(Meaning no.)* Umm.

CAROLEENA: Why not?

EDDY: Because, because, because, because...because. *(He lights his cigarette.)*

CAROLEENA: I'm in love with someone who will never love me. Ssss. It's a hopeless, doomed situation. And yet I feel so happy today. Look at me. Can you tell?

(Eddy nods at her and returns the lighter. Kate Spoon enters. She is dripping wet.)

KATE SPOON: I tried to drown myself, but at the last minute I threw the rocks out of my pockets. I thought I didn't really want to die in a lake and be nibbled on by fish. The way they look at you when you can't look back. Tell me, am I really such a fool for trying after twenty years to resurrect a dream?

EDDY: Why ask us? We don't know.

KATE SPOON: If only I didn't have to go back to St. Louis and face Otto and my children. Four out of five aren't speaking to me.

CAROLEENA: Well. Talk is cheap.

KATE SPOON: What does that mean?

CAROLEENA: Nothing. It was just something to say to make you feel better.

KATE SPOON: Why make me feel better? I suppose Jasper has reinstated your position at RLT and now you're feeling sorry for me.

CAROLEENA: (Shaking her head, no.) Jasper's looking for me. He wants to kill me, I think. He stole my car keys. I think if I think about it I was trying to be nice so you would give me a ride back to Chicago.

KATE SPOON: Oh.

EDDY: Could I have a ride as well? I'm trying to remove myself from a situation.

KATE SPOON: Did you really remember having a drink with me all those years ago and saying we were kindred?

EDDY: I'm afraid no. Actually, that's a lie. I did remember. Vividly. Does it make a difference...I mean concerning your giving me a ride back to Chicago?

KATE SPOON: No.

EDDY: Then no, I'm sorry I did not remember you after all. And I hope you'll never ask me again.

(A crumpled note is dropped from the tree.)

CAROLEENA: What's that?

(Eddy picks up the note, opens it and reads it.)

EDDY: "I am up in the tree. I would like to have a truce so I could come down and we could scatter Dash's ashes and leave this place. Sincerely, Jasper Dale."

CAROLEENA: *(Looking up and spotting Jasper.)* Jasper!

KATE SPOON: He threw an apple core at me.

EDDY: Yes, but still. Can we deal with a truce?

CAROLEENA: Yes.

KATE SPOON: Yes.

EDDY: Truce!

(Jasper climbs down the tree.)

JASPER: Hello.

EDDY: Hello.

JASPER: *(To Eddy.)* Could I have a cigarette?

EDDY: Of course.

(Jasper takes a cigarette.)

JASPER: Light?

EDDY: She has one.

(Jasper looks at Caroleena and extends his hand.)

CAROLEENA: You promised Dash you'd stop.

JASPER: I promised Dash the memorial would go smoothly; I promised Dash the theatre would not close; why not go whole hog? Have a Winston!

CAROLEENA: What do you mean, the theatre's closing? Isn't Victor—

JASPER: No. Vickie's had a change of heart.

KATE SPOON: Well, don't come crawling to me.

JASPER: Alright.

EDDY: Where is she? Victor, I mean.

JASPER: Don't worry, Ed-o. She doesn't want you; she's eloping with the cartoon kid.

EDDY: That fuckwit?

JASPER: Yes.

EDDY: Victor, my God. She is so insincere. She could ransack your heart if you trusted her for one minute. How can you believe someone who can't even... It's diabolical. I mean she passes out love like sticks of stale gum.

JASPER: Yes, she's fickle.

EDDY: I do not regret that I have no heart left to break.

(Bob enters carrying a lily. His T-shirt is bright yellow; his face is beaming.)

BOB: Hello! Hi! What a nice sunset.

CAROLEENA: Your T-shirt is yellow.

BOB: Yes.

CAROLEENA: It means you're feeling good.

BOB: Uh-huh.

KATE SPOON: Why would you be feeling good?

BOB: Timothy Harold's asked me to do the voice of Gumbo in his new movie. He's flying me out to Hollywood next week. I'll make an excellent salary. I can pay off all my debts.

CAROLEENA: Wow! That's great! Gumbo's my favorite!

KATE SPOON: Well, I'm the one. I told you you had a distinctive voice.

JASPER: Yes, it's all just wonderful. Any minute I'm going to grab my banjo and go out dancing in the streets. But first let's find Victor and sling this soot.

BOB: Victor told me to tell you, they had to go.

JASPER: Oh.

BOB: She sent this flower.

JASPER: Touching. *(Jasper drapes the flower over the cutout of Dash, then picks up the can of ashes and opens it.)* Alright. Here. Now. I suppose everyone just reaches in and grabs a handful. *(He holds the can of ashes out to the mourners.)* Just take what you want.

KATE SPOON: I don't want any. Dash didn't think I had talent. He wouldn't approve.

JASPER: Fine.

BOB: Is this the last thing we do?

JASPER: Yes.

BOB: So now do I do my piece?

JASPER: Well, that was supposed to be earlier, but why stand on ceremony? Now can be the time. Do it now.

BOB: Alright. *(Bob grabs a handful of ashes and stands on the stage clenching the ashes tightly in his fist.)* It's from a play of Danny's I saw over and over again when we were little. Except he didn't know I saw it because I never said I did.

(Throughout Bob's recitation, the others throw their ashes. Jasper slings his from side to side like a hapless, desultory farmer. The last bit he tosses carelessly over his shoulder like spilled salt. Caroleena flings her ashes with a magical delicacy, as though they were fairy dust. Eddy lets his ashes drift slowly through his fingers like helplessly departing grains of sand.)

BOB: Little man, Little man

Hold my hand, hold my hand.

Run with me, dance with me

Play and sing your tune.

But cry if you must

Cry if you must

Cry if you must.

(Kate Spoon starts to cry.)

EDDY: Strange how little we weigh.

JASPER: Oh God.

CAROLEENA: What?

JASPER: I should have…Why didn't I…I could have saved my ashes and given them to Earl Bell. But I threw them away.

CAROLEENA: Earl Bell?

JASPER: Yes, because I can see he would have wanted to have some.

CAROLEENA: I'd give you mine but I tossed them all away.

JASPER: I know. I know you would. Oh. Oh. Oh.

KATE SPOON: *(To Jasper.)* Why don't you go on and cry? Maybe you'd feel better if you could just cry.

JASPER: And maybe you'd feel better if you could eat a bug.

KATE SPOON: Well, I just...Well.

BOB: *(Offering Jasper his handful of ashes.)* Here.

JASPER: What?

BOB: Take mine. *(Bob pours the ashes from his hand into Jasper's hand.)*

JASPER: Thank you.

BOB: Uh-huh.

JASPER: I—I'll put them...I'll save them in this can.

CAROLEENA: *(Pretending to sling more ashes.)* Poof! Poof! Poof!

KATE SPOON: I just feel like if people feel like crying, they should go on and cry.

EDDY: Bones. There were bones. I felt bits of them. The knuckles.

BOB: Look how it's changing. The colors up there.

JASPER: Yes, I know. Such a sunset. Dash's last.

CAROLEENA: Poof, Poof, Poof, Poof. Poof...

> *(The sunset deepens to a multitude of unbearable, beautiful colors. Lights fade to black.)*

END OF PLAY

L-Play

FOR BELITA
WITH LOVE, LANGUOR, LUNACY, LEPROSY, LATEVER...

Nicole Bradin and Jennifer Thomas
in Berkshire Theatre Festival's 1995 production of
L-Play.

photo by Neil Hammer

ORIGINAL PRODUCTION

L-Play was produced by the Berkshire Theatre Festival in Stockbridge, Massachusetts, in 1995. It was directed by Eric Hill; set design was by Gary M. English; lighting design was by Phil Monat; costume design was by Pamela Scofield; sound design was by James Wildman. The cast, in order of appearance, was as follows:

Actress A . . . . Allyn Rose
Actress B . . . . Jennifer Thomas
Actress C . . . . Nicole Bradin
Actor A . . . . John Lenartz
Actor B . . . . Duane Noch
Actor C . . . . Jonathan Uffelman

A benefit performance of *L-Play* was produced by the Met Theatre in Los Angeles, California, in 1996. The cast, in order of appearance, was as follows:

Actress A . . . . Alfre Woodard
Actress B . . . . Holly Hunter
Actress C . . . . Amy Madigan
Actor A . . . . James Gammon
Actor B . . . . Ed Harris
Actor C . . . . Bill Pullman

THE CAST

The play requires three actresses and three actors:

ACTRESS A   plays Monica, Lunatic

ACTRESS B   plays Joan, Granddaughter, Small One, Lucheea

ACTRESS C   plays Gertrude, Grandmother, Shelly, Middle One

ACTOR A   plays Price, Malcolm, Ben, Big One

ACTOR B   plays Jay, Wes, Shoe

ACTOR C   plays Various Parts, Learner, Narrator

THE SCENES

Scene I   Loneliness (Monica, Joan, Price)

Scene II   Linked (Jay, Gertrude)

Scene III   Loser (Malcolm, Various Parts)

Scene IV   Lunatic, Part One (Lunatic)

Scene V   Learner, Part One (Learner)

Scene VI   Lost (Ben, Wesley, Shelly)

Scene VII   Lunatic, Part Two (Lunatic)

Scene VIII   Leaving (Grandmother, Granddaughter)

Scene IX   Learner, Part Two (Learner)

Scene X   Life (Narrator, Big One, Middle One, Small One)

Scene XI   Lunatic, Part Three (Lunatic)

Scene XII   Learner, Part Three (Learner, Lucheea)

NOTE: The idea of this piece is that each scene is brought vividly and singularly to life through lights, costumes, sound, style, and tone. However, the fragmented nature of the play necessitates production elements be selective and sparse, so that the play keeps moving.

SCENE I
LONELINESS

Sounds: Winter winds, distant train, dogs barking, church bells clanging.
Time: Christmas Eve, the past.
Place: Pitt's Diner, South Louisiana.

Lights up slowly on Monica Fench, thirties, an attractive but worn-out woman wearing a faded waitress uniform and talking into a black phone.

MONICA: *(Into phone.)* 'Cause Mama doesn't want me. She doesn't want me. No, because remember last year?…Well, did she say she wanted me?… Uh-huh, well then, she doesn't want me. Anyway, Lou Ellen, it doesn't matter 'cause I can't 'cause I'm working. I got to stay here and serve people… Sure. Three old ladies just left. They left me a fifteen cent tip. I swear I'm holding three nickels right here. *(She gestures with an empty hand.)* …No, baby. Mr. Pitt's not here. He had to spend Christmas Eve with his wife, ex-wife, and kids…I didn't wanna go. Their house smells like lavender piss…No, everything's real wonderful. I'm expecting Mr. Pitt's gonna give me a ring for Christmas…Of course you'll be invited to our wedding, you're my own sweet child…I don't know about afterward. Maybe you could visit us some…I said maybe; look, Lou Ellen, I got some people here… She does? Alright… Merry Christmas, Mama, how're you?… Well, of course I'm gonna send Lou Ellen something for Christmas. I looked. I'm still looking. I just can't seem to pick out what's right…No, I've got a job. Still working at Mr. Pitt's Diner…Well, it's better than scraping shit at Parchment Penitentiary… What you don't understand is I've already made something out of my life. I've been somebody and done some things and that's just what I'm trying to recover from…Uh-huh, I know that's how you think… You're gonna tell Lou Ellen what? You'll tell her the wool muffler's from me? Well, thanks, Mama. What color is it? Just so I'll know… Okay. 'Bye. *(She hangs up.)* Yellow's not her color. She'll never wear it.
(Joan Wells, fourteen, enters the diner. She is bundled up in secondhand winter wear. Her face is flushed from the cold.)
JOAN: Merry Christmas.
MONICA: Have a seat. There's a Christmas Eve special.
JOAN: I don't have any money.

MONICA: Well, none of the stuff is free.

JOAN: That would be funny. I mean, if it was.

MONICA: Well, then I guess it ain't funny.

JOAN: No, I know it ain't. I come t'see William Pitt.

MONICA: He's not here.

JOAN: 'Cause I'm his granddaughter, Joan Wells. I've arranged to come stay with him after the New Year, but I come on early so as not to miss Christmas.

MONICA: I've heard about you. You've been in trouble.

JOAN: Not much. Some.

MONICA: He had to sign some paper to keep you out of some big trouble.

JOAN: I come on early because of Christmas I guess is what happened.

MONICA: He's not even sure you're his granddaughter. He never married that woman.

JOAN: I know.

MONICA: So you're a bastard.

JOAN: No, ma'am, my mama was a bastard. Me, I just don't have any family. Except for this one grandpaw.

MONICA: His name's Mr. Pitt.

JOAN: Mr. Pitt. He used to visit them I know. One time he took them to the state fair and no one could guess his age.

MONICA: I don't know how happy he's gonna be about you coming here. Before you were expected. Where're your things?

JOAN: I left them behind.

MONICA: Are you on the lam?

JOAN: No, ma'am.

MONICA: I don't like this.

JOAN: It's how it is, I guess.

(Price Summers, thirties, enters. He is dressed for the cold weather. There is something unsettling and inappropriate about his genial exuberance.)

PRICE: I come for the Christmas Eve special.

MONICA: Alright.

PRICE: Do I know you?

MONICA: Uh-huh.

PRICE: *(To Joan.)* Do I know you?

JOAN: Maybe. I don't know.

PRICE: Well, something seems familiar.

MONICA: What would you like to drink?

PRICE: Milk.

MONICA: Small, medium, or large?

PRICE: Large, I believe, let's have a large. No. A small.

(Monica exits.)

JOAN: *(To Price.)* Would you like me to pray for you? Every day three times a day all through next year for just one dollar?

PRICE: What would you pray for?

JOAN: Whatever you like, mister. You name the bill. I'll fill it.

PRICE: I don't believe in church.

JOAN: Prayers ain't church.

PRICE: How 'bout fifty cents? How much would that get me?

JOAN: Same. I'd pray for you the same.

PRICE: Do it then. *(He tosses her a fifty-cent piece.)*

(Monica enters with a small glass of milk.)

MONICA: Here's your milk.

JOAN: I'd like one too, miss.

MONICA: Costs money.

JOAN: *(Showing her the coin.)* Here.

(Monica exits to the kitchen.)

PRICE: Those curls don't flatter her. She used to be an attractive woman. She doesn't remember me. We worked together on Senator Emiling's campaign. He was a great man, Senator Emiling. He knew everything about life. All of its ins and outs. Most people aren't versed in the important things, but he was. He knew. He could make things stick.

JOAN: That's good.

PRICE: A whole crowd of us would put in hours of volunteer labor. Mailing out flyers, handing out buttons, nailing posters up on telephone poles. I had twenty-seven bumper stickers on my car. It was a united front. We'd work late and have to order in sandwiches from a restaurant. Monica was one of the ringleaders. She was awfully pretty back then.

(Monica enters with a medium glass of milk.)

MONICA: *(To Joan.)* I brought you a medium.

JOAN: Thank you, ma'am.

PRICE: Monica. You don't remember me. We worked on Senator Emiling's campaign together. You'd always want a tuna fish sandwich, that was your favorite. And an ice tea. Lots of sugar.

MONICA: You want white meat, dark meat? You can get mixed on the special.

PRICE: Get it mixed?

MONICA: Yeah.

PRICE: The Senator hung himself over her. She turned him in to get leniency and he hung himself with a necktie.

MONICA: You got that wrong.

PRICE: Did it with the necktie she gave him.

MONICA: Had nothing to do with me.

PRICE: He was a great man. Had plans for change. He saw hope and goodness where others did not.

MONICA: Hey, I don't wanna serve you. Now why don't you go?

(Price threatens her with a gun.)

PRICE: I've been waiting to kill you for what you did to him. It tore everything apart. Say you're sorry.

MONICA: I'm sorry.

PRICE: Do you mean it?

MONICA: Yes, I'm sorry.

PRICE: You have to tell people what they want to hear or they don't come back. *(He shoots her.)* I had to do it. I had to do it. See if she's dead.

(Joan goes over to the body.)

JOAN: She's dead.

PRICE: Shake her. Make sure. Shake her.

(Joan shakes the body.)

JOAN: Uh-huh, she is.

PRICE: You. You're a bad luck penny.

JOAN: I know.

PRICE: Pray for me. You owe it.

JOAN: Heavenly Father, accept our thanks for this food and all our many other blessings. In Jesus' name, we pray. For Thou art the kingdom, and the power and the glory...

(Price exits. Joan kneels beside Monica's body.)

JOAN: Don't worry. I'm not gonna pray for him. Far as I'm concerned, he's wasted his money.

SCENE II
LINKED

Sounds: Back alley noises, vague flamenco music, cat screeching, traffic, infant crying, a neighbor's hacking cough.
Time: Late night.
Place: L.A., a cheap apartment.

Gertrude, thirties, paces around the apartment perspiring from the heat. She wears cut-off shorts and a T-shirt. Her sweat-drenched hair knotted on top of her head. Jay, thirties, sits at a table scribbling on a torn grocery bag. Both of them have been drinking sherry.

JAY: *(Writing maniacally.)* One moment, okay? One moment...Okay, continue.

GERTRUDE: *(Listening to the awful coughing emanating from the alley.)* It's impossible. Do you believe that? She's literally dying of smoker's consumption—hacker's cough.

JAY: Shut the window.

GERTRUDE: I can't, it's over a hundred degrees or something.

JAY: It doesn't affect me. I must be numb. Continue, please.

GERTRUDE: *(Yelling out the window.)* I wish you would die! Why don't you cough yourself into a coma and die!?

(The coughing subsides.)

GERTRUDE: Oh, if only I could breathe or think or know anything, where were we?

JAY: *(Reading.)* "Even though I care for you, I have to admit you're unseasoned."

GERTRUDE: Oh, right. *(Dictating.)* Even though I care for you, I have to admit you're unseasoned... *(A beat.)* In a few years, perhaps after some hours on the couch, you may possibly evolve into a semblance of a human being. *(A beat.)* In the meantime, I must seek a spiritually and sexually fulfilling relationship elsewhere among the living. *(Beat.)* Sincerely yours, Jay S.

JAY: *(Writing quickly.)* Alright, good. Good. Good. This is good, I think. I'll have to recopy. Bloodstains. I mean because she didn't even give me time...All my things... The things I left. I didn't see it coming, but it was, you see, in retrospect I remember things. And she kept suggesting to me, for my New Year's resolution, she kept suggesting I should try to become a more authentic person.

GERTRUDE: Well, you are authentic.

JAY: I think so. But women, they can make you doubt the nose on your face. I mean I actually went around for several days trying to be more authentic, but I'm sorry, I'm sorry, I didn't know how.

GERTRUDE: It's a blessing she threw you out. It's hard to see now, but in the long run you'll understand this is your lucky day.

JAY: I know you're right. I just can't see it. She had such a great body.

GERTRUDE: But she wouldn't fuck you.

JAY: Right.

GERTRUDE: She withheld sex. You had to beg; you had to plead. And still she said, "No." Now do you want me to tell you something awful that will make you feel a whole lot better?

JAY: Yes.

GERTRUDE: She's going to be fired.

JAY: Really?

GERTRUDE: The Research Center is making major cutbacks and it's no secret she's got serious attitude problems.

JAY: Katrina's being fired?

GERTRUDE: Next week.

JAY: Who will make my car payments?

GERTRUDE: I'll help.

JAY: If it wasn't for you, Gertrude, I'd think all women were bags of remorseless shit.

GERTRUDE: And yet I'm so lonely.

JAY: Didn't you go out with Alan? How did that go?

(Gertrude reacts with mad abandon: retching and gagging and pulling at her hair.)

JAY: What? What? He's not so bad. He lent me money and one of his ties...

GERTRUDE: Oh, stop, stop! Please! I have to beg you. Because I would never...Alan! Really! Didn't I tell you? We were out—this is so horrible—at this restaurant and he couldn't get over it because I had ordered a BLT with fries and he had ordered a Spanish omelette and hash browns and, oh my, he went on and on just on and on about how he wished he'd ordered the BLT and the Spanish omelette was made with canned tomatoes and couldn't he have just one of my fries because the hash browns weren't even crisp, until I thought I would...No, really, shoot me if I ever...I mean he ate half the plate of fries which were practically unsalvageable because he had salted with such ferocity...

JAY: He salted your French fries?

GERTRUDE: That's the kind of person...

JAY: Well, no, you're right.

GERTRUDE: And we are not talking moderate salting. I mean this was... *(She mimes reckless dumping of salt.)*

JAY: Yes, I know. But still I think, I think still, your standards are too high.

GERTRUDE: Too high? How can they be too high? I was with you, wasn't I?

JAY: Yes, but I wasn't so bad back then.

GERTRUDE: You were worse. Please. No, please. Here, let's make a list. Let's make a list of men I should date. Men who are worthy of me.

JAY: Alright.

GERTRUDE: How about…how about Jasper Johns? I love how he finds the divine in the ordinary.

JAY: I think he's dead and he's gay. But I'll put him down.

GERTRUDE: How about Ad Reinhardt? I love all those black paintings. The variations, the depth…

JAY: Dead.

GERTRUDE: Well, you think of someone.

JAY: Sugar Ray Leonard.

GERTRUDE: Hmm. Maybe. Is he married?

JAY: We could check. At least he's alive.

GERTRUDE: This is depressing. "Only connect." "Only connect." Who said…?

JAY: E.M. Forster.

GERTRUDE: Dead.

JAY: Very.

GERTRUDE: Right.

JAY: But you shouldn't give up.

GERTRUDE: No I won't. I'm a Capricorn. They don't give up. I hate it when people give up; after that there's so little left to do.

JAY: God, do you think Butch and I still have a chance?

GERTRUDE: Butch?

JAY: That's what I call Katrina. Sometimes I call her Butch.

GERTRUDE: Really?

JAY: Yeah.

GERTRUDE: I thought you didn't like nicknames. You said nicknames demean a person's dignity. They infantilize relationships. Turn people into pets.

JAY: I said that?

GERTRUDE: Yes. Remember, you wouldn't let me call you Ding.

JAY: I didn't like you calling me that. It always sounded obscene. It made me want to cover your mouth and go Ssh! Ssh! Ssh!

GERTRUDE: Butch! I mean what did you say? What did you say? That she didn't know the difference between ephemeral and diaphanous. Or she mistook opaque for translucent?! God! If you think about it, I mean just don't think about it too hard or you might regret. Big, big, big! Regret! Remember when you told me I reminded you of my dog?

JAY: How much have you been drinking?

GERTRUDE: I don't know.

JAY: Oh.

GERTRUDE: Why do you ask?

JAY: It's just your family are all alcoholics. You have the genes. You're suscep-
tible, I believe. Wasn't your mother a drunk?

GERTRUDE: She always liked you. She said you reminded her of an old Dutch
uncle, how you'd sit in the corner and ignore everyone.

JAY: Remember when you fell down all those stairs at the Ahmanson and I
had to wash off your knees in the pond...

GERTRUDE: Fountain.

JAY: That was a warning sign. You should have taken heed.

GERTRUDE: You are really making me want to drink very badly. But look at
this! You've hogged the sherry. It was mine. A gift from a dear friend.
Brought back to me from Spain. Spanish sherry. You can't even get it
here.

JAY: Who do you know that went to Spain?

GERTRUDE: I met someone who went to Spain.

JAY: Oh.

GERTRUDE: Nothing serious...a fleeting speck.

JAY: It doesn't... Believe me, it doesn't...I mean there is no residue.

GERTRUDE: I know. Oh, I know. That's why we're such good friends. But I do
want to save the bottle. Put a candle in it. Let it drip. Different colors.
Let them drip.

JAY: I've seen bottles like that. I used to have one.

GERTRUDE: Yeah.

JAY: Nice those.

GERTRUDE: Yeah.

(Loud sounds of an old woman's horrendous hacking cough.)

GERTRUDE: God, she's still alive. Isn't it awful?!

JAY: Yes.

GERTRUDE: God, it's awful.

JAY: Yes, yes, yes, it is.

SCENE III
LOSER

In the following scene, all of the parts except Malcolm are played by the same actor. The actor wears dark, neutral clothing and distinguishes each character by the use of a large, white handkerchief. Malcolm, the loser, wears an overcoat and funny shoes.

Sounds: Street noises, including horse hooves hitting pavement, horns beeping, traffic, vendors. Fractured light scatters, swirls across the stage.
Time: Later than you think.
Place: Street, Chatwick's home, the street.

Malcolm comes to center stage. A pinlight illuminates his face.

MALCOLM: Shoe Boy! Shoe Boy! Shoe polish!
  (Shoe Boy appears. He begins to polish Malcolm's shoes with a white rag.)
SHOE BOY: Today's your party day.
MALCOLM: Yes, I have an invitation. Mr. Chatwick has invited me. It's an intimate affair. From what I understand, Mr. Umpton was not included.
SHOE BOY: *(Completing his job.)* Good as new.
MALCOLM: Thank you, Shoe Boy.
  (Shoe Boy exits.)
MALCOLM: Now what can I do to make this a wonderful day?
  (Mrs. Pepper appears wearing a white kerchief around her head.)
MRS. PEPPER: Hello, Malcolm!
MALCOLM: Mrs. Pepper! How are you?
MRS. PEPPER: Back in my own backyard, eating peppers from my pepper tree.
MALCOLM: Everyone to his own taste! *(Then to himself.)* Or whatever one says to get down the road. *(Back to Mrs. Pepper.)* I'm off to a party at Mr. Chatwick's. I'll have some news for you when I return.
  (Mrs. Pepper exits.)
MALCOLM: Imagine this, my heart is beating. Strange the reactions we have when we're about to have a wonderful experience.
  (He knocks. Loud sound of knocking. A beat.)
MALCOLM: Perhaps they didn't hear. No, I knocked loudly. Sufficiently loud, I believe. *(A beat.)* Perhaps not. *(He knocks again.)*
  (Deafening sound of knocking.)
MALCOLM: I hope I didn't overdo it. I don't want to appear anxious. Wouldn't

look good. I hope I've come at the proper time. Perhaps it was another day. It's possible to make such errors. Such idiotic blunders. *(Frantically, he searches for his invitation. He produces it and reads it over carefully.)* No. Here. I'm correct; I should be here; I'm expected. My invitation. My invitation. What's this? A bell. A bell, of course. *(He rings.)*

(Unspeakably loud clanging of bells.)

MALCOLM: I'm overheated. These shoes say too much. They're not subtle. I'll change. But is there time? They might be coming to the door. What do you expect? You just rang the bell! Please, stand here, please stand here, stand here, please, and don't think about your feet.

(A Butler appears with a white napkin draped over his arm.)

BUTLER: Good day. Won't you come in?

MALCOLM: Thank you.

BUTLER: Shall I take your coat?

MALCOLM: Not at the moment. You see, I have some things in my pockets.

BUTLER: Would you like a drink?

MALCOLM: Whiskey.

BUTLER: Certainly.

MALCOLM: Oh, Butler. Where are the other guests?

BUTLER: Milling in the parlor.

MALCOLM: Has Umpton arrived?

BUTLER: Mr. Umpton has not been invited. *(Butler exits.)*

MALCOLM: Not been invited, I see. Whereas, I am here. Perhaps my clothes are somewhat shabby underneath this coat. And my shoes are vivid, ostentatious, even vulgar. Yet I am invited. I'm included in the gathering.

(A woman appears waving a white handkerchief.)

WOMAN: Have you been in the gallery?

MALCOLM: No.

WOMAN: Imagine Chatwick inviting us all over here to try and sell us his terrible little paintings in those vilely expensive frames. Crass is the word. And the subject matter!

MALCOLM: I haven't seen.

WOMAN: Ditches. Green ditches, brown ditches, yellow ditches. Variation: tree trunks crossing bigger, greener, browner ditches. Chatwick is such an ass. Don't you agree?

MALCOLM: Off the record, of course.

WOMAN: Oh, you are clever. Have we met?

MALCOLM: No.

WOMAN: Good. I'm going to walk right out this door and wait for you in the rose garden. I'll be waiting for you completely naked, so don't be long. I'll be standing among the damask variety. *(She exits.)*

MALCOLM: I knew it would be like this when I made it to the top. Just as I planned. Only better.

(Butler enters.)

BUTLER: Your whiskey, sir.

MALCOLM: Thank you.

BUTLER: Mr. Chatwick will now see you in his study. This way, please.

(They proceed to spiral endlessly around the stage.)

BUTLER: Ha, ha, ha, ha!

MALCOLM: What?

BUTLER: Pardon me, sir, I was remembering a funny I heard in the cook's quarters.

MALCOLM: Keep it to yourself.

BUTLER: Apologies, sir.

MALCOLM: Umph.

BUTLER: We have arrived. Mr. Chatwick will be with you in a moment.

(Butler exits.)

MALCOLM: I have arrived. The inner sanctum. I have arrived. A view. Look. A view. The water. The mountains. Sky. Standing here with my whiskey among comfortable furniture; admiring the view.

(Chatwick enters wearing a white bow tie. A crisp white handkerchief sticks out of his breast pocket.)

CHATWICK: Malcolm, very good.

MALCOLM: Mr. Chatwick. So kind of you to invite me.

CHATWICK: Of course. Now may I tell you something? A piece of information that will serve you for as long as you live.

MALCOLM: Oh yes. Please do, sir. Please do.

CHATWICK: You must always tell people what they want to hear or they don't come back.

MALCOLM: Very good. Very wise.

CHATWICK: A practical fact.

MALCOLM: It shall be my motto.

CHATWICK: A shame you didn't learn it sooner. Possibly I would have been able to renew your contract.

MALCOLM: My contract? You're not renewing my contract.

CHATWICK: No.

MALCOLM: I'm slightly confused. Then I—I'm getting a new contract with the promotion?

CHATWICK: Umpton's getting the promotion. He doesn't want you on his team.

MALCOLM: Then I...I...

CHATWICK: Yes, you shall be fired.

MALCOLM: But Mr. Chatwick, I beg you, please, reconsider, please. I've worked for you for seventeen years. I'm devoted to your firm. I love our organization. Every day I am happy to go there and work my hardest. I promise I've learned my lesson. From now on, I shall always only tell people what they want to hear. If I have a doubt as to what that is, I shall ask them specifically and make certain. It was—I know—the Stillers. I told them what the costs were actually going to be; I should have—I know this now—I should have told them the costs were what they wanted them to be. Yes! Very careless of me. Wrong, wrong! Shame! Shame! Go to the back of the class!

CHATWICK: Calm down now, Malcolm. Calm down. Rest assured, the Stillers are reasonable people. The objection there was a shaved pimple on your neck.

MALCOLM: Where?

CHATWICK: It's gone now. It's healed. But there was one. We saw it.

MALCOLM: Yes, well, I see.

CHATWICK: Very good then. It's settled. Let's go down and join the party.

MALCOLM: I believe I'll decline.

CHATWICK: But I've invited you. You're expected.

MALCOLM: I...Excuse me, sir, but wasn't I just asked here to be fired?

CHATWICK: Malcolm, you do amuse me. Would I invite you here just to fire you? Heavens, no! Why, I've bet on you!

MALCOLM: What?

(Sound of people partying.)

CHATWICK: Everyone crowd around! Gather round! Here he is! The man who makes funny noises, disgusting noises! All emanating from his armpits!

MALCOLM: Mr. Chatwick, I hardly think...

CHATWICK: Don't let me down now. I've bet on you. Yorkshire's bet me ten Z that such a feat is not possible. Ten thousand Z! Now go on, boy. But first you must remove your coat.

(Loud chants from the crowd. Malcolm removes his coat, revealing near nakedness covered by shabby rags. The crowd goes silent. Malcolm begins making flatulent sounds from underneath his armpits. At first, the noises are polite popping sounds. Slowly, they grow into loud, cracking, giant sounds. The crowd roars with laughter and applause. Malcolm completely commits

to playing the fool. *The whole episode builds to a mad crescendo, then abruptly ceases. Malcolm picks up his coat and puts it on wearily. Mrs. Pepper appears.)*

MRS. PEPPER: Hello, Malcolm. How was the party?

MALCOLM: A colossal event.

MRS. PEPPER: Would you like a bucket of peppers from my pepper tree? Something to take home with you?

MALCOLM: A bucket of peppers indeed! *Pah! Pah! Pah!* A bucket of peppers indeed. *(He stomps past her, furious with indignation.)*

SCENE IV
LUNATIC, PART ONE

Sound: Daytime television talk shows. Flicker of blue screen TV light.
Time: Now.
Place: Suburbia.

The Lunatic appears holding a dirty mop. She is dressed as a frumpy house-wife.

LUNATIC: At home, in my living room, I watched the brand-new mothers being interviewed on TV because bearing children had left them very, very fat. They had no self-esteem. It was a fact because of fat they didn't like themselves. And they weren't even happy with the young ones. They didn't say so, but I bet they wanted to smother them or something worse.

All of their husbands were skinny and had jobs where they worked. Up on the TV screen they showed pictures of the mothers before and after the nippers. Before they looked a lot thinner and much more fun-loving.

Most of the husbands I wouldn't want. A baby would be nice if it had personality and didn't make you fat. But they seem to, and then you might lose your self-esteem and have to look to your husband to be supportive.

Then it happened. I needed some products from the supermarket. I was buying a mop. It was poking out of my cart because of its length. I hadn't eaten all day. Actually, I'd had a fat-free muffin, but the point is I was light-headed and was driving the cart with some lack of caution and managed to swing the mop into the nose of a woman looking down at meat prices. She obviously had osteoporosis or some other fragile bone disease because her nose crumbled right on the spot, and now it seems I'm culpable.

There were other more chilling incidences. One morning I woke up with a start. I was in bed with a man or a woman. I couldn't guess who or where we were.

I was wearing roller skates and there was fruit all over the bed. Apple cores, oranges, pineapples, dates. I was shocked to see I had part of a banana up my "vagina," as they call it on the six o'clock news. Part of it seemed to have been eaten but this is, of course, conjecture. It was snowing outside, which was odd because the last thing I remembered was swatting flies in summer.

(Sound of flies swarming, swatting noises. Colored lights flicker. Blackout.)

SCENE V
LEARNER, PART I

Time: Now.
Place: College campus, Urbana.

Lights up on the Learner, a pale, emaciated young man with glasses, sitting pensively onstage, thumbing through a slim volume of poetry.

LEARNER: I'm taking a class in Modern Poetry. Today I was happy to find "A poem can be anything." Apparently, a poem doesn't have to rhyme or even be words. It could be X's on a page. That would be a concrete poem. I thought it was more complex, more technical, something I wouldn't be able to grasp.

Another thing Professor Billings said, "T.S. Eliot is overrated." I considered that good news because I don't understand him anyway. There was this girl though…the girl who wore the back brace. When she heard the recording of the "Proofrock" poem, soundless tears streamed down her face, her terribly red, blotchy face. But maybe it wasn't the poem. Maybe she'd had a romantic disappointment. Maybe she'd gotten bad news about the back situation. I wanted to, but I was afraid to speak to her. Afraid to eat the peach, or whatever.

I looked at her, then looked away. I started playing with a rubber band, twisting it around my fingers, snapping it ruthlessly.

Then she rose to leave the classroom, and I realized, I noticed, she was struggling with her books, her papers. Because of the back brace, balance was difficult to coordinate. I went to her rescue. Her name was Lucheea.

Every day I would meet Lucheea; I would help her with her books. Many books. Big, thick, heavy tomes, volumes. I suspected she wasn't reading them thoroughly. Perhaps she was checking them out to impress a certain other. But I don't know for certain. You never know for certain who has read a book. How much of it they have actually covered.

All the same, I loved her. Why should I care what she has or has not read with her brown eyes that won't look at me? Always protected by lids and lashes.

How I wanted to hold her pale face with my bony hands and stare into her eyes (brown her eyes!) until I would know her and she would see me too.

And then one day her back brace was removed. She was free to ambulate without obstruction. She claimed she no longer needed me to carry her books. She no longer wanted to walk slow and converse with me. I had to run after her. She could move very swift, even with all of those books. "What's that you're reading? Ah, Dostoyevsky. *The Idiot*? One of my favorites. The Volga. Gooseberries! Troika!"

Did she know I had never read it? Did she suspect that I have trouble reading the longer books? Holding them up with my frail wrists, reading the tiny print with my bad eyes. So many words I don't understand and I do not look up because dictionaries…well, just try to wrench one of those from a bedside table.

Lucheea, wait! I'm writing a poem! A poem inspired by you! Your name. Lucheea. The music of it. The music of you. Lucheea, Lucheea. My coy one! Lucheea!

(*Lights quickly fade to black.*)

SCENE VI
LOST

Sounds: Pool hall, pinball machine, beers sliding down a bar, country jukebox.
Time: Summer.
Place: Low-down bar.

Two men, Ben, older, and Wes, younger, stand drinking local beer from bottles. A bar stool sits between them.

BEN: How do I know? How do I know? I looked.

WES: You looked?

BEN: Don't you ever look?

WES: It's usually dark.

BEN: Light a match. Shine a light. Get her in the morning. Plan ahead. Nothing like it. Her vagina; Shelly's cunt. When she orgasms it turns purple, deep purple like a monarch butterfly, then flutters into a hot, sweet pink. Like nothing you've ever seen.

WES: Sounds good.

BEN: You should get you some.

WES: She's not interested in me.

BEN: She could be.

WES: Yeah?

BEN: If you spend money on her, she'll come right around.

WES: Yeah.

BEN: My bet.

WES: How much would it take?

BEN: The less the better.

WES: Yeah?

BEN: She likes little things. Little thoughtful things.

WES: Like what?

BEN: A rubber duck for the bath. A plastic flower so "It will never die." A barrette that has her name on it.

WES: If I don't get to fuck her, it won't be worth the trouble.

BEN: Trust me, I know.

WES: But she's in love with you.

BEN: Because of my thoughtfulness.

WES: Right. Yeah.

BEN: So be a little thoughtful.

WES: Why do women expect so much?

BEN: Because, I figured it out, it's because their fathers never loved them. Or maybe nobody ever loved them. But their fathers didn't for sure.

WES: Did you know her father?

BEN: I don't have to know the father, but I do know him.

WES: And he didn't love her?

BEN: No, I'm telling ya, that's basic. She was lucky he didn't kill her.

WES: And now I gotta, 'cause of him, I gotta buy this stuff. Be thoughtful.

BEN: Only if you want to get laid.

WES: Well, I do.

BEN: I figured.

WES: It just seems like…I mean, she's not buying me presents. Where's equal opportunity?

BEN: In your bad dreams.

WES: Well, it ain't fair.

BEN: What're you saying? You want a fucking rubber duck?

WES: No, but I'd like something. Maybe a pocket knife or something.

BEN: I'm seeing the Bradly in you, boy. That's your Bradly genes talking.

WES: Don't start in…

BEN: I wasn't but I will. I got the capabilities.

WES: Just 'cause Maw's down on 'em. Always talks down on 'em 'cause she's done so much better.

BEN: Living like a queen.

WES: Like to think she was. Won't help me out none. Tells me some days I'm not worth talking to 'cause I won't get a job and couldn't pass band and melted down all her food standing in front of the refrigerator. Even though she knows if I don't stay cool, I get this big rash. I guess it's my fault. I'm allergic to my own sweat. Nobody cares. Just let him scratch.

BEN: Look, here's five bucks, go get Shelly some fucking trinket and let's see if she'll fuck you.

WES: Why're you helping me like this to fuck your girlfriend?

BEN: We don't know that she's my girlfriend. If she fucks you, she's not my girlfriend. Just a girl I fucked for trinkets and helped you to fuck too.

WES: *(Taking the money.)* I'm not good at picking presents.

BEN: Hey, I can't wipe your ass for you.

WES: I know.

BEN: You're nice looking. Stop acting like a loser.

WES: I'm not. I'm not.

BEN: Then go get her a present.

WES: I'm going.

BEN: I'm telling ya, you can do this.

WES: I know it. I know I can. One thing for sure, I look better than you.

BEN: So show me you can fuck her.

WES: I will. *(Wes exits stage left.)*

(Ben finishes his beer with the helpless gusto of the very lost and exits stage right. Shelly comes down center stage and sits on the bar stool. She carries a shoulder bag and wears a barrette with her name on it. She is sexy, in an old fashioned, kittenish way. She sits on the stool, notices the static in her skirt, takes out Static Guard and sprays it. Wes enters with a brown sack.)

WES: Hi, Shelly.

SHELLY: Oh! I was just…my static.

WES: How ya doing?

SHELLY: Real good. Real good. Have you seen Ben?

WES: No.

SHELLY: He'll probably be here soon, ya think?

WES: I don't know.

SHELLY: He's mad at me.

WES: Yeah?

SHELLY: Uh-huh. Maybe.

WES: What'd you do?

SHELLY: I was dumb.

WES: Oh.

SHELLY: Don't tell anybody, but Ben made this pie, a lemon icebox pie, and I think he squeezed in too many lemons or didn't remember how many eggs, because overnight it didn't gel. It just stayed real liquidy. And I said don't worry, we'll just say it's custard; but he said it's supposed to be a pie. So we went on and took it to the Rodeo Picnic and set it out on the dessert table, and nobody ate it. I should of gone by and taken some pieces just to be nice, but there were all these other really good desserts: cherry cobbler, fudge brownies, homemade ice cream. At the Women's Crisis Center, they try to teach you it's healthier not to pretend to eat pie and secretly sling it in a trash barrel just to make somebody like you. But I think I'd be happier if Ben wasn't mad at me and I didn't feel like I was awfully mean and selfish not to even go by and take one piece of his pie. He worked hard making it. He wanted it to turn out good. It broke my heart because he pretended like it didn't matter when he came back and found out his was the only dessert on the whole table no one had even touched. I'm sorry I was talking fast, I been eating candy; I better shut up.

WES: *(After a beat.)* Hey, I got something for you.

SHELLY: You do?

WES: *(Giving her the sack.)* Here.

> *(Shelly opens the sack and takes out a small dime-store bottle of cologne.)*

SHELLY: Perfume.

WES: Yeah. It's a gift.

SHELLY: Tiger Rose. Thank you.

WES: Want to put some on?

SHELLY: Okay. *(She opens the bottle and smells.)* Mmm…nice. *(She dabs the cologne on her wrists.)*

WES: Why ya putting it there?

SHELLY: When ya put it on the veins, the scent goes into the bloodstream and carries it over your whole body.

WES: *(Amazed.)* Huh.

SHELLY: *(Continuing to dab cologne.)* I also like t'put it behind my ears; so I can smell it. And back here on my neck so I smell good from behind. I mean all around.

WES: Uh-huh.

SHELLY: Thank you, Wes. I love presents.

WES: Glad you like it.

SHELLY: It's not my birthday or anything though.

WES: I know.

SHELLY: Why'd ya get it for me?

WES: I don't know. I thought you'd like it.

SHELLY: That's so thoughtful. That's so sweet.

WES: You're sweet.

SHELLY: No, I'm not.

WES: I think you are.

SHELLY: You do?

WES: I can't stop looking at that beauty mark you have.

SHELLY: Where?

WES: Right here on your neck.

SHELLY: That's just a mole. I might have to have it checked for cancer if it changes colors or grows a whole lot bigger.

WES: Looks like a beauty mark to me.

SHELLY: That's sweet.

WES: Shelly?

SHELLY: Yeah?

WES: You want me to buy you a beer?

SHELLY: Buy me a beer?! Wes, I swear, why are you being so sweet to me?

WES: I don't know. You deserve it.

SHELLY: No I don't.

WES: I think you do. How 'bout a beer?

SHELLY: Alright, just one. Whatever they got on tap.

WES: Want some potato chips or pretzels?

SHELLY: Oh, stop it now! Just a beer, that's plenty.

WES: Be right back. *(He exits.)*

(She sits, lost and nervous for a moment, then looks down at the tiny bottle of cologne; her face glows.)

SCENE VII
LUNATIC, PART II

Sounds: Hospital noises: sirens, gurneys being rolled, oxygen being pumped, X-rays being taken, doctors being paged, ominous drilling, etc.
Time: Morning.
Place: An asylum.

The Lunatic appears in a hospital gown. A shadow of bars falls across her.

LUNATIC: I told them I only eat meat. Dog meat. Most people have something to say about that. Everyone wants to wag a finger. But I say "Free country." No one ever argues with that. Although when you ask yourself "What's free about it?"…the question is a stumper.

You have to tell people what they want to hear or they don't come back.

And so it is my lot to be a lunatic. Walking upright or on all fours, depending on the day and if I've been fed dog meat or snack packs.

I would puke from it if they would allow me. I can't anymore. You see, it's this program. This no puking program.

They want you to be fat. But you don't have to clean your plate. They don't force you to clean your plate.

Imagine, making people eat. Making them keep it down. That's the part. Keeping it down.

After meals, we have recreation and crafts. *(She removes a large, damp, grey puzzle piece from her pocket.)* I have a puzzle to solve. Pieces of piecemeal. Fragments, shards. It is all I can do to sit still and hold a grey section. Someone, I don't know who… *(Pointing to herself.)* …(but

I could put on my thinking cap and guess) has mixed up the pieces and I'm very much afraid the Pastoral Scene and the Arc de Triomphe have been mixed up with the Jigsaw Mutant and Picasso's *Guernica*. Also to make things more unpleasant, someone... *(Points to herself.)* ...(I wonder who?) has spilt cider over a big pile of pieces and the sticky ones got tossed out and are now lost for good.

So this puzzle is a big mess. A big mess to take on.

And, of course, there's a time limit which has to be strictly enforced, but the rules are no one knows for sure what it is. It varies for each player. That's how it's all kept fair.

I'm sure though. I'm sure. As soon as I put everything together, all together, I'll be set free to leave.

And I wonder when I leave where I should go first...the porno store or the mall? Which would be more degrading?

SCENE VIII
LEAVING

Sounds: Haunting violin music that fades into a ceiling fan turning, a rocking chair creaking; a needle on a record that has stopped playing.
Time: Late afternoon, as night is falling.
Place: A decayed boudoir.

The Grandmother, a sickly woman with one hand missing, lies on a chaise longue. Her Granddaughter sits next to her. Both wear half-masks. The Grandmother's mask is ancient, decadent, and decayed. The Granddaughter's mask is defiantly neutral. They are both very still. A green-blue light washes over them. The Granddaughter brushes her Grandmother's hair. All of the movement in this scene should be choreographed in a stylized fashion.

GRANDDAUGHTER: Grandmother, will you tell me?
GRANDMOTHER: What?
GRANDDAUGHTER: Who was your lover that summer?
GRANDMOTHER: Which?
GRANDDAUGHTER: That summer you cut off your hand.
GRANDMOTHER: I put it in a velvet box and gave it away. A gift. Decorated with rings.

GRANDDAUGHTER: I wanted to know about it.

GRANDMOTHER: I've forgotten that story.

GRANDDAUGHTER: You said one day you would tell me.

GRANDMOTHER: Yes. I will. I'll tell.

GRANDDAUGHTER: *(Stops the brushing.)* I wanted to know.

GRANDMOTHER: Did they come? Did anyone come?

GRANDDAUGHTER: Not yet.

GRANDMOTHER: When are they expected?

GRANDDAUGHTER: They've sent regrets.

GRANDMOTHER: All of them?

GRANDDAUGHTER: Yes.

GRANDMOTHER: They've responded?

GRANDDAUGHTER: Yes.

GRANDMOTHER: No one is coming?

GRANDDAUGHTER: They sent regrets.

GRANDMOTHER: Finally then. Get my jewels. I want to wear some of them.
(*The Granddaughter gets the Grandmother's jewels and opens the case.*)

GRANDMOTHER: Beautiful.

GRANDDAUGHTER: Yes.

GRANDMOTHER: *(Pointing to an opulent necklace.)* That one.

GRANDDAUGHTER: Yes. *(She takes out the necklace and puts it on her Grandmother.)*
Grandmother? Tell me something.

GRANDMOTHER: I don't know anything.

GRANDDAUGHTER: My father. Your son. What was he like?

GRANDMOTHER: I don't remember.

GRANDDAUGHTER: Please.

GRANDMOTHER: He didn't take care of his teeth.

GRANDDAUGHTER: Ah.

GRANDMOTHER: *(Pointing to a jeweled bracelet.)* This one.

GRANDDAUGHTER: Yes.

GRANDMOTHER: *(Lifting her twisted hand very slowly, wearing the heavy
bracelet.)* My hand. It mortifies me with its stillness. It's hard not to feel
self-pity when your fingers are too withered to wear rings. Lovely rings.
Such a collection. *(About the case of jewels.)* Take that away.

GRANDDAUGHTER: Yes. *(The Granddaughter removes the jeweled case.)*

GRANDMOTHER: You have always been my favorite.

GRANDDAUGHTER: I know.

GRANDMOTHER: Of course I loved them all. They may not have known it.
But they were all loved. Will you tell them?

GRANDDAUGHTER: Yes.

GRANDMOTHER: They won't believe you.

GRANDDAUGHTER: No.

GRANDMOTHER: Then don't. Don't then. Don't tell them.

(*The light has slowly changed to a deep blue-green.*)

GRANDMOTHER: It frightens me.

GRANDDAUGHTER: What?

GRANDMOTHER: The light. How it changes, this time of day, when it begins to get dark. Give me the medicine.

GRANDDAUGHTER: Now?

GRANDMOTHER: Yes. Be a good girl.

GRANDDAUGHTER: Yes.

(*The Granddaughter takes a brown bottle from the bedside table. She carefully pours into a teaspoon.*)

GRANDMOTHER: Careful, don't spill.

GRANDDAUGHTER: No. (*The Granddaughter gives her Grandmother the spoonful of liquid.*)

GRANDMOTHER: Done.

GRANDDAUGHTER: Yes.

GRANDMOTHER: I feel good now. Better.

GRANDDAUGHTER: All I want...I just want to know. That summer, your lover, who was he?

GRANDMOTHER: Look in the drawer, you'll find what I've left you. A remembrance.

(*The Granddaughter opens a drawer in the bedside table. She takes out a limp red balloon.*)

GRANDMOTHER: Don't take it outside to play. It's dangerous. If you swallow the rubber, you could choke on it and die. Play with it in here.

GRANDDAUGHTER: Alright. (*She begins pulling on the balloon.*) Grandmother. Do you believe in anything?

GRANDMOTHER: Yes, I do. Of course I do.

GRANDDAUGHTER: What is it?

GRANDMOTHER: Sophistry.

GRANDDAUGHTER: Ah.

GRANDMOTHER: Blow up the balloon.

GRANDDAUGHTER: Yes. (*She starts blowing up the balloon and then stops.*) Grandmother, one more thing.

GRANDMOTHER: I'm tired now.

GRANDDAUGHTER: Please. Who was he? (*She continues to blow up the balloon.*)

GRANDMOTHER: A red balloon.

GRANDDAUGHTER: Who was your lover that summer? *(She blows slowly into the balloon.)* Try to remember.

GRANDMOTHER: I've given you the balloon. *(The Grandmother quietly dies.)* *(The Granddaughter sucks air from the balloon, blows it back in, sucks it out, blows it back.)*

GRANDDAUGHTER: If only you could tell me something, something. Please. *(Air rushes from the balloon, which shrivels in her hand.)*

GRANDDAUGHTER: Something that you know.

(The lights turn blue, violet, red, black.)

SCENE IX
LEARNER, PART II

Sounds: Branches whacking against windowpanes, howling winds, water boiling.

Time: A snowy winter night.

Place: The Learner's garret apartment.

A pinlight illuminates the Learner's bony hand as it picks ball of lint from his trousers.

LEARNER: Lucheea. Poem. Lucheea. Poem. Poem. Poem. Poem.

(The lights brighten and we find the Learner lying on his side with a pensive look on his face.)

LEARNER: In trying to use my brain...In trying to use my brain, I find there are gaps.

I lie on my side wearing black trousers with hairs that arrived from I know not where, clinging to the fabric, giving me something to ponder and pick.

Progress is eventually made and the pants have less straying hair but, strangely enough, there are always some.

Lucheea. Poem. Lucheea. Poem.

And, by the way, there's food as well on the pants. Old food on the clothes. Why don't you toss them in the laundry? Do a load.

I'll have to go to the laundromat. It's snowing in Urbana tonight. Better put on your galoshes. Galoshes. Haven't had galoshes since the fifth grade. They were yellow and they're gone. I could put paper bags around my foot. Tie them with string, rope, tape…Walk out in the snow; walk out in the snow…

Is there no idea!? No idea that will come to me?

Lucheea. Poem. Lucheea. Snow. Lucheea.

Such a beautiful name. Are you a true dunce, a complete fool that nothing comes to you? Nothing flows forth? The sound alone. La, la, la. El. The sound of L alone…

Let's do some research. *(He picks up a mammoth dictionary.)* Scholars often do, do research. A common practice among them. Here we have it. The L's…

Look. All of these words. Loaves of them, loaves of them.

Labyrinth, lack, larceny, lark, lassitude, lacerate, lorn, liquescent. Lost, loser, lethargy, let, liberation, light, liquescent. Liar, life, lobotomy, load, lubricate, loyalty, lupine, liquescent…

L-words. Limitless. They are limitless. Yet there is a limit. You have a unifying element. A pattern in the universe, something to hang your hat on—the heartbeat of the L.

And it comes to me. An idea. An idea as big as candy in the hands of children. As big as the miracle that is spring.

The L-poem. I shall write the L-poem. Then she will…then Lucheea, she will love me. Love! Ha! See there! Love! Lucheea! Love!

Loneliness, linked, loser, lunatic, learner, leaving, lost, life, love, life, lost, love, life…

SCENE X
LIFE

Sounds: Drumbeat, heartbeat, falling water, vague distant chant—"life, life, life, life," etc.
Time: Dawn of man.
Place: Earth.

We hear the Narrator's amplified voice but do not see him.

NARRATOR: There once were three Ones. A Big One, a Middle One, and a Small One.
(The Ones emerge each from their own hole. The Ones are covered with dark mud. Their facial features are highlighted with rich earth colors.)

NARRATOR: They were at large together.

(The Ones circle each other, dazed and stupefied, staring at various body parts of their own and each other.)

NARRATOR: But they were bored and boring Ones. They never celebrated occasions and failed to share or savor the moment, or even bare their teeth and indulge in inappropriate behavior.

(The Ones stop and stare dumbly at the ground, shuffling their feet.)

NARRATOR: Then one day the Ones were given a gift.

(A fanfare. The Shoe enters, dressed in black, decorated with a dazzling red shoe string and a crisp white tongue. The Shoe soft-shoes around the stage.)

NARRATOR: The gift was a big shoe. The Ones were primitive beings and they did not know the beginnings about a thing such as a shoe. The Shoe was a shy shoe and was at a loss as to how to please six feet.

(The Shoe soft-shoes around the Ones. The Ones are confused and horrified. They scatter and regroup, surrounding the Shoe with menace.)

NARRATOR: The Big One decided they must build a cage for the Shoe.

(The Big One pulls down a web of string and, with the help of the others, surrounds the perplexed Shoe.)

NARRATOR: The Shoe objected. Things got uglier and uglier. And finally the shoe was tied up.

(The Shoe is wrapped in the web and, though it tries to escape, cannot. The Big One swaggers, bangs its chest and yells out guttural cries of victory. The other two Ones stand by and watch, nodding their heads impressed.)

NARRATOR: The Big One decided the Shoe would be butchered at daybreak.

(The Big One acts out the butchery of the trembling Shoe. The other Ones are ignited by this passion.)

NARRATOR: Blood lust was in the air. Wild revelry ensued.

(Music plays. The three Ones do a dance of blood lust.)

NARRATOR: Inappropriate behavior abounded.

(The dance builds to animalistic debauchery.)

NARRATOR: Sleep descended to quell the raging blood of the Ones.

(The lights dim and the spent Ones return to their holes to sleep.)

NARRATOR: The Shoe felt heartsick and sighed. Moonlight shuddered at the ache of the sound. And the Small One awoke.

(The Shoe twists itself with grotesque anguish and cries out. The night lights shimmer. The Small One comes out of its hole and approaches the caged Shoe.)

NARRATOR: The Shoe looked at the Small One and smiled in an attempt to break the ice. The Little One had never seen a smile and was frightened.

(The Small One cowers. The Shoe laughs and yelps. The Small One becomes angry and tortures the Shoe in its cage. The Shoe cries. The Small One is amazed to see such a thing as tears and reaches into the Shoe's cage to touch and taste the tears. The Small One likes the bitter taste and attempts to get more tears. The Shoe kicks the Small One and comes out of its cage. The Small One cries. The Shoe struts some, then thinks better of it and gives the Small One comfort. The Shoe kisses the Small One with many soft, quick kisses. The Small One is bedazzled and quickly kisses the Shoe, then begins to giggle with high-pitched delight. The Shoe and the Small One roll around the stage laughing themselves sick.)

NARRATOR: Suddenly, the Middle One awoke to the noise.

(The Middle One comes out of its hole and gestures to the Small One with severe displeasure. The Small One scampers back to its hole.)

NARRATOR: The Middle One commanded the Shoe return to its cage.

(The Middle One stops, wags its arms at the Shoe and bellows. The Shoe gives it a surly grin.)

NARRATOR: The Shoe was feeling frisky out in the night air under the stars. The Shoe wanted to dance.

(Music plays. The Shoe dances elegantly around the stage, then extends a hand to the Middle One, imploring it to join. The Middle One folds its arms around its head.)

NARRATOR: The Shoe produced a bright yellow branch and touched the Middle One's heart with it.

(The Middle One sighs a sigh so strange we cannot begin to fathom where it comes from. The Shoe uses the yellow branch to conduct the Middle One in a mysterious, beautiful dance. The Middle One dances across the forest elated. The Shoe joins the Middle One in the enchanted dance. A burst of red stars explodes across the sky.)

NARRATOR: Never having danced, it was a great occasion for the Middle One who fell in love with Shoe and wanted to save it from all harm forever.

(The Middle One caresses the Shoe, begging it to run and escape. They twist together and claw apart, trying to discover which direction they should go. Daylight begins to break. The Big One stirs. The Middle One panics at the rumblings of the Big One and takes the Shoe by its tongue, twists it and pulls it off in the direction of day.)

NARRATOR: Daybreak arrived. The Big One awoke with the swell of blood in its mouth.

(The Big One comes out of its hole slurping and rolling its head. It looks to the Middle One's hole and finds it is empty. The Big One rushes to the Shoe's

cage and frantically searches through the empty web. Covered in the spidery net, the Big One rages back and forth, bellowing in disbelief. The Small One appears from its hole, wiping sleep from its eyes.)

NARRATOR: There was nothing to do but ransack the Small One.

(The Big One pummels the Small One, beating it nearly to death. The Small One lies gasping for breath. The Big One is chilled by a dreadful moment of despair and self-loathing. It goes to the Small One and kicks it gently. The Small One pleads for mercy. The Big One wraps the Small One up in the web, picks it up, and carries it off through the woods.)

NARRATOR: Meanwhile, the Shoe and the Middle One have danced themselves ragged, past lust and to the bone.

(The Shoe and the Middle One appear. They show distinct signs of exhaustion and decay. The branch the Shoe holds is no longer bright yellow; it has turned blood-brown.)

NARRATOR: Too many nights under the stars can burn you.

(The Shoe looks at the Middle One and haphazardly waves the branch. The Middle One gives an uninspired wag of its foot. The Shoe shrugs as if to say, "not bad.")

NARRATOR: One day they fought over a trifle.

(The Shoe motions for the Middle One to go ahead. The Middle One defers and motions to the Shoe, "It's okay, you go ahead." The Shoe declines, insistently giving the right of way to the Middle One. The Middle One declines, and so forth, until wild gesturing erupts. A poke and a shove follow. Then a series of horrible huffs.)

NARRATOR: But later they blamed it all on the location of the moon.

(The Shoe and the Middle One begin shrugging their shoulders. The Middle One points out the moon with the branch. They both nod in agreement and shake their heads at the moon in disgust. The Middle One breaks the branch across its knee and slings part of it off into the woods. They exit aimlessly.)

NARRATOR: And, on the other side of things, the Big One and the Small One felt a loss.

(The Big One and Small One enter side by side. They come stage center and stare out across the audience.)

NARRATOR: They knew that they must search for the Middle One.

(The Big One turns and the Small One follows. They circle around the stage in a plodding manner.)

NARRATOR: Although most of the time they felt their search was useless.

(They stop and circle in the opposite direction, then exit. The Middle One enters stage right, chewing on the half branch that is now white with age.)

NARRATOR: Secretly, the Middle One felt a loss but told no one.

(The Shoe enters stage left slumped with despair. The Shoe and the Middle One stop center stage and stare at one another.)

NARRATOR: The Shoe was heartsick and wanted to leave.

(The Shoe holds out his hand for the Middle One to shake. The Middle One covers its mouth with its hands. The Shoe waves farewell. The Middle One puts the stick in its mouth and falls to the ground bereft.)

NARRATOR: A horrible loss of dignity ensued.

(The Middle One silently rolls around the stage with the stick in its mouth. Finally, it stops at the Shoe's feet. The Shoe sadly pats the head of the Middle One.)

NARRATOR: It was decided that the Shoe would stay.

(The Middle One and the Shoe sit together but apart. Eventually, the Middle One takes the stick out of its mouth and jabs it into its heart; the Shoe winces with untold anguish.)

NARRATOR: One day the Small One appeared.

(The Small One enters and begins to amuse the Shoe with strange antics, such as quick little kisses and flapping its arms as wings. The Shoe responds and they begin to play together.)

NARRATOR: Then came the Big One.

(The Big One enters with a giant jagged sword. Sounds of drums beating, violins scraping. The oppressive shadows of prehistoric birds fall chaotically across the stage. The Small One moves away from the Shoe. The Middle One does a fierce, stylized dance to barricade the Big One from the Shoe. The Big One looks at the Middle One, gestures majestically, then freezes in a horrific pose that both demands and begs. The Middle One steps aside.)

NARRATOR: And the Big One cut the Shoe to shreds, while the Small One laughed with a horror that filled the forest, and the Middle One watched silently and smiled a sick smile.

(The Big One takes the knife and viciously rips the Shoe to shreds. Cries of wild animals and human infants.)

NARRATOR: It was a ghastly occurrence. And ended unceremoniously.

(The Shoe dies. The Big One cuts off steaming parts of the Shoe and hands them to the others. They eat the victuals, blood dripping from their mouths.)

NARRATOR: The three Ones looked at each other baring their blood-caked teeth.

(Music plays. The three Ones circle each other baring their crimson teeth.)

NARRATOR: They knew they had been through something. A bright yellow branch. Branch. Yellow branch. A branch. Yellow branch.

(White stars ignite the sky. Fade out.)

SCENE XI
LUNATIC, PART III

Sounds: Piped organ merry-go-round music plays.
Time: Now.
Place: Here.

The Lunatic appears in a tattered circus dress with a full net skirt. A worn pouch hangs from her waist. One of her legs is missing. She hobbles haltingly on bright-colored crutches.

LUNATIC: It was a setback. A minor setback. Often they occur.

Uh-oh! There's no more milk in the refrigerator! I'll have to eat my cereal dry.

Trash day! Trash day! Look who didn't put out any garbage cans!

And then there are other more severe setbacks. Like the mop to the nose, waking up with fruit, or believing your leg is filling up with rat-dirty-water-excrement and you try to hack it off with garden clippers, but the thigh bone, the femur, is too thick. And ugly complications arise.

Later you have to learn to walk on crutches, which is harder than it looks. Setbacks can eat up your life.

It's best to be prepared for emergencies. I have a pouch full of emergency equipment: candy, tweezers, stuffed toy, silk panties, razor blades, can opener, family picture, maps of places, canteen, Vaseline, keys, round-abouts, clean socks, a daily calendar, and valentine. At one time there were Tic-Tacs, but they disappeared. Guess who? *(A pause.)*

You have to tell people what they want to hear or they don't come back.

You have to tell people...you have to tell...you have to tell...tell people...tell people...tell...tell...tell.

(Pretending to write in the air.) Dear Blank, Blank. I'm feeling now...feeling now...like I am circling the pit. A final walk on the rim. *(She circles around the stage on her crutches.)* Look, Maw, no hands! No hands to grab, to save, to wave, to blow a kiss good-bye.

How long does my solo act last? I appreciate the space you've given me to fill on this bill, but are there no other performers? No one to share the finale with?

(A long beat, filled with a horribly sweet need and loneliness.)

LUNATIC: Accentuate the positive. Accentuate the positive.

Open space is a wonderful asset. A miracle of possibilities.

And my life is completely empty. Wheat fields of emptiness.

Like a vacant ballroom waiting for whatever I choose.

Waltzes and champagne, sardines on crackers and the theme of the ball will be everyone must wear green and whisper secrets into strangers' ears. And the stories that are told will be revealed at midnight and prizes will be given. And no one, no one, no one will ever leave empty-handed. *(A spotlight hits the Lunatic. A waltz plays. She twirls around the stage on her crutches, then comes to a stop.)*

LUNATIC: When will they arrive, I wonder? All the guests? My company? I must prepare: invitations are to be sent; food will be cooked; decorations; musicians. Yes, good, good, good. I smell the smell of…fresh baked bread. Fresh baked bread from the kitchen.

The kitchen? Where's the kitchen? Has there always been a kitchen? *(Desperately, she seeks to follow the scent. The trail leads her higher and higher. Finally, she is sniffing upwards, her nose high in the air. From above, warm, friendly kitchen sounds: wooden spoons mixing batter in bowls; oven doors opening and closing; water running; lettuce being torn; soft, friendly voices chattering.)*

LUNATIC: Oh. Oh. Oh. Ah, up there.

It's very true. I do not look up enough. I do not raise my head and eyes to look at the sky. Note its color, the time of day, the weather conditions. I do not look up enough. I have always been more comfortable with a bowed head. *(Sniffing as she gazes upward.)* Pumpkin bread. Beef stew. A bowl of apples. How I'm looking forward to supper tonight. Supper with the others up there in the kitchen.

SCENE XII
LEARNER, PART III

Time: Now.
Place: College campus.

A pinlight comes up on the Learner's hand, holding a crumpled sheet of paper on which a poem is written.

LEARNER: Today in class my L-poem was read.
(The lights come up as the Learner walks toward the audience uncrumpling the paper.)

LEARNER: If one were to believe in the grading system of a third-rate university, then we would have our conclusions drawn for us. *(Reading.)* The concept of your poem is, to say the least, absurd. To write a poem based on the letter L suggests an immature nature found suspect beyond the age of three. "Daddy, don't you think eights are better than twos? Blue's my favorite color. I bet rhinoceroses are the biggest animals…" Etcetera, etcetera and so forth.

D plus. The plus is nice. Plus what? Plus pity? Plus pain? Plus pustules?

But I wholly reject and disregard this classification. Nothing is not minute enough to describe what it means to me.

It is she. She. Lucheea. Who held my grade. Held it in her eyes (brown her eyes).

When my poem was read. She did not cry like with Proofrock. But chewed cowlike on a red pencil. Teeth tapping innocuously on the eraserless tool. Her brown eyes floating across the fluorescent ceiling, lost in private reverie. Unchanged by my bon mots, heart's surges, brain struggles, soul's pourings.

After class I went up to her…

(Lucheea, a beautiful young girl with auburn hair, appears. She carries a tower of books, effortlessly.)

LEARNER: Was it tasty?

LUCHEEA: What?

LEARNER: The pencil? The red one?

LUCHEEA: Sorry, I don't have an extra pencil.

LEARNER: Well, I don't need one. I have many pens.

LUCHEEA: Oh.

LEARNER: I wanted to ask you about my poem.

LUCHEEA: The one heard in class today?

LEARNER: Yes. That one. What did you think? I want an honest reaction.

There's no point in not being utterly frank. Speak what your heart tells you.

LUCHEEA: I didn't know where it was going.

LEARNER: Oh no, of course not. Certainly I planned that. Any other remarks?

LUCHEEA: It made me think…of other things.

LEARNER: Right. Good. *(A beat.)* May I help you with your books?

LUCHEEA: I haven't got that many today. Thanks all the same. *(Lucheea exits.)*

LEARNER: And so she was gone, walking down the hall with her skyload of books.

And I kept watching her, waiting for her to trip. Trip with all of those books and bruise up her knees and elbows and cry like a little girl thrown out on the pavement.

But she kept on walking, a shaft of light across her. On out the door where sunlight gallantly burst through her auburn hair.

And I felt sick with…sick from…the trail of her smell. And I knew I would excavate all the…every tomb of the alphabet to discover…in search…eternal search of the word, the letter, the breath that would please her.

(Hold a moment. Blackout. Sound of Dean Martin singing "That's Amoré.")

END OF PLAY

IMPOSSIBLE MARRIAGE

DEDICATED TO PATRICK,
WHOM I LOVE AN IMPOSSIBLE LOT.
FOREVER AND EVER.

Holly Hunter
in Roundabout Theatre's 1998 production of
Impossible Marriage.

photo by Joan Marcus

ORIGINAL PRODUCTION

Impossible Marriage was produced by Roundabout Theatre in New York City, New York, in 1998. It was directed by Stephen Wadsworth; set design was by Thomas Lynch; costume design was by Martin Pakledinaz; lighting design was by Peter Kaczorowski; sound design was by Dan Wojnar. The cast was as follows:

Sidney Lunt	Daniel London
Floral Whitman	Holly Hunter
Kandall Kingsley	Lois Smith
Jonsey Whitman	Jon Tenney
Pandora Kingsley	Gretchen Cleevely
Reverend Jonathan Larence	Alan Mandell
Edvard Lunt	Christopher McCann

THE CAST
(In order of appearance)
SIDNEY LUNT: 20s, son of the groom
FLORAL WHITMAN: 30, older sister of the bride
KANDALL KINGSLEY: 50s, mother of the bride
JONSEY WHITMAN: 30s, brother-in-law of the bride, married to Floral
PANDORA KINGSLEY: 20, the bride
REVEREND JONATHAN LARENCE: 20s–50s, the reverend
EDVARD LUNT: 50s, the groom

THE SETTING
The entire play takes place in Kandall Kingsley's garden on her country estate somewhere outside of Savannah. The garden has many entrances and exits: some leading to the manor; some into the woods.

THE TIME
Mid-May.

NOTE: The play is performed without intermission.

PART I

A young man, Sidney, with a beard and wire glasses, enters. He carries a stick and walks across the stage rather menacingly, as he talks to himself and the gods. He stops, looks at a row of flowers, whacks them with his cane, laughs, reflects, twirls his cane, and exits. Floral, thirty, enters from the manor. She is dressed in lace, acutely pregnant, and severely distraught.

FLORAL: How will it end? *(Floral unbuttons the top button of her blouse, fans herself with a handkerchief, mops her forehead with it, looks down at her belly, moves around in a circle, and sits down on a bench; she rocks and sings a song to soothe herself, something like "I'm Young and Healthy." Kandall, fifties, a beautiful, elegantly coiffed woman, enters from the manor.)*

KANDALL: Why must you run off and cry?

FLORAL: I'm not crying.

KANDALL: You knocked over the Reverend's tea.

FLORAL: I did not.

KANDALL: What is it, Floral? What has upset you?

FLORAL: Nothing, Mother. Please.

KANDALL: Tell me, darling.

FLORAL: I swept up all these leaves and no one noticed. No one thanked me. I do my best to help, but nothing I do makes an impression. They're all ungrateful.

KANDALL: It's a good job. Yes. You've done a very good job with the leaves, but you shouldn't be lifting rakes.

FLORAL: Now you turn on me.

(Jonsey, thirties, an almost embarrassingly handsome man, enters from the manor.)

JONSEY: *(To Floral.)* There you are, dearest. Why did you run off? Were you crying?

FLORAL: No.

KANDALL: The leaves, she raked them up. You should be ashamed letting your wife, in her condition, lift and tote like a day laborer. I'm surprised at you, Jonsey. You ought to have more sense.

FLORAL: Don't blame him. He doesn't know any better.

JONSEY: I apologize to everyone. Forgive me, forgive me. There now, it's settled. It's all settled. Here, I've brought you some chocolate wrapped in gold. *(He hands them to Floral.)* She eats all the time. She has such cravings. Now about these leaves, I'll sweep them up.

FLORAL: *(Eating chocolate.)* I've done them all. They're raked. No one else thought of it but me. The wedding's tomorrow and I'm the only one who considered the leaves.

KANDALL: Have we heard anything further from the groom?

JONSEY: No word, I'm afraid.

FLORAL: He's probably not coming, the dog. I kill myself over these leaves and he leaves her screaming at the altar.

KANDALL: Don't be melodramatic. He's coming. I'm sure he's coming.

FLORAL: What makes you sure?

KANDALL: It's such a very bad match.

FLORAL: You'll get no arguments there. And, I am forced to say, Reverend Larence is a ridiculous-looking man. I had to restrain myself from patting him for luck on the head like a hunchback.

KANDALL: Don't be wicked. I don't like you when you're wicked.

FLORAL: You'd like me if I stopped this wedding.

KANDALL: How would you do that?

FLORAL: Wickedly.

JONSEY: They're coming. The Reverend, Pandora. Sssh.

(From the manor, Pandora, twenty, the image of youthful exuberance, enters with Reverend Jonathan Larence, a strange-looking man with an innocent aura that can be alternately interpreted as idiotic and wise.)

PANDORA: Here, Reverend, under the trellis we'll be wed.

REVEREND: A beautiful spot.

PANDORA: Red roses grow all through the vines. After the ceremony everyone will throw scarlet petals in our path. Poor Mama's upset because the groom is late. She thinks he's not coming.

KANDALL: No, no, I'm sure he's coming. His son's arrived.

PANDORA: Which son?

KANDALL: Sidney.

PANDORA: How wonderful! Ever since the divorce none of Edvard's children have spoken to him.

KANDALL: Please, I'd rather we didn't mention the scandal.

JONSEY: Yes, no.

PANDORA: Sssh! It's all a secret.

(Pause.)

REVEREND: Lovely day.

KANDALL: Yes.

REVEREND: Gentle breeze. I see congratulations are in order.

FLORAL: What?

REVEREND: *(To Floral and Jonsey.)* I see you're expecting. Congratulations.

FLORAL: Is it really that apparent? I'm carrying extremely small for my size. I really didn't realize my condition was noteworthy.

REVEREND: Forgive me.

JONSEY: No, no. We're very proud. Very pleased. We've hoped for this ever since the day we were wed.

FLORAL: Yes.

JONSEY: We had the perfect wedding.

FLORAL: Yes.

JONSEY: The day was perfect.

FLORAL: I was happy.

JONSEY: Everyone was transformed by our love. It was effortless.

PANDORA: I'm going to wear blue wings for my wedding.

REVEREND: Really?

(Everyone nods with dismal restraint.)

PANDORA: Edvard once asked me what gift I would most like in all the world, and I told him, "Blue wings." He put it in his book that I said it. It's something I really said and he put it in his book. I am the girl in his book…No one but Edvard has ever understood me.

KANDALL: Reverend, how was Nigeria?

REVEREND: Much squalor. Much sadness.

PANDORA: You're such a good man.

REVEREND: I'm afraid I'm not. I'm not. No, no. But I thank you for the thought.

PANDORA: You are good, really.

JONSEY: Very good in my book.

KANDALL: Let's go in and have refreshments.

JONSEY: Yes.

REVEREND: How nice.

JONSEY: Reverend, have you ever been married?

REVEREND: Yes, I mean no, no!

(Jonsey, Reverend, Kandall exit to the manor.)

FLORAL: Pandora. Wait here a moment. I have something…Let them go. Let them get out of range.

PANDORA: What is it?

FLORAL: I love you.

PANDORA: Yes, I love you too.

FLORAL: I wanted you to know, in case you had any doubts. Having said that, I must ask you, why are you marrying this man?

PANDORA: He divorced his wife of twenty-three years and all of his children just for me.

FLORAL: Ask yourself ponderously, does that speak well of his character?

PANDORA: His character's not important. He's an artist.

FLORAL: So you have no doubts about your future? No gnawing concerns? I mean, the fact that he is over twice your age, myopic, rumored to be a drunkard, decidedly a philanderer, and has been known to wear a pony-tail, makes no matter to you?

PANDORA: Not really, no.

FLORAL: Very well, as you wish.

PANDORA: Thank you, but you mustn't be concerned. He's everything I've ever wanted, all my heart desires, I couldn't be happier, if only he were more my age.

FLORAL: What can you do? He won't grow younger. I presume just older.

PANDORA: I wouldn't mind it, if only...

FLORAL: What?

PANDORA: His hands have spots.

FLORAL: Age spots, liver spots. Death spots.

PANDORA: Little brown ones. And there are grey hairs all over him. On his chest even. Another thing, he cries when he looks at me.

FLORAL: You're going to be his nursemaid.

PANDORA: I'm too young to be a nursemaid.

FLORAL: And yet it's your fate.

PANDORA: Oh, help me. You're my older sister. Please, save me. Make every-thing alright again. I'm too young for all this.

FLORAL: Alright. I'll tell him. I'll break it off for you.

PANDORA: He's going to be so angry.

FLORAL: Then so he shall be...You must not sacrifice your life to some dod-dering relic, simply because he turned you into a silly legend.

PANDORA: I like being a legend.

FLORAL: But is it worth a bad marriage?

PANDORA: You have a bad marriage.

FLORAL: Why do you say that? Jonsey and I are very happy.

PANDORA: You seem to despise him. Yesterday you and I were going out to get malts, Jonsey asked to join us and you changed your mind immedi-ately, saying you had no interest in a malt. When we returned with our malts, you cried, saying you had wanted one all along. Jonsey offered you his, but you shoved it away with such a force that it fell and splat-tered all over the cobblestones.

FLORAL: I suppose I simply did not want a malt after all. You don't understand being pregnant. There are cravings you cannot explain. These cravings are very deep and reason does not speak to them. Now shall I call off your wedding or not?

PANDORA: What do you think I should do?

FLORAL: Why ask me? It's your decision entirely. This will make or break your life and I won't be held responsible, only you can decide.

PANDORA: Ooh. Ooh. I don't know. Why ask me? Let's pull the petals off this flower. Whatever it says will be so. *(She picks a flower from the yard.)*

FLORAL: That is a childish way to make up your mind, a foolish solution.

PANDORA: I think it'd be fun to do it this way.

FLORAL: Fine. It's your life.

PANDORA: *(As she plucks petals from the flower.)* Yes, I'll marry; no, I'll not. Yes, I'll marry; no, I'll not. Yes, I will. No, I won't. Yes. No. Yes, no. Yes, no. It stopped.

FLORAL: Fine.

PANDORA: But my heart.

FLORAL: Too late. Live by the flower, die by the flower. The wedding is off.
(Kandall enters from the manor.)

KANDALL: Refreshments are being served.

FLORAL: Mother, Pandora has something to tell you.

KANDALL: *(To Pandora.)* What?

FLORAL: There'll be no wedding.

KANDALL: Really?

PANDORA: Yes, she's right. She's right. He's repulsive. I never should have agreed to marry such a hairy old goat. After all, the flower would have told me the truth.

FLORAL: Nature doesn't lie.

KANDALL: There will be no marriage. The marriage is off.

PANDORA: What must we do?

KANDALL: Pick up the wedding cake immediately. I refuse to have the whole town viewing it as an emblem of our impetuous hearts.

PANDORA: I'll go with you. I want to see all the roses and swirls and turtle doves.

KANDALL: Are you very unhappy?

PANDORA: No. I'm very happy. Very, very happy indeed.
(Pandora and Kandall exit to the manor.)

FLORAL: Well now, there's my good deed for the day. *(A beat as she breathes in the beauty of the garden.)* How it worries me. How it has me worried.

(Jonsey enters from the manor.)

JONSEY: Ah, Floral! Mr. Edvard Lunt has finally arrived. Where's Pandora?

FLORAL: She's breaking off the engagement.

JONSEY: But, why?

FLORAL: Obvious reasons.

JONSEY: How shocking.

FLORAL: Bring him to me at once. I must explain the unfortunate situation.

JONSEY: Pandora's left it to you to break her engagement to this man?

FLORAL: An unpleasant chore. But I'll manage.

JONSEY: Did I tell you I love you today?

FLORAL: Yes.

JONSEY: Tonight I'll pour sweet oils for your bath and rub your belly and feet. My wife. My cherished mother-to-be.

FLORAL: Please bring him.

JONSEY: I love you, my love.

FLORAL: I love you, I love you, I love you too.

(Jonsey exits to the manor.)

FLORAL: All this waiting.

(Edvard Lunt, fifties, enters from the manor. He is an extremely appealing though decadent-looking man.)

EDVARD: Edvard Lunt. I've come in search of Pandora. I'm terribly late.

FLORAL: So lovely to meet you, Mr. Lunt. I'm Floral Whitman, Pandora's sister.

EDVARD: Yes, yes. You must forgive me. I was in a hotel fire. My cat was burnt. My documents destroyed. I thought of calling, but I would have missed the next flight and been even later.

FLORAL: Don't worry. It's never too late to do what's right. Don't you agree?

EDVARD: I do not. In fact, I believe we are defined by the things we can no longer feel, dream, or accomplish. The man who is no longer capable of scaling the mountain is quite different from the boy who has yet to try. Ah, indeed, if it were never too late to do anything, life would hold no meaning whatsoever.

FLORAL: Life hold no meaning. There are schools of thought which adhere to that philosophy.

EDVARD: A gravely unimaginative conclusion to these mysteries we behold. I adamantly reject the notion of meaningless existence.

FLORAL: Famous people generally do. Otherwise, the value of their fame would evaporate.

EDVARD: It's true, fame does help give meaning to life. In fact, fame helps a good deal.

FLORAL: On the other hand, I find it untragic that I have never done anything of use with my life. A big waste it has been. But that's not unusual. Most of us, most people are in that boat. It's a very full vessel. I'm afloat with a mob.

EDVARD: I don't know you. I can't say. You are having a child.

FLORAL: Another passenger on board.

EDVARD: You have a way of looking at things.

FLORAL: How kind you are and how polite. Did it ever occur to you my sister may be far too young for you?

EDVARD: No. I love her madly. What else matters?

FLORAL: That she comply. You'll forgive me for being rude, blunt, and the bearer of bad news, when I tell you Pandora wants to call off the marriage. She feels it was a hasty decision, and now she has decided against it firmly.

EDVARD: Are you serious?

FLORAL: Quite.

EDVARD: Where is she? I must speak to her.

FLORAL: She never wants to see you again.

EDVARD: I can't. Please. Pandora! Pandora, my darling! Pandora! Where is she? Pandora! My life! My love!

(Pandora rushes in.)

PANDORA: Edvard, my love! You've come! How I've missed you! How I feared you would never come!

EDVARD: Please don't toy with me. I can't. It's too awful. I'm too old.

PANDORA: Don't cry. Don't cry. You mustn't.

EDVARD: Your sister says you're having doubts about the wedding.

PANDORA: Just some jitters. Nothing of any matter. She doesn't know me. How can she tell what is in my heart? (To Floral.) Look how he's crying. Aren't you ashamed?

FLORAL: I have disgraced myself for you. I divorce you as my sister.

PANDORA: She's very jealous of me. What can I do? Everyone says I'm the beauty. And she's the plain one. Where have you been? Why are you so late?

EDVARD: I was in a hotel fire. My cat was burnt. My documents destroyed.

PANDORA: How I love the sound of your voice. Come, let me kiss off your tears. Such a wicked sister I have.

(They exit to the woods. Kandall enters.)

KANDALL: She threw herself out of the moving car when she heard him shout her name.

FLORAL: Pity she didn't break her neck.

KANDALL: Please. We'll have to be happy for her now, when she gets married, and sad for her later, when she is married.

FLORAL: Divorce is an option.

KANDALL: People don't get divorced in our family. There's no precedent. Besides, a divorce would be so vulgar.

FLORAL: Yes, true.

KANDALL: Oh, if only he'd die soon.

FLORAL: I must say, he looks even older in person.

KANDALL: Really? Oh my.

(Sidney enters.)

SIDNEY: Good afternoon.

KANDALL: Hello, Sidney.

SIDNEY: I heard my father has arrived.

KANDALL: Yes, he has. What a lovely wedding it will be. We're all so thrilled.

SIDNEY: Marriage is an evilly antiquated institution. A suffocating environment where banality is bred.

KANDALL: So many opinions and yet so young.

SIDNEY: Indeed.

KANDALL: Tell me, Sidney, what of love? Do you regard love?

SIDNEY: Perhaps. Perhaps not. Love has yet to avail itself to my scrutiny.

KANDALL: There's been no one?

SIDNEY: In fact no. Not really. There was this one girl I liked. We would chat and talk about ice cream selection. She worked behind the counter and offered me unlimited free samples in small midget spoons. Often I couldn't make a decision, or up my mind, and would ask for her recommendation. Her preference. I would put it to her like this, "Which flavor would you get?" I always enjoyed whatever she selected or chose, until one day she picked Pistachio. I wasn't pleased with it. It wasn't up my alley. I told her this and she gave me a new cone. The Rocky Road. She took the Pistachio from me, threw it in a canister, and said I was not to pay her for it. I knew she couldn't be giving out free cones. I was aware the price of the second cone would be deducted from her small wages. So I left money for it. The cone. Too much money really, but I could not stand to wait for change. I never came back, of course, because it may have been an uncomfortable situation. Anyway, it could never have been the same.

FLORAL: This is a silly person.

SIDNEY: I didn't know you were listening.

FLORAL: I'm not a post! Mama, get a gun.

KANDALL: Let's go find your father so you can say, "Hello."

SIDNEY: Very well. Except he doesn't want to see me.

FLORAL: Please. Then why come?

SIDNEY: I have a message for him.

FLORAL: What message?

SIDNEY: A private message.

FLORAL: God, I would never have given you a free ice cream cone.

KANDALL: Please, Floral, try to be gracious. Let's go find your father. I'm sure he'll be delighted you've come.

FLORAL: I'll just stay here and pick at my wart.

KANDALL: Lovely. *(To Sidney.)* There are allowances you make for women in her condition.

(Sidney and Kandall exit to the manor.)

FLORAL: *(About her stomach.)* My God. It's frightening. The growth. The undulations.

(The Reverend enters. He walks clumsily onto the scene.)

REVEREND: Floral.

FLORAL: Reverend.

REVEREND: I…

FLORAL: What?

REVEREND: I'm…so happy for you.

FLORAL: And I for you.

REVEREND: Me?

FLORAL: A great trip you have had.

REVEREND: Something of a pilgrimage.

FLORAL: And all this time I have not missed you.

REVEREND: You've been very busy.

FLORAL: Not in the least. Nothing much has happened. Not a thing.

REVEREND: Your sister's marriage…

FLORAL: I cannot be held responsible.

REVEREND: She professes deep love.

FLORAL: Meaningless protestations. Vaporous vows.

REVEREND: Sincerity is difficult to discern.

FLORAL: I'm in complete agreement.

REVEREND: It's kind of you to say.

FLORAL: I hope you don't mind, but I have so many things to do. *(Floral exits.)*

(Pandora and Edvard enter from the woods. Kandall, Sidney, and Jonsey enter from the manor.)

KANDALL: Floral, Jonsey says…

PANDORA: Mother! He's here! Edvard, my beloved. He's come. I said he'd come, and he's come.

KANDALL: Mr. Lunt. What a great honor to make the acquaintance of a man of such global renown.

EDVARD: My pleasure entirely. I'm terribly sorry to be late.

KANDALL: Not at all. Everyone is just so thrilled about the wedding. And isn't it wonderful Sidney came all this way?

EDVARD: Sidney. Yes. So nice to meet you.

SIDNEY: We've met before.

EDVARD: Have we? Yes, of course. I remember the face very well. Where was it we met exactly?

(An awkward pause.)

SIDNEY: My name is Sidney. I am your eldest son. You are my father.

EDVARD: Sidney? Oh no, no. You're far too old.

SIDNEY: Nevertheless, and be that as it may, I am Sidney Raymond Lunt, your eldest son.

EDVARD: Your voice has changed. Your face is different.

KANDALL: Perhaps he had a growth spurt.

EDVARD: Yes, at one time he was much younger. It's just there were so many offsprings. Eight altogether.

SIDNEY: Seven.

EDVARD: I exaggerate. It's my temperament. Well, I'm glad you've come after all. Very pleased indeed. I didn't think you children were speaking to me.

SIDNEY: We're not. I've come only to deliver something to you from Mother.

EDVARD: *(To Pandora.)* As long as it's not a poison cloak for Pandora. *(Laughs, then to Sidney.)* Well…what is it?

SIDNEY: I'd prefer to give it in private.

KANDALL: I'm off to pick up the cake. Pandora, Floral, please come assist.

JONSEY: Reverend, let me show you where the cardinals gather in the grove.

(Kandall and daughters exit. Jonsey and Reverend exit to the woods.)

EDVARD: So you're Sidney, my son.

SIDNEY: Yes.

EDVARD: Amazing what time does.

SIDNEY: Yes.

EDVARD: Remember me reciting "Lament" to you?

SIDNEY: No.

EDVARD: I did for a while. Every night when we lived in Pittsbur[

SIDNEY: We left Pittsburgh when I was two.

EDVARD: Is two too small to remember?

SIDNEY: I don't know. In any case, I don't.

EDVARD: Well, you should read it some time. It's an excellent poem.

SIDNEY: I'll look it up.

EDVARD: Do.

SIDNEY: Mother sent this note to you.

EDVARD: Thank you. *(Edvard takes the note, opens it; his eyes fill with tears.)* The way she writes, so small and blunt, workmanlike. No curlicues and with a pencil. This simple, terrible handwriting touches me to the heart. *(He returns the note to Sidney.)*

SIDNEY: Do you see what she says?

EDVARD: What does she say?

SIDNEY: She's going to kill herself if you marry Pandora. I'm to let her know as soon as the vows are exchanged, and she's throwing herself out the attic window.

EDVARD: She's not serious.

SIDNEY: She clawed her face with a nail. She'll do anything.

EDVARD: I cannot hear this.

SIDNEY: Please, do not force M'amie to jump from the attic. I could not live without her because of how I love her.

EDVARD: God.

SIDNEY: What are you thinking?

EDVARD: I wish you loved me the way you love her.

SIDNEY: You hardly ever lived with us. It's been years since we have spoken.

EDVARD: I don't know what to say to children.

SIDNEY: Of course, it's not your fault. Just please don't make my mother die.

EDVARD: I don't know what to do. A dark veil descends over the proceedings. If I call off the marriage, I'll be the victim of a coarse and scurrilous blackmail worthy of Pandora's eternal scorn. Yet if I marry, Margaret will kill herself. How could I live with her blood caked all over our marriage vows? What will I become? A coward? Or a killer? Oh God, this is an impossible way to start a marriage! Hand me that letter. I must see it once more.

(Sidney hands him the letter.)

EDVARD: How I am tormented by this measly handwriting. Don't tell Pandora. Tell no one. I must bear the burden alone.

SIDNEY: I'll bear it with you.

EDVARD: What can you do? You're no help. Go away from me with your glasses and beard. I pray I never grow as old as you. *(Edvard exits.)*
(Jonsey enters from the woods.)

JONSEY: There were three cardinals in the grove. Bright red they were and in high spirits.

SIDNEY: I spoke with my father.

JONSEY: Nice to have a living father. My father's been dead for twenty-seven years.

SIDNEY: My father is a good man. Only he doesn't know what to say to children.

JONSEY: It was a boating accident. I watched him drown. You never really get over that shock. That shock of losing a parent.
(A beat. Lights fade to black.)

PART II

Night. Pandora enters. She runs down the hill and begins dancing.

PANDORA: I'm dancing in the night. Everything's in bloom and I'm dancing in the night. All alone. Out here. Come look at me! Everyone, I'm dancing all alone out here in the night. I'm spinning under all of these stars and I can't stop! I will not stop. No one can ever make me stop. Never. Never…Where is my lover?

EDVARD: *(Offstage.)* I cannot see.

JONSEY'S VOICE: *(Offstage.)* We're coming! Don't trip! Mr. Lunt, watch yourself!

KANDALL'S VOICE: *(Offstage.)* Light the lantern. The Reverend will bring candelabras. The light.

FLORAL'S VOICE: *(Offstage.)* I wonder if I got these warts out here touching frogs.
(Jonsey, Kandall, Floral, and Edvard enter from the manor. Jonsey carries a bottle of champagne. Kandall and Edvard carry champagne glasses. All have been drinking.)

JONSEY: How lovely! What a vision you make!

PANDORA: Edvard, look at me. My hair has come unbound. Dance with me.

EDVARD: I do not feel the urge. I've just eaten too much.

JONSEY: I'll dance with you.

PANDORA: Ooh, Jonsey!

(Pandora and Jonsey dance beautifully together.)

PANDORA: Jonsey is the most wonderful dancer in the county. All the women seek his company. He's acclaimed.

KANDALL: Yes, everyone says he's a very good dancer.

FLORAL: And handsome. They all say it and it's true. My husband's a handsome man.

KANDALL: *(To Floral.)* Why don't you join in?

FLORAL: How can I? My feet are swollen. I can't be expected to twirl.

KANDALL: Why don't you rest? We'll get you a chair. Jonsey!

JONSEY: Pardonnez-moi, Mademoiselle. *(He rushes to Floral.)* There, dear. Let's remove these shoes. I'll massage your precious feet.

(Pandora continues dancing alone.)

PANDORA: Look at me. I can't stop spinning! I can't stop spinning! *(She twirls herself into Edvard's arms.)* Hold me in your arms before I lose myself altogether. Wait. Wait. Where's the music? Wasn't there music playing? Violins. Harps. String instruments.

EDVARD: There's no music out here.

PANDORA: But I heard it all so clearly. Could it have been in my head? All in my head? How flustered I am with excitement. Tomorrow I will be wed. Tonight is the last night I stand on this planet a solitary person. I will never be alone again. Marriage is the most wonderful state. Never to be alone.

JONSEY: I've never been lonely a moment, since the day I said, "I do." Not one instant.

PANDORA: All of this love, it will last and last and last.

JONSEY: Yes.

EDVARD: Not necessarily. I mean my first marriage didn't last forever.

PANDORA: But it wasn't a good marriage.

EDVARD: For a time it was. In the end it fell apart. I met you.

(The Reverend and Sidney enter carrying candelabras.)

REVEREND: We've brought the candelabras. I found kind assistance.

KANDALL: Ah, Sidney! Where have you been?

SIDNEY: I thought it best to keep my own counsel.

KANDALL: But you missed supper. Pheasant was served.

SIDNEY: I had a package of peanuts that was given to me on the plane.

REVEREND: Where would you like the candelabras?

KANDALL: Over here. And there.

EDVARD: There's something terribly sad about the way this evening is progressing.

PANDORA: What's sad? Tell me.

EDVARD: It's not something one can explain, but it is very sad indeed. *(Edvard walks away from Pandora.)*

JONSEY: *(Rubbing oil into the palm of his hands.)* Now for the primrose oil. A special blend all my own.

REVEREND: *(To Floral.)* Have you hurt your foot?

FLORAL: Not in the least. He does this regularly.

REVEREND: Oh.

SIDNEY: *(To Edvard, with great intensity.)* Have you given further consideration?

EDVARD: Don't plague me. Enough! Enough.

(A moment of silence. The golden light created by the candles is breathtaking.)

KANDALL: Magnificent candelabras. The mood created.

PANDORA: I feel like the girl Edvard wrote about in his book. Brimming with sadness and longing under flickering lights.

FLORAL: You mean Sandra in *The Zookeeper?*

PANDORA: Yes.

FLORAL: I suppose I'm not literary. Although I am a voracious reader, psychologically astute, and a keen observer of human behavior, still I don't see the likeness. The girl in the book, she has a job. She feeds animals at the zoo.

PANDORA: Yes.

FLORAL: Well, Pandora, as most of us know, has never had a job of any sort. The only pets she ever had was a bowl of five unfortunate goldfish. The largest swiftly starved to death because she never fed them. When I pleaded with her to remove its rancid carcass, she refused, in a state of high hysteria. The remaining fish swiftly perished and the stench permeated our entire property. Only then was she finally forced by the household to flush the malodorous mess down the sewer.

PANDORA: I could not understand why I should throw out a fish because it was dead. It had done nothing wrong or unnatural, I still loved it. It was still my fish. Why should I toss it down the drain?

FLORAL: Because it stank.

EDVARD: Listen to her. Her heart is bigger than all of ours together. She teaches me so much. *(To Pandora.)* I thought my life was over, then I met you.

SIDNEY: What does this mean? Tell me, what are you saying?

EDVARD: She is my bride, for better or for worse.

SIDNEY: Is that your final answer?

EDVARD: Yes.

SIDNEY: Do you understand what this means?

EDVARD: Your mother makes her own decisions. I can't be held responsible.

SIDNEY: It's only because she loves you that she is killing herself.

PANDORA: Who's killing herself?

KANDALL: Let's have dessert.

EDVARD: My wife has threatened to jump to her death the instant our marriage vows are spoken.

PANDORA: Your marriage to me will kill her?

EDVARD: Only if she's crazy and only if she's told.

KANDALL: I do not like scandal. I will not invite it into my home.

EDVARD: Forgive me, I did not want the situation revealed. I knew it would cast a shadow. Yet it's unavoidable how truth seeps out of its hole and crawls toward the light.

KANDALL: It certainly is not unavoidable. I've never heard of such a thing.

PANDORA: *(To Edvard.)* How you must love me to go through with our marriage under such tragic duress.

SIDNEY: *(To Edvard.)* Just so you'll know. After M'amie kills herself, I plan to take my own life with an unsharpened hatchet. I feel certain my fellow brothers and sisters will follow suit and do the same.

KANDALL: No, no. No, no, no. We cannot have a scandal of this magnitude in my garden. What a pity the wedding is called off.

PANDORA: Mama, please. Everything is prepared. It would break my heart. The whole town will whisper I've been jilted. Think of the shame.

KANDALL: Reverend, advise us swiftly. Give us your wisdom.

REVEREND: I have so little.

KANDALL: Don't dally with me. This is your vocation.

REVEREND: I believe you must seek to be with those you love and of whom you are beloved.

(Floral swoons, Jonsey attends to her.)

SIDNEY: At any price? A whole family slaughtered?

REVEREND: To slaughter yourself in any sense is a sin. We must find love in our hearts, no matter how meager the supply.

SIDNEY: How grateful I am to have forsaken organized religion of any sort.

PANDORA: Mama, I want to have my wedding.

KANDALL: Let's wait a bit. We'll wait.

PANDORA: It's mid-May and everything's in bloom. I can't wait. Now is the time. If we must, we'll run off tonight and I'll never see or speak to you again. How I will miss you.

KANDALL: Pandora, don't do this to me.

PANDORA: Don't make me. I beg of you, do not make me.

KANDALL: Very well. The wedding will proceed as planned.

PANDORA: Yea!

SIDNEY: Then all must die. *(Sidney exits to the woods.)*

KANDALL: More champagne, please.

PANDORA: Thank you, Mama. We're going to be happier than anyone has ever been in all the world. Except perhaps for you and Daddy. My parents were very, very happy. Weren't you?

KANDALL: We were.

FLORAL: And Jonsey and I are very much in love. We're having a child together. Our first child. Tonight we'll pick a name. One for a boy and one for a girl.

JONSEY: Floral.

FLORAL: What?

JONSEY: To hear you speak of the child. Our child. You hardly ever do.

FLORAL: Why illuminate the obvious? Look at me. I'm gigantic! Elephantine even! Choo! Choo! Choo! Choo! Choo! Choo! *(She dances around like a comedic pig.)* I could accommodate a circus under this tent!

PANDORA: *(Laughing.)* I believe she could.

FLORAL: Three rings at least!

EDVARD: *(Overenthusiastic.)* Oh, I don't doubt your prowess in the slightest.

FLORAL: Nor should you. Nor should you!

REVEREND: Excuse me.

KANDALL: Reverend, where are you going?

REVEREND: Off.

PANDORA: What for?

REVEREND: To pray. *(Reverend exits to the manor.)*

PANDORA: He's such a very good man.

FLORAL: Everyone isn't always what they seem.

PANDORA: What do you mean?

FLORAL: Everything isn't always as pictured. Frankly, I'm carrying around a huge, empty frame with no walls to hang it on. A rectangle of steel. It weighs two thousand tons. My back aches, my shoulders burn, even though it's empty—the damn thing is heavy! As usual, no one knows what I'm talking about. They just wait for the noise to stop. I'm going to go roll down a hill. Can anyone understand that?

PANDORA: You're forgetting your shoes.

FLORAL: My feet will no longer fit in them. *(Floral exits to the woods.)*

KANDALL: Her moods swing, it's her condition. Our dessert is long overdue. Cherries jubilee. I'll retrieve it from the pantry.

PANDORA: Wait, Mama, I'll go with you. You'll need me.

KANDALL: What do you mean?

PANDORA: You'll see.

KANDALL: See? I don't want to see. I can't stand any more surprises ever again in my whole life.

(Pandora and Kandall exit to the manor.)

JONSEY: A fine night.

EDVARD: Yes.

JONSEY: Glorious weather.

EDVARD: Umm.

JONSEY: I have been wondering, is it yours?

EDVARD: What?

JONSEY: The child Floral is carrying.

EDVARD: Excuse me?

JONSEY: I beg your pardon. My mind plays tricks. I'm a very handsome man.

EDVARD: Why would you make such a remark?

JONSEY: I don't mean to boast. It's simply true, don't you agree? I am handsome.

EDVARD: I suppose, yes, your face is well structured.

JONSEY: Regrettably, sex holds no interest to me. It doesn't even repulse me. I'm that flaccid, I'm afraid. But what makes it a tragedy, which is my point, is the fact that I am so very, very handsome.

EDVARD: I see.

JONSEY: I love Floral. I love her because she struggles so hard. But I have never had sex with her. Something is absent. That longing. I run her bath, massage her feet with oils, dab her wrists and neck with fine perfumes. I powder every crevice of her body and feel only calm. I flirt with other women to proliferate the myth that I am a cad. There are whispers about my prowess and endless adulteries. But nothing is ever revealed. There are no revelations to make. Nothing is hidden, all is illusion, misdirection and palming.

EDVARD: Whose child is it?

JONSEY: I don't know.

EDVARD: What does your wife say?

JONSEY: We pretend it's mine.

EDVARD: How?

JONSEY: I don't know, but we do.

EDVARD: That's very terrible.

JONSEY: I thought it was admirable.

EDVARD: It's chilling.

JONSEY: We're talking about the same thing. We mean the same thing. We're just using different words. I feel like a stroll, will you join me?

EDVARD: I'm very tired today. I was in a hotel fire. My cat was burnt, my documents destroyed.

JONSEY: Well, certainly, you must get your rest.

(Jonsey exits to the woods. Kandall and Pandora enter from the manor with Cherries Jubilee.)

KANDALL: If you had asked me, I would have said, "Impossible!" That I should live to see this day! A grown daughter of mine. *(To Edvard.)* Mr. Lunt, I'm mortified…Floral has carved into your wedding cake.

PANDORA: She took a giant piece, leaving a lopsided mess.

KANDALL: I fear she must have eaten cake with her hands. Such grotesqueries. What have I raised?! God, what have I raised?!

EDVARD: But it really is a small matter.

KANDALL: Not if your mind works in metaphor! A deliberate desecration.

EDVARD: Are you certain it was Floral?

PANDORA: I saw her, after all, I watched her take it.

KANDALL: Did she? Did she eat it with her fingers?

PANDORA: Mother.

KANDALL: Tell me.

PANDORA: Yes.

KANDALL: My God.

PANDORA: And she has warts, Mother. She has warts on her fingers.

KANDALL: If this continues, we'll soon be searching for distant places in which she can be put out of our sight for long periods of time along with other criminals, lunatics, and barbarians. I blame it all on Jonsey. She would not live in such a rageful state, if only he could be faithful.

PANDORA: Jonsey has not been faithful?!

KANDALL: You never heard me say that. It did not come from my lips! Erase! Erase!

PANDORA: I knew it all along. The whole town whispers.

KANDALL: *(Drinking more champagne.)* I hoped having a child would make a difference. And it has made him even more horribly attentive. Unfortunately, the more attentive he becomes, the more unbearable her behavior. It seems he cannot give her the one gift she craves, so all others are fruitless.

EDVARD: What gift does she crave?

KANDALL: Faithfulness.

EDVARD: How strange.

PANDORA: She went into counseling at the church. No one in our family had ever gone into counseling. There was no precedent. She had a session every week with the Reverend.

KANDALL: For a time she seemed happy.

PANDORA: Then he left for Nigeria.

KANDALL: Afterwards she became pregnant.

PANDORA: Or was it right before?

EDVARD: I'm very tired. Forgive me.

PANDORA: His cat was burnt earlier today.

KANDALL: How dreadful.

PANDORA: Won't you come in now, Mama?

KANDALL: No, no. I want to be out here and breathe some…air. Good night.

PANDORA AND EDVARD: Good night. *(Pandora and Edvard exit to the manor.)*

KANDALL: A wedding. A wedding in my garden tomorrow with these people. Impossible.

(Sidney enters.)

SIDNEY: Forgive me.

KANDALL: For what?

SIDNEY: For being in your line of vision.

KANDALL: Really, Sidney. Please don't be odd. Won't you come in with me and have some cherries jubilee.

SIDNEY: I beg you, stop treating me kindly. I am not here as a friend of these proceedings. I've come only to disrupt and annihilate.

KANDALL: In any case, you can still have jubilee.

SIDNEY: Forgive me, I cannot.

KANDALL: As you wish. You know, Sidney, we are not on opposite sides. I too would like nothing better than to see this engagement broken. Confidentially, I do not believe the match to be at all suitable. Champagne?

SIDNEY: I don't drink.

KANDALL: Why not?

SIDNEY: I like to keep a clear head.

KANDALL: What for?

SIDNEY: To deal with—the day—my business…I'm not clear on that.

KANDALL: Yes, I understand how confusing it often is—being rational.

SIDNEY: Mind-boggling really. Now that I hand it a thought. Pass it a glance. And so…champagne, please. This could, after all, be my last night on earth. My last look at the moon.

KANDALL: Such a nice one.

SIDNEY: And stars.

KANDALL: Glittering, glittering, glittering. All in all, a fine last night. Cheers.

SIDNEY: Yes.

(They drink.)

SIDNEY: Do you really think I'll be dead tomorrow?

KANDALL: Only if you have not a modicum of sense, and prove to be a completely ludicrous person.

SIDNEY: I understand your ridicule. But every time I shut my eyes I see…

KANDALL: What?

SIDNEY: My mother's body falling. I could not live without my mother.

KANDALL: And yet you would.

SIDNEY: How would I?

KANDALL: You would breathe. You would breathe.

(Sidney breathes.)

SIDNEY: Breathing helps.

KANDALL: Sidney, I want to tell you something.

SIDNEY: What?

KANDALL: A secret. Will you keep it?

SIDNEY: Yes.

KANDALL: I'm not well anymore.

SIDNEY: What?

KANDALL: Just that.

SIDNEY: You're ill?

KANDALL: Precisely.

SIDNEY: How ill?

KANDALL: Very much.

SIDNEY: Very much ill? I'm so sorry.

KANDALL: Fortunately, it's hopeless. There's more dignity that way, don't you agree?

SIDNEY: I don't understand. You look well.

KANDALL: Thank you. I make an effort.

SIDNEY: Have you told your daughters?

KANDALL: I feared it would cast a shadow.

SIDNEY: How can this be? I don't understand. You look so well. So very well. My heart has stopped. It…stopped.

KANDALL: Breathe.

SIDNEY: I cannot.

KANDALL: Breathe. Breathe. Breathe. I've had a life. My husband's buried. Both daughters married. A grandchild on the way. That will have been enough of a life. What else is there to do? Endless travel? An old lady alone on a steamer, draped in wool, watching fog drift by, sipping tea. Remembering...what? My first kiss.

(Sidney kisses her with passion.)

KANDALL: Good heavens.

SIDNEY: I love you.

KANDALL: You've kissed me on the lips. What in the world?

SIDNEY: Forgive me. I'm a young upstart, worthy only of contempt, to be thoroughly despised and roundly horsewhipped. *(He kicks down a row of toadstools.)*

KANDALL: Don't do that! You must stop! Foolish, stupid boy.

SIDNEY: What have I done?

KANDALL: You've destroyed the fairies' houses. Fairies live under toadstools. Tonight they will have no place to sleep. They will come home and be lost.

SIDNEY: No one ever told me about the fairies. No one ever came to take my teeth.

KANDALL: What a dreadful night this has turned out to be.

SIDNEY: I'm sorry I didn't know about them, the fairies. I would never have done it had I known. I have never meant to hurt anyone.

(Kandall exits to the manor. Sidney tries vainly to repair the fairy homes. Floral enters from the woods covered in dirt and grass and leaves. Her hair is wild.)

SIDNEY: What has happened to you?

FLORAL: I've been rolling down hills. My heart has been dragged all through these woods, leaving a trail of red you can follow with your eye's closed because of the stench.

(Sidney exits in confused horror as the Reverend enters.)

REVEREND: Floral, I'm so very grateful to have come upon you. I have some information to impart. Nothing noteworthy. In fact, a matter of no importance to anyone. I have come to the conclusion this evening that I must leave the church. It is not much, but it is all I have to sacrifice for my hypocrisy. I'm not a talented or impressive man. All I had to give the world was a few good deeds. I took the woman with no legs an Easter bonnet; I taught the blind child to sing; I allowed mosquitoes to suck my blood with impunity. All of this motivated by a desperate wish to have some value. And yet I betrayed it all. *(He looks away from her.)* The meaning of my life and the woman I esteem above all others. I beg her forgiveness. I do not expect it. In fact, I firmly believe forgiveness must never be granted. But I do crawl at your feet on my hands and knees now and always, and forever.

FLORAL: Please. Penitence is not necessary. Understand I am quite happy with my husband. We are having a family. All goes well. All is intact.

REVEREND: I'm relieved and joyous to know that your spirit survived the evil I perpetrated. You came to me for guidance and I carried you to iniquitous grounds.

FLORAL: Ridiculous man, I seduced you.

REVEREND: No, no, no. I seduced you.

FLORAL: You are quite incapable of seducing a harlot in Dante's inferno.

REVEREND: Oh, I am, I am, I most definitely am. I am not good at all.

FLORAL: You are good and you must not leave the church. Just as I must not leave my marriage.

REVEREND: No, you must not.

FLORAL: Why do you say that to me?

REVEREND: Because it is the right thing to say.

FLORAL: Is it? Is it?

REVEREND: Yes, it is.

FLORAL: Very well. *(A beat.)* Jonathan.

REVEREND: Yes, Floral?

FLORAL: Jonathan.

REVEREND: Floral…

FLORAL: I feel romance all in the air. It's ripping through me like flowers blooming through my skin.

REVEREND: I cannot bear this.

FLORAL: Do something.

REVEREND: You are another man's wife.

FLORAL: I was before.

REVEREND: And now with his child.

FLORAL: There it is. You think I'm unpleasantly large.

REVEREND: No, I think you're very pleasant in shape…Really quite…in total. Your shape, I find…My tongue has departed.

FLORAL: In bed you're so different.

REVEREND: I spark fires.

FLORAL: Yes.

REVEREND: It's all because of you. Only because of you. It would not be possible with anyone else.

FLORAL: Take me.

REVEREND: Where?

FLORAL: Wherever.

REVEREND: I have to go.

FLORAL: I will kill you.

REVEREND: Do. It would be a blessing.

FLORAL: How should I kill you?

REVEREND: However.

FLORAL: With my claws, my teeth, my body and soul.

REVEREND: Yes, yes, all that.

FLORAL: Until there is nothing. Nothing left but shreds, shreds, shreds.

REVEREND: I have to take you. There is no stopping me. No stopping this onerous affliction. *(He runs his fingers through her hair, pulls her head back, and kisses her neck.)* I can't. I can't. This is impossible. Impossible. *(He moves away from her.)*

FLORAL: Is it? Is it? Is it? I never cared for you at all. I am happily married. Happily, happily, happily. My child will come from a good home. Without any hint of scandal. *(To her child.)* And everything will be possible for you. My dear, my most secret dear. It will all be possible.
(Jonsey enters from the woods. He does not see the Reverend.)

JONSEY: My God! I was looking for you.

FLORAL: I have been rolling down hills. Won't you bathe me, wash my hair, and soak me in fine scents? *(Floral grabs Jonsey in her arms.)*
(The Reverend exits to the woods.)

FLORAL: How I love you, my love.
(Floral kisses Jonsey desperately on the lips. They slowly pull apart and regard each other with profound sadness.)

PART III

The following morning. Decor such as flowers, flowing lace, a harp have appeared, indicating the wedding is imminent. Kandall, dressed in a discreetly elegant mother-of-the-bride ensemble, stands dropping rose petals over the crushed toadstools. Floral enters from the manor in a flowing gown. She wears an ostentatious hat, huge earrings, a cumbersome necklace and bracelet. Throughout the Act these various accessories are removed.

FLORAL: Mother.

KANDALL: Oh my.

FLORAL: I read a book that suggested one emphasize accessories in the later stages of pregnancy. Is it too much?

KANDALL: It's perfect. For the occasion. *(She returns to dropping rose petals.)*

FLORAL: *(A beat.)* I'm sorry I lurched into the wedding cake. I was so hungry. I couldn't stop myself. There's no excuse. Just an overwhelming craving I could not control.

KANDALL: Forgive me, I thought we were civilized human beings, not animals. *(Kandall starts to exit.)*

FLORAL: Where are you going?

KANDALL: To get the show on the road.

(Sidney enters.)

KANDALL: Good morning, Sidney.

SIDNEY: Forgive me.

KANDALL: As you wish.

(Sidney and Kandall exchange a look. Kandall exits to the manor.)

FLORAL: She can do so much with the tone of her voice. Why do you wear that awful beard?

SIDNEY: My fresh face is gruesome to me. Innocence repulses me on every level. I can't watch children playing in a school yard without experiencing revulsion.

FLORAL: Nevertheless you should shave.

SIDNEY: How can I? When under this growth is the despicable face of a pasty coward. After all this morning my father marries; my mother dies. That simple and I'm eating a muffin.

FLORAL: They are good, aren't they? May I have some?

SIDNEY: Yes. *(He gives her some of his muffin.)*

FLORAL: Now, in my opinion, if you were a man of character and truly loved your mother as you profess, you would not sit here impotently eating a muffin. You would take action.

SIDNEY: What should I do?

FLORAL: Stop him. Shoot him. Do something that would slow him down.

SIDNEY: Shoot my father?

FLORAL: To save your mother. If you don't have a pistol, I'll tell you, there's one in the kitchen hidden in the yellow sideboard, bottom left-hand drawer beside the silver trivets.

SIDNEY: Alright. I'll go. It is my fate. *(Sidney exits to the manor.)*

(Floral remarks after him.)

FLORAL: And bring more muffins! The ones with raspberries. How will it end? I see no end. No end.

(Edvard enters from the manor dressed as a groom. He is distracted and ill at ease. He carries his dress shoes and socks which he puts on in the following scene.)

FLORAL: Edvard Lunt.

EDVARD: Yes.

FLORAL: Last night there was a little misunderstanding between us that I must rectify. When I said there could be a circus performing under my skirt, I was implying—it was meant to be a joke. I was attempting to indicate, I was wearing a tent, a large, billowy dress. Because of the pregnancy I was so big and wearing such large garb, i.e., tents, that a circus could or would be capable of performing underneath. You (I assume) assumed I meant I could service a whole circus, I mean an entire company of clowns or whatever could come under my skirt with their lascivious little ladders and horns and party, party, party or whatever. Actually, it was a joke I could have phrased more carefully. Still your interpretation was not warranted.

EDVARD: In attempting to follow your amorphous train of thought, I seem to have derailed.

FLORAL: In any case, I'd like you to know I'm extraordinarily particular about who I see privately. I'm not a virgin, but other than that, I am wholesome in the extreme. Having said that, I beg you to leave.

EDVARD: How can I leave? I'm to be married in three minutes.

FLORAL: You're in danger if you go through with this wedding.

EDVARD: Yes, yes. I have my doubts. I'm already suffocated by all of this ceremonial paraphernalia. When Margaret and I wed, it was simple. Everyone brought a dish and danced without shoes.

FLORAL: You could be shot.

EDVARD: No, no, in every sense I shall keep my shoes on and be civilized.

FLORAL: Being civilized is a rot.

EDVARD: I disagree. Without the tormenting friction between the civilized and the primitive, life would be bereft of its most rapturous flavor.

FLORAL: What flavor is that?

EDVARD: Erotic abandonment. For there is no eroticism in a wholly primitive world and no abandonment in a wholly civilized world.

FLORAL: Yes, yes, I see. Table manners are important. So that when we eat berries with our fingers and let the juices drip down our lips, a statement is made.

EDVARD: You have a way of looking at things.

FLORAL: How kind you are and how polite. Now to save your life rush immediately to the station, get on the first train that comes, and go wherever it takes you.

EDVARD: Oh. To be free of all marriages forever. I will go. No, I love her. I cannot. And yet…

(Jonsey enters from the manor.)

JONSEY: More drama. The Reverend was not to be found this morning. Servants went to search for him across the property and discovered him in a ditch. His clothes had to be laundered. Kandall was very cross.

EDVARD: What was he doing in a ditch?

JONSEY: Crying is what I heard. I'm holding the rings. I've Pandora's here. I'll hold yours as well.

EDVARD: Yes. I—I…It's not here. I did not bring it. I left it. I'll retrieve it at once. *(Edvard exits.)*

FLORAL: I don't believe he'll be back.

JONSEY: Nonsense. They're very much in love. And a beautiful wedding is just what we need today.

(Reverend enters.)

JONSEY: Good day, Reverend.

REVEREND: Mr. Whitman.

JONSEY: The groom went off, nervous nanny. He forgot his ring. An odd fellow. I believe he's European or his family was European or he's been to Europe. Excuse me, I'm such a torrential bore. I don't know how my wife puts up with me. I'm content with things going on and on the way they are. I never wanted an interesting life. I prefer a few familiar things: my estate, my yachts, my trusted staff and crew.

(Kandall enters.)

KANDALL: We're ready to begin. This really should not take long. *(Indicating that Floral should begin the music.)* Floral, the harp.

FLORAL: Mama, not everyone is here.

JONSEY: The groom is absent.

KANDALL: You mean for good?

(Edvard enters with the ring.)

EDVARD: It was in my pocket all along. But the wrong pocket. Not the one I thought.

JONSEY: Yes, naturally. Stand here. Hand me the ring.

(Floral plays beautiful music on the harp.)

EDVARD: Has anyone seen my son, Sidney?

JONSEY: Shh. The bride.

(Pandora enters in a blue gown wearing blue diaphanous wings, and carrying a bouquet of blue and violet flowers. Everyone looks at her and reacts accordingly. Sidney enters silently. He watches a moment, then raises his pistol, pointing it at Edvard.)

REVEREND: Dearly beloved…

SIDNEY: Stand back, all of you. I'm going to shoot my father.

(Everyone freezes.)

KANDALL: Good heavens.

SIDNEY: There will be no marriage. The marriage is off.

EDVARD: My God, how mortifying. *(To Kandall.)* I'm terribly sorry.

SIDNEY: Everyone except my father will leave here at once.

FLORAL: Perhaps we should all go.

PANDORA: *(Running to Edvard.)* I won't leave you! Never, never!

EDVARD: Pandora, please.

SIDNEY: Get away from him. Stay away.

PANDORA: Write about how I died protecting you with my blue wings.

SIDNEY: Don't be so sure I'll not blast those wings!

REVEREND: Hand me that gun, you ridiculous maniac. How dare you endanger these people?! *(The Reverend walks toward Sidney.)*

SIDNEY: Halt! Halt!

FLORAL: Halt!

REVEREND: Please, do you doubt for one instant I would not relish a bullet to the brain? Better yet, the heart. Blast it to shreds, all to shreds.

SIDNEY: You are mad. Be reasonable. I will shoot.

FLORAL: No!

KANDALL: Sidney, if you shoot that Reverend, I'll never speak to you again!

SIDNEY: Kandall, please don't say that! *(Sidney accidentally shoots his own foot. He falls to the ground.)*

(Everyone is aghast.)

FLORAL: My God, he's been shot.

KANDALL: Yes, he has.

SIDNEY: I'm such a failure, a failure, an abject failure.

PANDORA: You saved us, Reverend. You're such a very good man.

SIDNEY: I don't know what to do. I'm bleeding. Help me. Reverend, help.

REVEREND: Don't ask me for help. I'm through giving help. Here, take this collar. Have it. It's more fit for a beast than a man. I'm sick from answering prayers and doing good deeds. It has turned me into a raving lunatic and left me with desperate, unquenchable desires. I want to spit on all altars for the remainder of my days. God, I am wretched. *(He exits to the woods.)*

SIDNEY: Someone, help me.

PANDORA: You got what you deserved.

SIDNEY: I cannot bear the sight of blood.

KANDALL: Mercy, mercy. Take him back to the manor, our house physician must tend his wounds.

(Jonsey and Edvard go to lift Sidney. Sidney winces in pain.)

SIDNEY: Oh Father. Father.

EDVARD: There, there. *(Reciting from Dylan Thomas's "Lament.")*
When I was a windy boy and a bit
And the black spit of the chapel fold
(Sighed the old ramrod,...

SIDNEY: ...dying of women)...

SIDNEY AND EDVARD: ...I tiptoed shy in the gooseberry wood...The rude owl cried like a telltale tit...I skipped in a blush as the big girls rolled... Ninepin down on the donkey's common...And on seesaw Sunday nights..."

(Pandora, Jonsey, Sidney, Edvard exit to the manor.)

KANDALL: Amazing. It all has gone off so much worse than expected.

... A surprising turn of events.

...wonder, Floral, how Sidney came across my grandfa-

KANDALL: What?

FLORAL: I confess I did not want things to go off smoothly; so I orchestrated a few bumps.

KANDALL: You wicked thing! To do this to your sister.

FLORAL: She'll be grateful. After all, marriage isn't for everyone. Once you are married you're stuck. Nothing ever changes. Every year there's a turkey at Thanksgiving and a goose at Christmas. Jonsey gives me one more letter opener for my collection and no one ever sends me any mail.

KANDALL: Tradition cements our sanity.

FLORAL: But if I wanted things to be different, would it all crumble?

KANDALL: Are you saying you want a goose for Thanksgiving?

FLORAL: I'm saying this is not Jonsey's child.

KANDALL: Dear. Dear, dear, dear, dear, dear.

FLORAL: What shall I do?

KANDALL: Don't tell Jonsey.

FLORAL: I haven't.

KANDALL: Good.

FLORAL: But I suspect he knows.

KANDALL: How?

FLORAL: We don't have sex.

KANDALL: Since when?

FLORAL: Ever.

KANDALL: Oh dear, dear, dear, dear, dear, dear. What does he say?

FLORAL: He says I'll make a wonderful mother. That all along he has wanted a child and we'll have a beautiful happiness…Something. I don't know.

KANDALL: This is all good.

FLORAL: I don't love him.

KANDALL: Of course. I see. You have a lover.

FLORAL: No.

KANDALL: But you did.

FLORAL: That one.

KANDALL: What does he say about the child?

FLORAL: I haven't told him it is his. He assumes it's Jonsey's.

KANDALL: This is really quite a mess. And on the day of your sister's wedding. It reminds me of when you got that horrid green gum stuck in your hair on Confirmation Day. Well, we can't cut this out with scissors and cover it with a wide-brimmed hat.

FLORAL: *(Weeping.)* No.

KANDALL: Don't cry. Well, do if it helps.

FLORAL: Nothing helps. You see, all along all I have wanted was to emulate you and Father. How you loved each other.

KANDALL: We didn't love each other.

FLORAL: You always said you did.

KANDALL: Yes, because we didn't want you children to know how much we suffered. You might have gotten the wrong idea about marriage.

FLORAL: We might have gotten it all wrong.

KANDALL: I couldn't let that happen.

FLORAL: No, no. I love you, Mama.

KANDALL: I love you too.

FLORAL: Tell me what to do.

KANDALL: Think of it like this. Eventually, we'll all be dead. Your travails will have ended and you can rest in peace, knowing you have experienced the pain, confusion, and various contretemps that give life girth.

FLORAL: But what about the scandal?

KANDALL: It shall be monumental. All will be raked over coals and publicly crucified without mercy.

FLORAL: I'm so sorry.

KANDALL: Oh, after all, who gives a damn?

(They embrace. Pandora enters from the manor. She wears her wings over her honeymoon suit.)

PANDORA: Mother, Edvard and I have decided not to be bullied and blackmailed by his deranged ex-spouse. We're driving over to Lordsley County, where we will be wed at once by the Justice of the Peace who awaits our arrival.

KANDALL: Darling, you are determined.

PANDORA: Yes, quite. And please do not suspect it is because I am in her woeful condition. I've no intention of ever having children. What they can do to you.

KANDALL: Yes, I know. I'm aware. How's Sidney?

PANDORA: A scratch, a flesh wound, nothing of note. He turned out to be entirely unremarkable.

(Kandall takes a breath of relief.)

KANDALL: I'll go in and wrap up the top tier of your wedding cake for you to take.

PANDORA: Thank you, Mama. Oh, isn't this romantic! We're running off to be wed outside the arms of the church.

KANDALL: Also some rose petals and champagne. *(She exits to the manor.)*

PANDORA: Yes, yes, yes, yes, yes, yes! What do you imagine happened to the Reverend? Such scandalous behavior.

FLORAL: Pandora.

PANDORA: Good-bye, Floral.

FLORAL: I love you.

PANDORA: I love you too.

FLORAL: Having said that, I must tell you, I am very jealous of you.

PANDORA: Of course you are.

FLORAL: I've plotted against your wedding.

PANDORA: I know you have.

FLORAL: My marriage is a morbid predicament without passion or hope. You have such brave gaiety, romantic notions, youthful daring, and translucent beauty.

PANDORA: Yes, but there's a terror to it.

FLORAL: What terror?

PANDORA: I play the lovely, joyous child everyone adores and is drawn to, but sooner than later my face will be less round, my eyes will dull, worry lines will cross my hardened brow, and I will become something that once was and now is not. My charms will not age well. Now is my time. I must take it.

(Edvard and Jonsey enter from the manor.)

EDVARD: My beloved.

JONSEY: Your car awaits.

PANDORA: Yes. I'll gather my fallen bouquet. Oh, beautiful blue flowers, blue…

(Throughout the following, Pandora picks up her flowers, smells them, and twirls.)

EDVARD: Look at her. So pleased with the newness of the day. A brand-new penny that has not been dropped down toll booths, handed to beggars, thrown into wishing wells, flipped for bets, or used in bad magic tricks.

PANDORA: Jonsey, dance!

JONSEY: Mademoiselle!

(Pandora and Jonsey dance.)

EDVARD: And yet I have my doubts.

FLORAL: Who doesn't?

EDVARD: Many don't.

FLORAL: Hated multitudes.

JONSEY: *(To Pandora.)* Oh, your rings! I'm holding your rings!

PANDORA: Give me! Give me!

(Jonsey gives Pandora the rings.)

EDVARD: Pestilence and hope were in Pandora's box. Hope was the salvation. Or was it the final pestilence?

FLORAL: An argument for the ages.

JONSEY: What are they talking about?

PANDORA: Nonsense. Good-bye, Jonsey. Our rings. Don't lose. *(Pandora gives Edvard the rings.)*

PANDORA: Good-bye, dear sister.

JONSEY: My most heartfelt congratulations to you both.

FLORAL: Pandora.

EDVARD: Farewell, all of you! Farewell. Auf Wiedersehen.

(Pandora and Edvard exit to the manor.)

JONSEY: An odd man. He thought jasmine were honeysuckle.

FLORAL: I want to ask you a question.

JONSEY: Naturally, I wish them well and hope they have a most pleasant life. People deserve such things.

FLORAL: Your lovers? Which ones have been your lovers?

JONSEY: Floral. How strange.

FLORAL: Everyone knows about your infidelities. I've known for some time. I suspect even my mother suspects.

JONSEY: But I don't have lovers. Darling, you, of all people, must know. You know I cannot...It's quite clear I cannot.

FLORAL: With me.

JONSEY: With everyone.

FLORAL: I thought only me. You flirt with so many.

JONSEY: So they won't know. So you won't be ashamed.

FLORAL: My. You see, all along I thought it was only me.

JONSEY: I beg your pardon. I thought it was all apparent. I assumed you knew that my attention to others was merely a guise to make us appear normal.

FLORAL: No. I missed that.

JONSEY: Now you understand.

FLORAL: Yes.

JONSEY: Good.

FLORAL: I think I have to leave you.

JONSEY: No. Impossible. You're my wife. That's my child.

FLORAL: It's not.

JONSEY: We'll say it is. I'll love it like it is.

FLORAL: Love can't make it so.

JONSEY: What can?

FLORAL: It has to be.

JONSEY: I see. I see. There's nothing I can do.

FLORAL: About what?

JONSEY: Anything. Everything. I give up. I surrender. Wrap me in a white flag and ship me toward death. Better than whining and wanting like an undignified dog. Don't you agree?

FLORAL: Well, I do believe it has been your character.

JONSEY: Best not be without character.

FLORAL: People can change.

JONSEY: Who told you that? They were lying.

FLORAL: I've seen it happen.

JONSEY: Well, best believe your own eyes.

FLORAL: *(A beat.)* What are you thinking?

JONSEY: I'm trying to recall if you said anything clever yesterday. Something I could compliment you on today.

FLORAL: Ah.

JONSEY: So rarely do I look people in the eye and wonder what they are thinking. What if it were something that could spoil the day? Because what
you are thinking is exactly the opposite of what I am thinking. It's dia-
metrically opposed. That's not to say I believe you to be wrong and me
to be right or vice versa. Truthfully, my belief system is lenient to a grave
degree. There is no point at which my spine is not wholly gelatinized.
And yet I'm so handsome.

*(Sidney enters from the manor. His leg is bandaged and he limps with his
cane.)*

SIDNEY: Hello.

JONSEY: Sidney Lunt. I was just explaining to Floral why it is that we have
such a very bad marriage. You see, she snores. I've never really been able
to abide it, that trait. I've kept it to myself all these years, but it is something that has disturbed me every night of my life and I can no longer
keep quiet about it. This is not to say, dearest wife, that I do not adore
you in many other respects. However, this grievance strikes a chord so
deadly deep that I must insist we seek a divorce at once. Don't you agree?

FLORAL: Yes, I agree.

JONSEY: Very good. You are our witness, Sidney. Good day. *(Jonsey exits.)*

SIDNEY: I have your muffin.

FLORAL: Yes.

(Sidney offers Floral the muffin. She takes it.)

FLORAL: Sidney, in retrospect, I must say the gun suggestion was a mistake.

SIDNEY: No question. No question. However, I was able to call M'amie and
report that the wedding did not take place. She was quite happy. For the
moment.

FLORAL: Hope.

(The Reverend enters from the woods.)

REVEREND: Hello, Sidney. Floral.

FLORAL: What has happened to you?

REVEREND: I have been rolling down hills and giving vigorous thought to the
question...The question: What is impossible? The answer is, a formidable lot. To dance from here to the stars, to eat a tribe of bees, to scream
down a forest, to remember when you were born, to know when you will
die, to stop breathing and live. Many things are impossible. Endless
things are impossible. Our life together is not quite that.

FLORAL: Not impossible?

REVEREND: Tricky, yes.

FLORAL: Jonathan. I must...Must I? Must I speak the truth? Oh. I feel as though I'm going to perish. If only I would perish.

REVEREND: Don't perish. Please. No.

FLORAL: This is your child I am carrying. I am in love with you. I want to be with you forever.

REVEREND: Impossible.

FLORAL: What will happen to us?

REVEREND: Many things. But not in this garden.

FLORAL: Where?

REVEREND: *(Touching his heart, her heart; then taking her hand and leading her out of the garden.)* Here. Here. Here. *(Gesturing to the whole world.)* Here. *(They exit to the woods.)*

REVEREND: *(Offstage.)* Here.

(Kandall enters. She holds raspberries in her hands and eats them with her fingers.)

KANDALL: Sidney, you have made a shambles of the day.

SIDNEY: I've behaved abominably. There's no doubt.

KANDALL: My children. My girls. Their little lives are just ruined.

SIDNEY: Things do not look promising. Floral has departed with the Reverend.

KANDALL: To seek counsel?

SIDNEY: No. It seems...Apparently...If I am not wholly mistaken...He is the father of her child.

KANDALL: *(Taken aback.)* Oh. I missed that. Is it too late for me to change?

SIDNEY: What would you change?

KANDALL: I would change my life.

SIDNEY: Yes, it's too late to change that.

KANDALL: The rest of it though. All the rest could be different.

SIDNEY: I believe so.

KANDALL: Kiss me, Sidney.

(A silence. He cannot.)

SIDNEY: *(Taking her hand.)* Forgive me.

KANDALL: For what?

SIDNEY: You see I am such an impossible fool.

KANDALL: Oh, I understand. I remember my first kiss. Far away in the garden under the arbor. I was seven and the boy was nine. He grabbed me by the puffs of my sleeves and pulled me to him. We kissed full on the mouth, I was terrified and ran away. Afterwards I felt wicked and was in a mood for days. At night, in bed, I'd remember the dark secret. My heart pounding my body trembling. How it was all so quick and slow.

SIDNEY: May I trouble you for one raspberry before I go?

KANDALL: Of course. I have plenty.

(She offers the berries to him. He carefully takes one and slips it into his mouth.)

SIDNEY: Mmm.

KANDALL: Yes.

SIDNEY: *(Not going.)* I'm off.

KANDALL: *(Offering him berries.)* It was lovely to have met.

SIDNEY: And so...

KANDALL: Yes.

(They stay eating berries together. Fade to black.)

END OF PLAY